PUZZLES about ART

An Aesthetics Casebook

Margaret P. Battin
University of Utah

John Fisher
Temple University

Ronald Moore
University of Washington

Anita Silvers
San Francisco State University

ST. MARTIN'S PRESS
New York

Text Design: Barbara Bert / North 7 Atelier, Ltd.
Cover Design: Darby Downey
Cover Art: Pablo Picasso, *La Femme-Fleur*
Cover Photo: Robert Doisneau / Rapho / Photo Researchers

Library of Congress Catalog Card Number: 87-60519

For information, write:
St. Martin's Press, Inc.
175 Fifth Avenue
New York, NY 10010

ISBN: 0-312-00307-2

Acknowledgments

William Carlos Williams, *Collected Poems, Volume I: 1909–1939.* Copyright 1938 by New Directions Publishing Corporation.

Excerpt from *Travesties* by Tom Stoppard. Reprinted by permission of Grove Press, Inc., and Faber and Faber Ltd. Copyright © 1975 by Tom Stoppard.

John Hospers, UNDERSTANDING THE ARTS, © 1982, pp. 227–228, 361, 271, 189. Reprinted by permission of Prentice-Hall, Inc., Englewood Cliffs, New Jersey.

John Hospers, UNDERSTANDING THE ARTS, © 1982, pp. 33, 271. Adapted by permission of Prentice-Hall, Inc., Englewood Cliffs, New Jersey.

Excerpted from PINCHER MARTIN, copyright © 1956, 1957 by William Golding; renewed 1984 by William Gerald Golding. Reprinted by permission of Harcourt Brace Jovanovich, Inc.

Copyright © 1985 by *Harper's Magazine.* All rights reserved. Reprinted from the July issue by special permission.

Elizabeth Gilmore Holt, ed., *Literary Sources of Art History: An Anthology of Texts from Theophilus to Goethe.* Copyright 1947, © 1975 renewed by Princeton University Press. Excerpts reprinted with permission of Princeton University Press.

Excerpt from "Public Art no Public Sentiment" by Alvin Lane, July 13, 1985. Copyright © 1985 by The New York Times Company. Reprinted by permission.

Excerpt from "Why Are All Those Swans Dressed in Black?" by Jack Anderson, July 13, 1986. Copyright © 1986 by The New York Times Company. Reprinted by permission.

Excerpt from "Richard Serra's Radical Message Is Rooted in Tradition," by Michael Brenson, March 16, 1986. Copyright © 1986 by The New York Times Company. Reprinted by permission.

From Steven M. Cahn and L. Michael Griffel, "The Strange Case of John Shmarb: An Aesthetic Puzzle," *The Journal of Aesthetics and Art Criticism,* XXXIV: 1 (Fall, 1975): 21–22.

From ON MORAL FICTION, by John Gardner. Copyright © 1978 by John Gardner. Reprinted by permission of Basic Books, Inc., Publishers.

CONTRIBUTORS

VIRGIL C. ALDRICH
    University of Utah
PHILIP ALPERSON
    University of Louisville
JAY E. BACHRACH
    Central Washington State College
ANNETTE BARNES
    University of Maryland, Baltimore County
MARGARET P. BATTIN
    University of Utah
PEGGY ZEGLIN BRAND
    Ohio State University
JAMES BOGEN
    Pitzer College
ALLEN CARLSON
    University of Alberta
DAVID E. CARRIER
    Carnegie-Mellon University
DONALD W. CRAWFORD
    University of Wisconsin/Madison
RANDALL DIPERT
    SUNY College at Fredonia
MARCIA MUELDER EATON
    University of Minnesota
JOHN FISHER
    Temple University
STANLEY GODLOVITCH
    Mount Royal College
BROOKE HOPKINS
    University of Utah
JOHN HOSPERS
    University of Southern California
GARY ISEMINGER
    Carleton College
W. E. KENNICK
    Amherst College
PETER KIVY
    Rutgers University
MICHAEL KRAUSZ
    Bryn Mawr College
FLO LEIBOWITZ
    Oregon State University

JERROLD LEVINSON
University of Maryland
MATTHEW LIPMAN
Montclair State College
ROBERT L. MARTIN
Cellist
RONALD M. MOORE
University of Washington
JULIUS MORAVCSIK
Stanford University
HOWARD RISATTI
Virginia Commonwealth University
STEPHANIE ROSS
University of Missouri/St. Louis
ANITA SILVERS
San Francisco State University
FRANCIS SPARSHOTT
Victoria College
LAURENT STERN
Rutgers University
ALAN TORMEY
University of Maryland, Baltimore County
JUDITH TORMEY
Temple University
DABNEY TOWNSEND
University of Texas at Arlington
BRUCE VERMAZEN
University of California/Berkeley
KENDALL L. WALTON
University of Michigan
PATRICIA WERHANE
Loyola University of Chicago
EDDY ZEMACH
Hebrew University, Jerusalem

PREFACE

There are, we believe, two different ways to approach the classical and contemporary problems of aesthetics. One, the well-used, familiar way, examines various aesthetic theories and then applies these theories to specific examples of art and aesthetic objects. The other, its reverse, which we introduce in this book, is the "case-driven" approach: here one *begins* with specific puzzle cases about art and aesthetic objects, and uses these cases both to develop insight into aesthetic issues and ultimately to test and challenge aesthetic theories. Aesthetic theories have always been plentiful, from the time of Plato and Aristotle to the present, but what has not been easily available is a literature of well-developed, diverse, trouble-causing puzzle cases with which to approach the central issues in aesthetics.

This volume presents a collection of puzzle cases contributed by thirty-eight scholars working in aesthetics or in closely related fields. These cases are intended both for classroom use and for extended discussion by working aestheticians. They represent both a new pedagogical technique and a new way of looking at the field. To be sure, there are many antecedents for such a volume, both in the work of major aestheticians discussing specific issues and in the use of case studies in law, medicine, and applied ethics—especially bioethics, business ethics, and the ethics of legal practice. However, recognition of the importance of the case-based approach to the issues in aesthetics is, we believe, quite new.[1]

THE ROLE OF PUZZLE CASES

Puzzle cases are designed to play an important role in both teaching and research in aesthetics. Their use in teaching illustrates how they function. Traditionally, the teaching of aesthetics has begun with the exposition of historically significant or influential contemporary aesthetic theories, which are then illustrated by reference to specific works of art. For instance, the instructor might assign Tolstoy's famous essay propounding his version of expression theory, and illustrate the lecture with slides or recordings of expressive works of art: Picasso's *Blue Bathers* or Debussy's *La Mer*, for example. In this way, students are

---

[1] Extended developments of some of the material in this Preface can be found in Margaret P. Battin, "Lessons from Ethics: Case-Driven Aesthetics and Approaches to Theory," in *Aesthetic Distinction—Essays presented to Göran Hermeren on his 50th Birthday*, ed. T. Anderberg, T. Nilstun, and I. Persson (Lund: University Press, 1988); Ronald Moore, "The Case Method Approach to the Teaching of Aesthetics," *APA Newsletter on Teaching Philosophy*, pp. 11–15; and Margaret P. Battin, "The Dreariness of Aesthetics (Continued), with a Remedy," *Journal of Aesthetic Education* 20: 4 (Winter 1986), 11–14.

brought both to be familiar with expression theory and to see what it is for a work of art to be expressive. But this procedure has a major pitfall. The artworks selected for illustration in this manner serve to reinforce the theory, not to challenge it, and even illustrations selected to serve as counterexamples—a comparatively inexpressive Ingres portrait, for example—work typically only to dismiss the theory. The exposition and illustration of theories do only half the work in teaching (and doing) aesthetics, and often the other half remains undone.

It is to fill this need that puzzle cases may be employed. Consider, for example, the following real-life case, based on an incident in the Vatican on May 21, 1972. A deranged young Hungarian-born Australian, claiming to be Jesus Christ, attacked Michelangelo's *Pièta* with a hammer, striking the statue 15 times before he was dragged away.

THE DAMAGE TO THE *PIÈTA*

A hammer-wielding attacker has damaged Michelangelo's *Pièta*, destroying the Madonna's nose, shattering her left arm, and chipping her eyelid and veil. You, as director of the Vatican Museum, must choose whether to preserve the sculpture as is or attempt to restore it. Suppose the options open to you are:

1. Do not alter the statue; do nothing to repair the damage other than clear away the rubble from the base of the statue.
2. Restore the nose, arm, eyelid, and veil as nearly as possible to their original appearance. You have available to you and your staff photographs and drawings of the *Pièta* made before the incident, as well as a plaster cast of the statue made 40 years ago, and you can use a polyester resin to reaffix any salvageable fragments and to form a ground-marble plaster where fragments are too small to be used. If your work is successful, the new parts will look just like the old, and viewers will be unable to tell which parts have been restored.

Forced to choose between these options, readers may find themselves torn. Those who pick option 1 will usually think that it would be wrong to substitute anything that wasn't Michelangelo's work, even if it might look a lot like the original, and that what is important is the authenticity of the piece: the fact that it is *Michelangelo's* work.[2] They will point out that the areas of damage could have been

[2] The *Pièta* case is based on one by Mark Sagoff. He provides a defense of the purist response in "On Restoring and Reproducing Art," *Journal of Philosophy* 75 (1978), 453–470.

still larger and that if attempts were made to restore the work, there would be no limit in theory to replacing virtually the whole thing. But the statue would then be of no greater value than the plaster cast made 40 years ago—an informative likeness, perhaps, but not Michelangelo's work.

Those who defend attempting to restore the *Pièta* (option 2), insist that the appearance of the work would suffer if it lacked the nose, parts of the eyelid and veil, and especially the left arm, which had been extended in a way integral to the balance of the composition, and that viewing it in this damaged state would interfere with one's aesthetic experience of the whole.[3] To be sure, they would admit, some important works, like the *Venus de Milo*, cannot be restored because we have no way of knowing what the original was like; but where we know the original and can replicate its appearance, it is imperative that we do so. They will grant that the restoration might be of poor quality, but claim that unless the job is botched, the statue will be of more profound aesthetic impact if some of its parts are not quite as they were than if they remain broken off.

In forced-choice puzzle cases such as this, what the reader must do, in analyzing and defending an answer to the practical problem the case poses, is to give a reasoned argument for the course of action he or she thinks appropriate. To be persuasive, reasons for a course of action must be based not just on immediate feelings, but must appeal to a more general principle. Thus a puzzle case like this requires articulation of the principle or principles which are held to make a given answer correct. Those who favor the purist policy 1, for instance, appeal to a principle of authenticity in art, that principle which is also appealed to when labelling forgeries and replicas inferior to their originals: this principle holds that it makes a difference whose work it is. Those who favor the integralist restoration policy 2 appeal to aestheticist principles about the appearance of an artwork and the importance of aesthetic experience: what is significant about a work of art is not so much who made it but how it looks.

Of course, many professional aestheticians would assent to *both* a principle of authenticity and a principle of aestheticism. This is what makes these puzzle cases dilemmatic: we want to have it not just one way or the other, but both ways at one. Yet a case like *The Damage to the Pièta* makes it clear that one cannot always have it both ways. This is so even if the case is revised to offer more sophisticated options which take account of both principles involved. Suppose, for instance, that there were two additional possibilities open to the museum director who must decide what to do with the damaged *Pièta*.

---

[3] A defense of the integralist response to the *Pièta* case is given by Michael Wreen, "The Restoration and Reproduction of Works of Art," *Dialogue* 24 (1985), 91–100.

3. Working from photographs, drawings, and the plaster cast of the *Pièta* made prior to the incident, restore the nose, arm, eyelid, and veil to their original contours, but use a resin lighter (or darker) in color than the original marble so that the viewer knows which portions have been restored.

4. Restore the damaged portions with a material that is visually indistinguishable from the original (i.e., follow option 2), but incorporate a tracer dye into the resin to permit X-ray identification of the restored portions.

If offered these two possibilities, many readers will again find themselves torn, though since both options 3 and 4 represent compromises, their discomfort may not be as intense as when they were faced with the choice between options 1 and 2. Nevertheless, the reasons they give for preferring 3 will still appeal primarily to the principle of authenticity and for 4 to aestheticist considerations. No solution permits them to have it both ways; either the statue no longer looks like the statue Michelangelo created, or some portions of what looks like the work are no longer his.

To resolve this case, then, one is forced not only to identify the principles to which appeal is made—these are usually stated as reasons in the explanations of why one course of action is to be preferred to another—but also to prioritize the principles that have been identified. Either authenticity gives way to aestheticist principles, or the other way around. The difference between those who pick 1 or 3 and those who pick 2 or 4 can be said to consist in a difference in the way they rank principles which are accepted by all. They feel the pull of both authenticity and of aestheticism as principles important in response to art, but assign them different weights relative to each other.

In turn, the way weights are assigned to competing aesthetic principles indicates basic allegiances to background aesthetic theories. Expression-based theories will give higher priority to authenticity, while formalist theories will give greater importance to the perceptual properties of the work. But different expression and formalist theories will try to tread this line in different ways, and it is here that prodding with a specific, forced-choice puzzle case makes the background aesthetic theory display, as it were, its true colors. Some theories even insist that there can be no intermediate principles at all. But if a theory is complete and consistent as an account of art, it should eventually decide hard cases such as these in one way or another, and if it is inadequate to do so, the theory will thus reveal itself to be in need of extension or repair. Thus, by using cases, we can identify and address difficulties within aesthetic theory itself, and thus reveal the sources of confusion as well as illumination in what we think about art.

USING THIS VOLUME

Each chapter in this volume is divided into two sections: an introductory essay outlining the background issues in aesthetics, and a group of diverse cases probing these issues. The background essay is provided to give the reader some footing in the major areas of aesthetics and to provide a conceptual framework for discussing the cases; the cases themselves serve to elicit the issues and to initiate the inquiry the reader is to pursue. The first five chapter essays each introduce a number of sample cases and show how further cases can be used to pursue problems raised by a preceding one; the final chapter examines at greater length a single actual case, the dispute over Richard Serra's *Tilted Arc.*

In teaching, puzzle cases are used both to provoke classroom discussion and to serve as bases for papers, exercises, and examinations. It is important that students understand that these are *hard* cases, cases which do not have "right" answers or answers which will be accepted by all. Quite the contrary, they are cases intended to stir up trouble and to show where further work in aesthetics needs to be done. Analyzing a case might consist in a comparatively brief diagnosis of the issues it appears to involve, perhaps contrasted with other seemingly similar cases; it might also involve extended, termpaper-length examination of the deeper, more complex issues raised by a single case. Not only may there be no single right answer to a case, but there is no single way in which these cases must be used.

The volume itself is designed to serve as a companion to the anthologies of theoretical papers which are the traditional reading matter of courses in aesthetics. In both teaching and in approaching research issues, puzzle cases will be most effective if they are explored *first,* before one turns to theoretical formulations of the issues at hand; this allows one to avoid being limited in advance by the partial picture a theoretical formulation characteristically develops, and permits one to arrive at an issue with a full conception of what it is that needs to be explained. The greatest pedagogical benefit is thus achieved by introducing an issue by means of puzzle cases, together with the background analysis the chapter introductions provide, and only then reading the anthology's more abstract, sustained analyses of the issues the cases have raised. This is a "problems first, solutions later" approach, an antidote to that familiar convention in aesthetics which first examines the theoretical solutions and then tries to get clear about what the problems may have been.

The Damage to the Pietà is a real-life case. Many of the cases in this volume are also real-life cases, based on historical events or current controversies. Some are hypothetical cases, constructed to press specific theoretical points or to appeal to various conflicting intuitions; these fictional cases generally present starker dilemmas than those posed by actual ones, since they often eliminate by hypothesis any convenient middle positions. Most of the cases in this volume involve the central arts of painting, music, literature, sculpture, dance, and drama, but there is also a sprinkling of cases from peripheral areas intended to exploit parallels to the central ones. The cases vary considerably in complexity; in some, the conflict which is central is immediately evident, while in others the tension is much more subtle and requires considerably more exploration to identify what it is. Many cases overlap with neighboring cases presenting slightly different issues, and they are arranged here to emphasize these overlapping relationships. Most importantly, virtually all the cases involve multiple issues, and while they are grouped here under six chapter headings, a great many could have been placed in other chapters with almost equal plausibility. Exploring those issues suggested for a case by the chapter designation within which it falls may not exhaust the issues it presents, and a great many of these cases can be profitably discussed by considering them under various different chapter headings in order to highlight different features of the case.

The cases in this volume raise a very broad range of issues in aesthetics, and inasmuch as they have been contributed by number of working aestheticians, they present issues of continuing professional interest to this distinguished group. Cases are attributed to the individual who supplied them for this volume, but of course many of the problems on which they are based have been circulating in a variety of forms within the aesthetics literature for years, and their precise point of origin cannot be identified. They have been formulated in a way that seeks to stress the issues raised, even if some of these puzzles may have seemed to be resolved.

The authors would like to acknowledge the editorial contributions of Nancyanne Moore; library assistance from Hikmet Dogue; the secretarial assistance of Teri Finnerty and Cindy Allen; the very helpful suggestions of Peggy Brand, Randall Dipert, Patricia Werhane, Peter Kivy, Dabney Townsend, and Steven Sverdlik, the latter five as readers for St. Martin's Press.

M.P.B.
J.F.
R.M.M.
A.S.

CONTENTS

Chapter 3.   MEANING and INTERPRETATION   60

Chapter 6.   CRITICAL JUDGMENT

The Dispute over *Tilted Arc*

Index

CHAPTER 1

ART and ARTWORKS

I.

THE CHIMPANZEE PAINTER

Betsy the Chimpanzee in the Baltimore Zoo is given some paints and some paper; with them she creates various products, some of which might be called paintings. Even if Betsy's works are not masterpieces, they are undeniably interesting and appealing in their own way. Selected pieces from Betsy's "oeuvre" are displayed for a month at the Field Museum of Natural History in Chicago. Suppose that the next month the same pieces are exhibited at the Chicago Art Institute, and that at both exhibitions, Betsy's works are greatly admired by the viewing public.

Is Betsy's work art? Is it art only under certain conditions of display (e.g., at the art museum, but not at the natural history museum)?[1] If it is (at least sometimes) art, whose art is it?

When we are trying to decide whether something is an artwork, what sorts of considerations should we have in mind? Should it matter whether its creator is human? Should it matter whether its creator intended it to be received or understood as art? Should it matter whether the object in question is, in our judgment or in the judgment of others, an excellent one of its type? Should it matter where, when, and by whom it is seen, if by anyone? If by chance Betsy creates a composition that is indistinguishable from a work universally acknowledged to be a work of art, would that make her work an artwork? What difference will it make whether we determine Betsy's compositions, or any other things, to be artworks? What changes, if any, are required in the way we deal with and think about such objects when we make this determination?

2. "CALL IT *DRIFTWOOD*"

Suppose a well-known artist happens to be vacationing in the small community where you are curator of the local museum. One day you see him walking along the beach, and you tell him that your museum—although it is almost without funds to purchase new works—would be greatly honored to be given a work by him. He pauses, smiles in an indecipherable way, and bends over to pick up a piece of driftwood that is lying on the beach. "Here," he says with a glint in his eye, "take this. Call it *Driftwood*."

As curator, do you exhibit the driftwood or not? (Your gallery would be greatly enhanced by acquiring a genuine work by this famous artist.)

When we say that something is art, or a work of art, do we mean to say at the same time that it should be understood or appreciated in a certain way, or taken seriously in a particular fashion? And if so, do we think that the seriousness in the audience's response is an acknowledgment of deliberation and creative concern on the part of the artist? How elastic are the boundaries of the concept "art"? Can effects that occur purely accidentally, like the ocean's polishing of the driftwood, become art? Or must there be some minimum infusion of the artist's special creative influence before the appellation "art" is warranted?

3. DON'T FORGET THE KETCHUP

In 1967, the Art Gallery of Ontario paid $10,000 for a work called *Giant Hamburger* (1962) by Claes Oldenburg: a hamburger complete with pickles on top, made of painted sailcloth and stuffed with foam rubber, about 52 inches high and 84 inches across. A group of local art students fabricated from cardboard a ketchup bottle on the same scale, and contrived to set it up alongside the hamburger, to the delight of the local newspapers and the annoyance of the museum management. The hamburger remains in the museum collection, but the bottle has not been seen since.*

This incident really happened. What are we to make of it? Should it be regarded as a gesture of disrespect to an eminent artist and a dignified institution, as a show of bad manners? Or should we see it as a satirical exposé of the facility and superficiality of the "pop" art of the time (as pop art sometimes was a comment on "serious" art of *its* time)? Was it a harmless joke, leaving things just as they were, with no aesthetic damage done? Or was something damaged, aesthetically or otherwise, by the prank? Was it simply a blunder? Did the students miss the point of Oldenburg's work and hence make the relation between their cardboard bottle and the Oldenburg mock-up aesthetically uninteresting? More to the point, should we say that the students had created a new artwork of their own, incorporating Oldenburg's work as part?

WHAT COUNTS TOWARD SOMETHING'S BEING ART?

There are cultures in which nothing is regarded as art; no object is spoken of as an artwork. This is said to be true of the Balinese, for example, who, according to one observer, claim, "We have no art; we do everything the best way we can."[2]

Possibly there is some advantage to this way of looking at things; for, by refraining from drawing a boundary around certain exclusive objects deemed worthy of the label "art," the Balinese may be more readily disposed to perceive and appreciate in all spheres of their activities those aesthetic values we find in artworks alone. In our culture we *do* draw such a line, and adult users of our language normally come to master the distinction between art and non-art for most practical purposes. We all can name a good number of standard examples of artworks—a Beethoven symphony, the *Mona Lisa*, Rodin's *Thinker*, and so on—even if we cannot say just what it is about these things that qualifies them as artworks. Usually we have no difficulty in determining whether a given object is an artwork because, in most cases, it will obviously fall within or outside of the class of objects that are, loosely speaking, "like" the standard examples. This familiar rough-and-ready management of the concept of art suffices perfectly well for most day-to-day uses. But now and then it becomes important for the average person to clarify or explain what it *means* to call something "art," or an "artwork." If, for example, some portion of public tax money is scheduled to be expended on art, the public will be

* Case by F. Sparshott.

interested to know whether an ice rink or a rose garden or a room full of dirt should be deemed art. Or if a high school art teacher were to devote a majority of class time to instruction in cooking, ice skating, or astrology (each of which has at times been spoken of as an art), the public might want to know whether the teacher should be disciplined for failing to teach *art*. It is this need to clarify the conceptual lines we have casually drawn and to make plain the basis of our classifications that motivates the philosopher's efforts to answer the deceptively simple question, "What is art?"

The somewhat outré candidates for the title "artwork" (or, equivalently, "work of art") mentioned in the preceding cases serve to highlight the utility of this question. For we cannot begin to decide whether a chimpanzee composition, a chunk of driftwood, or a giant ketchup bottle is a work of art without first making clear to ourselves what principles guide, or should guide, our considered use of the concept "art." Each of these items shares some features with paradigmatic artworks, that is, objects like the *Mona Lisa*, which we would insist are artworks if anything is. However, each of these items also differs from the paradigmatic artworks in unmistakable ways. Which are the telling ways and which the irrelevant ones?

The traditional philosophical method of answering this question has been to propose and defend one or another *real definition* of "art," or of "artwork." A real definition is a verbal formula that purports to identify features of a thing that are shared with all other things of the same title and that are, when taken together, peculiar to just those things. So, for example, if "female fox" is offered as a real definition of "vixen," the claim is thereby made that all and only things that are both foxes and females are vixens. A feature without which a thing cannot lay claim to a given title is called a "necessary condition," and a feature that, if enjoyed by a thing, ensures a given title, is called a "sufficient condition." In this definition, being a fox is a necessary condition of being a vixen.

Real definitions are called "real," as opposed to "nominal," because they identify necessary and sufficient conditions for usage on the basis of *discovered*, rather than stipulated, traits of the things in question. That is, the proponents of a real definition maintain that all and only these things *actually* share certain features and that this shared set of real features—their essence—warrants our calling them by a common name. For example, we arrive at the real definition discussed above by noting that a common thread runs through all vixens and nothing else: it is the complex fact that they are both female and foxes. Where we find this thread we call things vixens, and where we don't, we don't. We cannot produce a real definition by arbitrarily "sewing things together," designating whatever things we wish "female" and "fox" in order to constitute a membership class for "vixen." Instead, we must discover whatever it is that constitutes the essence of the thing. Philosophical theories of art from Plato's day forward often have sought to identify the essence of art and to use this discovery as the basis of clarifying and correcting discussions of art and its relation to other phenomena.

THE ESSENTIALIST TRADITION

Prior to the present century, from Plato's day forward, nearly all prominent art theories were alleged to have been based on discovery of the essence of art and to have captured it in a real definition. To be sure, Plato, the progenitor of this tendency, could not claim to have defined "art," for the simple reason that ancient Greek had no single term corresponding to our modern concept. But Plato did develop a metaphysics and theory of language, which hold that the meanings of terms, because they are abstracted from their referents, can be perfect and enduring in a way in which ordinary objects—the referents themselves—cannot. Plato thus held that the essences of particular things, such as beds or triangles, as well as abstract entities, such as beauty, are discoverable by a process of careful philosophical reflection. Art theorists since Plato have followed his metaphysical lead in attempting to discover the essence of art, and thus to formulate a definition of *art*.

Indeed, some later theorists have seized on the concept of the essence of art as an antidote to talking nonsense. Clive Bell, for instance, insists that

> either all works of . . . art have some common quality, or when we speak of "works of art" we gibber. Everyone speaks of "art," making a mental classification by which he distinguishes the class "works of art" from all other classes. What is the justification of this classification? What is the quality common and peculiar to all members of this class? Whatever it is, no doubt it is often found in company with other qualities; but they are adventitious—it is essential. There must be some one quality without which a work of art cannot exist; possessing which, in the least degree, no work is altogether worthless.[3]

Others seized on the concept of the essence of art as an antidote to the corruption of artforms in their time. Leo Tolstoy, for instance, complained that

> [a]rt, in our society, has been so perverted that not only has bad art come to be considered good, but even the very perception of what art really is has been lost. In order to speak about the art of our society, it is, therefore, first of all necessary to distinguish art from counterfeit art.[4]

And still others saw in it the prospects of uniting the fine and applied arts in the public consciousness and of recognizing the unity underlying art's enormous diversity of form. Thus, DeWitt Parker observed:

> Art is itself so complex a fact that a satisfying definition of it must also be complex, that is to say must involve many characteristics. As the mathematicians would say, the characteristics must be not only necessary but sufficient. They must penetrate deep enough into the roots of art to meet the challenge of the pluralists and show that there is, after all, a significant sameness in all the arts,—despite their differences in technique and media,—connecting the fine with the applied arts, so far as the latter are beautiful, and the realistic with the fanciful and the idyllic.[5]

The various rationales for aesthetic essentialism have, over the centuries, supported a tremendous profusion of definitions of "art" and of theories of art built upon them. Whole schools or movements of theory may be conveniently classified according to their acceptance of this or that feature or set of features as the defining characteristic of art. Thus, the so-called mimetic theorists of the Platonic tradition point to a relation of resemblance between the artwork and the object it imitates as the key to definition; the "expression" theorists of the more recent Romantic tradition point to the artist's emotion brought to one form of completion; the "aesthetic attitude" theorists point to a certain disinterested quality of mind the artwork invites; "formalists" point to "significant form"; "intuitionists" to some intuited quality or other; "hedonists" to objectified pleasure, and so on.

How is one to decide, in the midst of this confusing array of theories, which is most sound? It will not do simply to pick one's favorite feature of art or artworks and accept the theory that takes that feature to be a defining one. For it sometimes turns out that we are willing to acknowledge that some things are artworks although they lack the favored feature (we must conclude that this feature is not a necessary condition), or that some things that have it aren't art (we must conclude that the feature is not a sufficient condition). Historically, the battles among rival theories of art have been waged by capitalizing on the strategy of counterexamples these observations suggest. "Theory A can't be right," say the proponents of theory B, "because item X has the features theory A takes to be essential to art, but everyone will readily admit that X isn't art." And proponents of theory C may challenge theory D by saying, "Work Y is recognized by everyone as art, yet Y doesn't have some feature theory D takes to be essential." Recently, however, a more radical form of criticism has emerged. Some philosophers have argued that piecemeal attack on definition after definition of "art" is beside the point for the simple reason that art is, of its very nature, indefinable.

ANTIESSENTIALISM AND ANTI-ANTIESSENTIALISM

The immediate inspiration for the antiessentialist attack on traditional theories of art was the publication in 1953 of Ludwig Wittgenstein's *Philosophical Investigations*. There, the argument is made that, for a good number of important terms, Plato's insight was wrong: there is no one feature or set of features that is common to all members of the group sharing the name. Take the word "game," for example. What is it that is common to all games? Plato would have thought there *must* be something, or we could not legitimately call them all by the same name, "game." However, for any definition that one might wish to propose, there appear to be counterexamples, activities that everyone thinks of as games but that do not fit the definition, or activities that fit the definition but that no one thinks of as games. Suppose, for example, one proposed to define "game" as "competitive contest." This proposal fails because there clearly are competitive contests, such as wars, which we would not call games, and games, such as solitaire, that are not competitive contests. Instead of some common feature or features, Wittgenstein points out, what we find when we look at the actual usage of a concept like "game" is a set of overlapping features. A partial set of these features is shared by one pair of subgroups and another partial set is shared by another pair: "The strength of the thread [i.e., the concept, or name] does not reside in the fact that some one fibre runs through its whole length, but in the overlapping of many fibres." Wittgenstein called these nonessential bases for naming "family resemblances."[6]

Philosophers of art were quick to draw implications from Wittgenstein's theory of language. First Paul Ziff and then Morris Weitz applied the notions of conceptual overlap and family resemblance to the concept "art." Ziff observed that "so long as there are artistic revolutions, the phrase 'work of art,' or some equivalent locution, will continue to be used in many ways."[7] And Weitz carried the point farther:

> The problem of the nature of art is like that of the nature of games, at least in these respects: If we actually look and see what it is that we call "art," we will also find no common properties—only strands of similarities. Knowing what art is is not apprehending some manifest or latent essence but being able to recognize, describe, and explain those things we call "art" in virtue of these similarities.[8]

The point Ziff and Weitz were making is at once a claim about language and about the world. They argued that the historical diversity of artforms—radical changes in style, medium, material, critical vision, taste, and so on—makes it inappropriate to use the words "art" and "artwork" as though the concepts for which they stood were closed. An open concept is one for which the conditions of application are always emendable and corrigible. And art, as these antiessentialists saw it, is and ought to be such an open concept, for its openness is a precondition of creativity and novelty in the field.

More recently, antiessentialism itself has come under attack. George Dickie and others have argued that "art" is not indefinable after all. Indeed Dickie has proposed an irreverently new definition, one that has been hotly contested. Dickie's original version of this definition, known as the Institutional Theory of Art, went like this:

> A work of art in the classificatory sense (1) is an artifact (2) a set of the aspects of which has had conferred upon it the status of candidate for appreciation by some person or persons acting on behalf of a certain social institution (the artworld).[9]

Dickie has revised this definition into a "small dictionary" of the philosophy of art, a set of five deliberately circular definitions which, he says, reveals the "inflected" nature of art:

> 1. An artist is a person who participates with understanding in the making of a work of art.
> 2. A work of art is an artifact of a kind created to be presented to an artworld public.
> 3. A public is a set of persons the members of which are prepared in some degree to understand an object which is presented to them.
> 4. The artworld is the totality of all artworld systems.
> 5. An artworld system is a framework for the presentation of a work of art by an artist to an artworld public.[10]

Dickie's point, put as simply and uncontroversially as possible, is that a dynamic social institution—the artworld—rather than a static conceptual formula, is given the job of distinguishing things that are properly to be called art from those that aren't. As an institution, the artworld consists of more or less established practices and a more or less loosely organized core of personnel: artists, reporters, critics, art historians, philosophers of art, and others. Thus, what counts toward a thing's being an artwork is, in this view, a function of practices and decisions within the ever-changing context of the social institution that provides for art's continuing existence. No fixed conceptual formula is necessary; art is what the artworld takes to be art. Thus, Dickie's account will not tell us directly whether Betsy the chimpanzee's painting is art, or what perceptual features the driftwood must have, or, for that matter, what makes the *Mona Lisa* or a Beethoven symphony art; but it does tell us whom to ask—the members of the artworld. If *they* take these things to be art, then they are; if they do not, they are not. Furthermore, presumably, an object might cease to be an artwork if the artworld no longer regards it as one.

WHAT IS THE ARTWORK?

In the course of trying to answer the question "What is art?" we may find ourselves facing an equally challenging companion question: "What is the artwork?" A determination that an object or event passes the test by which we judge things to be art does not, by itself, tell us what feature, facet, or aspect of it is the appropriate focus of critical appraisal or appreciation. Strange as this may seem, we may well decide that a given work is art in advance of deciding just what the work *is*. After all, everything in the world can be described in countless ways, some of which are invariably more apt for certain purposes than others. A smile, for example, may be described by referring to the muscles it involves, the joke that provoked it, the amused reaction the smiler wishes the observer to see, and so on. Some of these descriptions, and not others, will be pertinent to determining whether the smile was sincere. Likewise, only some of the possible descriptions of art objects are the ones that fit those objects as *artworks*.

In Advance of the Broken Arm is the title of a composition by Marcel Duchamp, a twentieth-century artist particularly well known for his "ready-mades." The snow shovel so prominent in it is a real shovel, just like one that you might purchase at a hardware store. Consequently, many, perhaps most, correct descriptions of Duchamp's snow shovel fit your snow shovel as well. But it certainly does not follow that judging Duchamp's "ready-made" to be art requires judging your snow shovel to be art too. For, here the descriptions that count—the ones that identify *In Advance of the Broken Arm* as an *artwork*—have to do with such features as the gesture of mockery involved in its display, the significance imputed to the snow shovel by the title, the receptivity of a certain audience to this kind of display, and so on.

The problem of deciding which descriptions characterize a thing as an artwork is no less severe for art objects that few people would confuse with everyday objects. Music critics overwhelmingly agree that Bach's last work, *Die Kunst der Fuge*, is art but disagree widely as to what exactly it is about this monumental composition that is the *work* of art. Is it the creative idea in Bach's mind as he composed the piece? If so, the artwork happened only once, centuries ago, and every rendition of it, even Bach's own manuscript notation, may only imperfectly express it. Is it instead the notation itself—the original, autographic musical manuscript? If so, ironically, this famous work can never be heard; for marks on paper are by their very nature silent. Is it the set of instructions those marks are conventionally taken to provide to performing artists? If so, the identity of the work will change over time as those conventions change, so that Bach, were he to reappear today or sometime in the future, might not recognize the work as his own. Worse still, because the conventions could change radically, any sounds could come to constitute a performance of any work. Finally, perhaps the work of art here is the set of its peform-ances, or the performances together with audience responses to them. But this view leads to especially awkward and unsettling results: Bach did not indicate instrumentation for this piece; consequently, it has been performed by an unusually wide variety of instrumental ensem-bles (solo organ, duo pianos, woodwind quintet, string orchestra, and so on). Are all of these quite different-sounding performances perform-ances of the same *work*? (We will return to questions of performance in Chapter 4.)

Puzzles of this kind concern the *ontology* of art. Ontology is that branch of metaphysics concerned with the systematic characterization of the stuff, or ingredients, constituting all of reality. The chief aims of ontological reflection are the delineation of *kinds* of thing, and the general description of the spatial and temporal situation of things of a given kind. The ontology of art thus aims to determine what kind of thing an artwork is and to provide the means of judging when and where artworks occur. Historically, these issues have proved to be every bit as controversial as the issue of the definability of "art."

When philosophers differ over the kind of thing an artwork is, their differences are sometimes traceable to divergent convictions regarding the nature of reality in general. Materialists, for example, will take the work of art to be something physical, perhaps a brain state in the mind of the artist, or a configuration of molecules, or patches of pigment on a canvas. Idealists will take an opposing view, maintaining that the work of art is a pattern of thought or emotion, perhaps a pattern shared in some way by artist and audience. Not all differences over kind are differences in background metaphysics, however. Two idealists might, for example, differ markedly in their views as to whether the art students' *joke* in juxtaposing the ketchup bottle with the Oldenburg *Giant Hamburger* was part of the artwork (if the resultant whole were taken to be art). Or they might differ as to whether the *juxtaposition*—that is the relation itself, apart from the things related—was part of the artwork. And again, they might differ as to whether *audience response* to the juxtaposed hamburger and ketchup bottle helped constitute the artwork or whether the artwork was complete in the minds of the pranksters.

In asking what an artwork is, we are sometimes asking more than what kind of a thing it is; we may also be trying to determine its boundaries—what it should and should not be taken to include. Questions of when and where the artwork occurs can be no less thorny than the ontological questions considered above. Even should we come to agree that *Driftwood* is art, we may differ as to *when* the artwork came into being. Was it with the glint in the artist's eye? Or when he said, "Call it *Driftwood*"? Or when the curator accepted it for exhibition? Or when he exhibited it, and it was actually viewed as art by gallery visitors? Or has the idea of such an artwork always existed, though it has only recently been actualized?

The same kinds of questions may reappear if we ask when the artwork is completed. If, years after first exhibiting it, the curator were to paint *Driftwood* black (following the artist's telephoned instructions), would he have created a new work, destroyed the old work, completed an unfinished work, or done something else? Similarly, we may differ as to *where* the artwork is, what its spatial limits are. If it is art, is the *Driftwood* artwork coextensive with the piece of driftwood, or does it take in the gesture of its presentation, its setting in the gallery, the range of reactions to it, and so on? Ontological questions such as these command our attention because their answers are preconditions to consistent communication about art. People who have in mind different kinds of things, or things in different places or occurring at different times, when they speak of artworks, will inevitably talk past one another. However acute their observations, they simply cannot mesh, and this will lead to nothing but confusion and frustration. No simple or sweeping policy seems likely to settle all such questions. Philosophers of art have held widely divergent views as to ontological policy, views so numerous and varied that we cannot hope to review and adjudicate them here. It is tempting to suppose that different ontological policies will reflect and accommodate differences among genres, styles, epochs, cultures, and so on. If this conclusion is sound, the distinctions we draw will, as much as anything else, reveal the people we are and the times we live in.

BEYOND DEFINITION: ART AND SOCIETY

Sometimes, the questions "What is art?" and "What is the artwork?" are not aimed at establishing credentials for these concepts. The questions may be seen as invitations to provide accounts not of the essence and ontology of art, but of the peculiar effects art has on us, the phenomena that surround and incorporate it, the value assigned to it, and the relations artworks bear to other elements in our experience. A good many theories of art are, in fact, less concerned ultimately with the definitional than with the contextual.

Once again the source of speculation in this direction may be traced to Plato. Plato held that the primary issues facing human beings concerned relations between the individual and what might be called the personality of the state. Art's role in human affairs was, as Plato saw it, both determined by the correct adjustment of these relations and subject to them. So, it was not only possible, but entirely appropriate, that certain forms of art should be subject to political control or suppression wherever they could be shown to disturb the correct relations between the individual and the state. Plato thus introduced the philosophical discussion of censorship as a practice to be employed wherever aesthetic values conflicted with political and ethical ideals. This issue (which will be considered more fully in Chapter 5) continues to arise wherever the possibility is raised that the effect of art on the individual or on human social life may be destructive as well as constructive.

We may not entirely agree with the way in which Plato and other theorists chose to delimit the social experience of art, yet we may wish to reach beyond the definitions proposed in traditional theories of art to find out what it is about art that makes it important enough in our lives to be worth theorizing about. A good many philosophers (e.g., Friedrich Nietzsche, John Dewey, Karl Marx, Susanne Langer) have addressed this theme at some length. So have a number of social scientists (e.g., Max Weber, Bronislaw Malinowski, Thorstein Veblen, Clifford Geertz). Although we cannot attempt to summarize here their widely disparate views, it is perhaps worth remarking that efforts to describe the social setting in which art exists may prove to be as useful as any definition in helping us to decide what to say about giant ketchup bottles, chimpanzee works, driftwood, and the *Mona Lisa* as well.

CASES ━━━━━━━━━━━━━━━━━━━━

What Is Art?

1-1. WILLIAM CARLOS WILLIAMS AND THE ICEBOX

The following is one of William Carlos Williams's best-known and most often anthologized poems:

THIS IS JUST TO SAY

I have eaten
the plums
that were in
the icebox

and which
you were probably
saving
for breakfast

Forgive me
they were delicious
so sweet
and so cold[11]

What, if any, difference should it make if someone discovered that Williams had not written this as a poem, that he had never intended it for publication, and that, in fact, it was just a note he had left on the door of a friend's refrigerator after eating all the plums?—J.B.

1-2. *PILE OF BRICKS*

Consider the following possibility, based on an exhibit at the Tate Gallery in 1976.[12] A person already known, perhaps even famous, as a "minimalist" sculptor buys 120 bricks and, on the floor of a well-known art museum, arranges them in a rectangular pile, 2 bricks high, 6 across, and 10 lengthwise. He labels it *Pile of Bricks*. Across town, a bricklayer's assistant at a building site takes 120 bricks of the very same kind and arranges them in the very same way, wholly unaware of what has happened in the museum—he is just a tidy bricklayer's assistant. Can the first pile of bricks be a work of art while the second pile is not, even though the two piles are seemingly identical in all observable respects? Why, or why not?—W.E.K.

1-3. MAN BECOMES ART (?)

In 1964, the Parisian performance artist Ben Vautier sat down in the middle of a street in Nice with a placard on his lap. The placard read, "Regardez moi cela suffit je suis art." ["Look at me. That's all it takes; I'm art."] He then had himself photographed in this position.

Was Ben right? Can a person be an artwork? If so, was Ben an artwork when he went home to shower? Would he remain an artwork were he to be drafted into the French army? Could he have been an artwork without his placard? Is asking whether Ben is art the best way of looking at his performance, and if not, in what alternative way could the placard and the performance be understood?—J.L.

Ben Vautier, 1964, Nice.
Photo: Copyright Ad Petersen.

1-4. PULLING POETRY OUT OF A HAT

In Tom Stoppard's play *Travesties*, Tristan Tzara, the well-known Dada poet, creates poetry by cutting up Shakespeare's sonnets, dropping the individual words in a hat, and then selecting and arranging the words drawn from the hat at random. In one scene, Tzara begins with the Eighteenth Sonnet:

> Shall I compare thee to a summer's day?
> Thou art more lovely and more temperate:
> Rough winds do shake the darling buds of May,
> And summer's lease hath all too short a date;
> Sometime too hot the eye of heaven shines
> And often is his gold complexion dimmed;
> And every fair from fair sometimes declines,
> By chance or nature's changing course untrimmed;
> But thy eternal summer shall not fade,
> Nor lose possession of that fair thou ow'st;
> Nor shall death brag thou wander'st in his shade,
> When in eternal lines to time thou grow'st:
> So long as men can breathe, or eyes can see,
> So long lives this, and this gives life to thee.

According to Stoppard, Tzara came up with:

shake thou thy gold buds
the untrimm'd but short fair shade
shines—
see, this lovely hot possession growest
so long
by nature's courses—
so . . . long—heaven!
and declines,
summer changing, more temporate complexion. . . .[13]

My seven-year-old daughter recently imitated Stoppard's Tzara, also by randomly selecting cut-up words from the Eighteenth Sonnet. Her work began as follows:

Death complexion see, declines,
summer's this as Rough changing eye course thee
more sometime not hot lives long fade
dimm'd; often eternal growest: May
Nor date. wander'st lines this temperate. lease
When eyes too is that his can brag to.

Is this poetry? Is Tzara's "creation" poetry, as Stoppard portrays it? Is either work original?—P.W.

1-5.   MODERN MASTERPIECE JUST DUCKY

In Liverpool, England, late in 1983, a wine merchant named Maureen Gledhill bought an abstract painting from Ernest Cleverley, a sculptor who also runs a pet shop. When Ms. Gledhill walked into the shop, the sculptor had been discussing the picture with Brian Burgess, an artist, and she believed it was one of Burgess's works. She paid $105 for the painting, thinking it a bargain, and displayed it prominently in her home.

But it turned out that the painting was the work of a duck named Pablo, who had escaped from his cage while Cleverley, the sculptor, was doing some painting, and had got his feet in the paint.

"I noticed that it made an interesting pattern, and it just developed from there," said Cleverley. "I tried him on canvas with different colors. He has a real eye for composition and flair for color."

Gledhill no longer displays the painting at her home, but she remarks, "I know it sounds corny. I don't know much about art, but I know what I like, and this was a painting I liked."

"The duck," said Cleverley, "is a natural."[14]

What would it help Ms. Gledhill to know about art in deciding what to think about the painting? Given that she has already acknowledged that she likes the painting, what plausible alternative reasons might she have for removing the painting from her home?—G.I.

1-6.   MALLARMÉ'S BLANK SHEET

In his essay "Minimal Art," Richard Wollheim writes:

> In a historic passage Mallarmé describes the terror, the sense of sterility, that the poet experiences when he sits down to his desk, confronts the sheet of paper before him on which his poem is supposed to be composed, and no words come to him. But we might ask, Why could not Mallarmé, after an interval of time, have simply got up from his chair and produced the blank sheet of paper as the poem that he sat down to write? Indeed, in support of this, could one imagine anything that was more expressive of, or would be held to exhibit more precisely the poet's feelings of inner devastation than the virginal paper?[15]

Wollheim claims that Mallarmé could not have produced a poem in this way, "For there is no structure here on the basis of which we could identify later occurrences as occurrences of that poem."[16] Is Wollheim right that *le vide papier* could not have served as Mallarmé's poem, could not itself have been a work of art?—R.M.M.

1-7.   DUCHAMP'S *FOUNTAIN*

In 1917, for the first annual exhibition of the Society of Independent Artists in New York City, French artist-in-exile Marcel Duchamp submitted a work entitled *Fountain*. The work, a simple porcelain

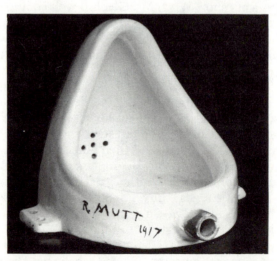

Marcel Duchamp, *Fountain*, 1917. Ready-made urinal. 24″ high.
Courtesy Sidney Janis Gallery, N.Y. Photo: Otto E. Nelson.

urinal purchased by the artist, hung at a 90° angle, and signed with the pseudonym "R. Mutt," was rejected by the society because it was judged to be not art but an immoral display.

Duchamp, Beatrice Wood, and H. P. Roche responded to this judgment in an article in *The Blind Man* of May 1917, saying:

> Now Mr. Mutt's fountain is not immoral; that is absurd, no more than a bathtub is immoral. It is a fixture that you see every day in plumbers' show windows. . . . Whether Mr. Mutt with his own hands made the fountain or not has no importance. He CHOSE it. He took an ordinary article of life, placed it so that its useful significance disappeared under the new title and point of view—created a new thought for that object.[17]

Should *Fountain*'s offensiveness to current moral sensibilities have counted against its being recognized as art? Do the facts that Duchamp *chose* this particular urinal and presented it in a certain way with a certain title constitute sufficient grounds for recognizing it as art? If you were a judge at the 1917 SIA exhibition, what would you have decided to do with this work? If you were a judge for an annual show of new works in a major American art museum *today*, what would you do with it, assuming it had never been displayed before?—H.R.

1-8. TATARKIEWICZ'S DEFINITION OF ART

The literature of aesthetics contains an embarrassment of riches when it comes to definitions of art. In "What is Art? The Problem of Definition Today," Wladyslaw Tatarkiewicz defines a work of art as follows: "A work of art is either a reproduction of things, or a construction of forms, or an expression of experiences such that it is capable of evoking delight, or emotion, or shock."[18]

Note that this sentence defines art *disjunctively* ("Anything is a work of art just in case it is A *or* B *or* C"), whereas most definitions are *conjunctive* ("Anything is a work of art just in case it is A *and* B *and* C"). Tatarkiewicz regards this as an advantage. But what this means is that there are three things (reproductions, constructions, expressions) and three reactions or responses they are capable of evoking (delight, emotion, shock), any one or more of which from each set is a logically *sufficient* condition for something's being a work of art. The only *necessary* condition is that a work of art must be at least one of the three things and must be capable of evoking at least one of the three responses.

Is this an adequate definition of art? Do some works of art fail to satisfy Tatarkiewicz's definition? Is there anything that is not a work of art that satisfies his definition?—W.E.K.

1-9. SONFIST'S *TIME LANDSCAPE*

Alan Sonfist is a contemporary artist who to some extent models himself on Marcel Duchamp, but with an important difference—Sonfist's "ready-mades" are natural objects. Sonfist, whom *New York Times* art critic Grace Glueck calls "nature's boy," says he is "not trying to alter" nature but is "trying to present it"; he wants to create art that makes nature "visible" and "directs" people to look at it. He claims: "I think nature is art and people have to realize this" and compares himself to Duchamp, saying: "He claimed man-made objects as works of art—I claim natural phenomena."[19]

Sonfist gives this basic idea extensive treatment in such works as *Time Landscape* (1965–1978), which consists of a network of sites throughout New York City where areas of land have been restored to the way they might have appeared before urbanization. Depending on the particular site, the land has been replanted with different varieties of trees, shrubs, and grasses in an attempt to recreate precolonial landscapes. As one art critic put it: "*Time Landscape* presents nature in an unadulterated, unmodified state as the fundamental content of the work."[20] Another critic claimed that in Sonfist's works, "Nature asserts itself as itself."[21]

If what these critics say about Sonfist's works is correct, why should any of them be considered works of art? If Sonfist's landscapes have been replanted, are they really "natural ready-mades"? What would be the difference between one of Sonfist's artworks and a garden, a botanical museum, or a historical arboretum?—A.C.

Alan Sonfist, *Time Landscape of New York,*
1965–78.
Courtesy of Alan Sonfist © 1978.

1-10. BAD ART OR NOT ART AT ALL?

In 1943, Theodore Adorno argued that we blunt our own critical weapons if we claim that Hollywood does not create works of art. Movie industrialists, he said, may wish to evade criticism on the grounds that they are engaged in a business, not in creating art, and that their only goals are profit and success; hence, they may try to claim that they are not subject to aesthetic criticism. But aesthetic criticism, Adorno continues, is criticism these movie makers richly deserve. Since they are using artistic means, they are creating art, even if it is *bad* art.

In 1969, Adorno argued that there is no bad art, and that the claim that a given artwork is "unsuccessful" is self-defeating. He claimed that although the notions of normal and revolutionary science make sense, it does not make sense to speak about "normal" art: either artworks are successful and revolutionary, or they are not art.

Did Adorno contradict himself in claiming, first, that there is such a thing as bad art and then that there is not? Does his 1969 view involve a rejection, a modification, or merely an elaboration of his 1943 view? Or could it be that Adorno did not change his mind but that the world changed between 1943 and 1969?—L.S.

What Is the Artwork?

1-11. THE CAPTIVE CAT

At Columbia University, a bronze statue of a cat stands on the floor at the head of a staircase. Presumably it is of some value, for university officials have fixed a chain around its neck and fastened the chain to the stair railing.[22]

Should the artwork be appreciated as a statue of a chained cat, or is it simply a chained statue of a cat? Because the chain is visible, is it possible to exclude it from one's aesthetic appreciation of the work? —A.S.

1-12. BIX BEIDERBECKE'S SOLO

In 1927, Bix Beiderbecke played a cornet solo for a recording of "Singin' the Blues," and it became one of the most famous and emulated solos in jazz for decades afterward. But the record was, alas, only a record, so in some sense no one after 1927 quite heard the solo. Musicologist S. L. Mismo decided to remedy this defect of time by notating Bix's solo in the smallest detail: pitch, rhythm, intonational nuance, volume. Then he got the classical conductor Gerard Schwarz, who also plays the cornet, to play from his music, and Schwarz got every detail right.

Mismo was there. Did he hear Bix's solo, unheard since 1927? Did he hear the same solo that everybody who listened to the record since 1927 had heard? Did Schwarz express what Bix expressed? Did Mismo, in notating the solo, express what Bix expressed? Would your answers to these questions be different if the record were by Wynton Marsalis, who plays both classical and jazz trumpet, and the artist whom Mismo used in the enterprise were also Wynton Marsalis? Would it make a difference if the solo had been notated in the same detail *before* Bix (or Wynton) played it the first time and Mismo's version (coincidentally) turned out to be identical to the original version?—B.V.

1-13.   SOL LEWITT'S WALL DRAWING

The Carnegie Institute in Pittsburgh owns a large wall drawing by Sol LeWitt. LeWitt provided instructions, indicating what lines were to be drawn, and the work was executed by local artists.

The museum plans at some future time to "move" the drawing, that is, to have it redrawn in another location. Can it justifiably claim that it will have the same work of art in its possession?

The drawing is beautiful; I would love to have it in my dining room. Suppose I have a second drawing made, using LeWitt's original instructions, but without his authorization. Would that work be a forgery? How would it differ from the first, given that it followed the same instructions? Suppose I hire the very artists and students who made the first drawing. Would that change the situation?—D.E.C.

1-14.   THE PAINTER AND THE PHOTOGRAPHER

Suppose an artist recognized both as a painter (of the photo-realist variety) and a photographer takes a photograph of a street scene. The artist then paints a picture of the photograph using an opaque projector to ensure that the painting is as accurate as possible. Finally, the artist photographs the painting. The three "works" are exhibited together. To the naive eye they all look alike, they all are exactly the same size, and they all appear to be photographs.

How many artworks, or kinds of artwork, do we have? Why? Should all these works be understood to convey the same meaning?

Suppose now that a West German art critic who is writing a book called *Photo-Realism in Painting* requests a photograph of the painting. By mistake the New York gallery that exhibited the three works sends him a photograph of the original photograph on which the painting is based, and this is used as a basis for discussion in the art critic's book. Realizing its mistake, the gallery sends the critic a photograph of the painting, but when the critic looks at the new photograph, he finds that everything he has said in interpreting the work is still applicable. The criticism appears unchanged in his book.

Has the critic been dishonest? How serious is the gallery's error? Should the critic acknowledge what has happened in his book?—A.B.

1-15. CHRISTO'S CONSTRUCTIONS

The recent projects of the contemporary artist Christo, such as *Running Fence, Valley Curtain, Surrounded Islands,* and *Pont Neuf Wrapped,* which consist of hundreds of thousands of yards of fabric or plastic draped or hung over natural features of the earth, have taken many years from conception to realization. To some extent this is because the projects are controversial and have required permission from various government and private agencies for their construction. But Christo is fully aware that his projects will raise these issues and insists that "the work of art is not merely the physical object finally attained, but the whole process—the surveys, the engineering, the leasing, the fabricating, the assembling, the hearings and the rest of it."[23]

Every complex work of art, from Michelangelo's sculptures to Steven Spielberg's films, requires a long process of planning and realization. Suppose Michelangelo had said that his sculptures were not merely the physical object finally attained but the whole process—

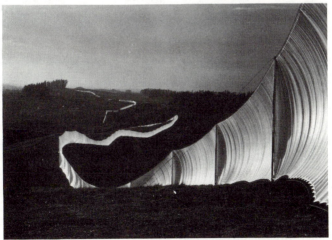

Christo, *Running Fence, Sonoma and Marin Counties, California, 1972–76.* Steel poles, steel cables, and 2½ million square ft. of woven nylon. Height: 18 ft. overall. Length: 24½ miles.
© Christo 1976. Photo: Wolfgang Volz.

cutting the marble blocks at Carrara, shipping them to Florence, and settling the controversies over the final location of the statue? Or suppose that Spielberg insisted that even a delay in filming due to a severe storm or a strike by the electrical workers was part of the work of art, part of the film he was making. Are these three cases essentially similar? Or can a case be made that Christo's work, unlike traditional art or even contemporary art in established media, "ceases to be the mere physical construction on a natural site, but a project with extended temporal boundaries, whereby the social context of its realization takes on aesthetic import"?[24]—D.W.C.

1-16. WHAT DO YOU READ?

> Polonius: What do you read, my lord?
> Hamlet: Words, words, words.[25]

A literary critic seems to disagree:

> A literary text, after all, in an objective sense consists only of a certain configuration of specks of carbon black on dried wood pulp. When these marks become words, when those words become images or metaphors or characters or events, they do so because the reader plays the part of a prince to the sleeping beauty.[26]

Do you read words, or marks on paper, or neither of these? What does the play *Hamlet* consist of—words, marks on paper, or something else?—L.S.

1-17. JOHN CAGE'S *4' 33"*

Among the most famous works of John Cage, a well-known contemporary composer, is his piece for piano entitled *4' 33"*. To perform that work the pianist goes on stage, sits at the piano, opens the keyboard, and remains seated for exactly 4 minutes and 33 seconds. At the end of that time the pianist closes the keyboard and leaves the stage.

Is *4' 33"* a work of art? Is it a piece of music? What if Cage insisted that *4' 33"* is a "listening experience" in which the audience is supposed to hear background noises—would your answer to the last question be different?

Suppose that during a recent concert of Cage's works, the pianist hired to perform *4' 33"* became ill at the last moment and had to withdraw. In desperation the stage manager himself performed the work.

Would this be a performance of Cage's work? Would it be a musical performance?—P.W.

1-18. THE CASE OF THE MOTIONLESS DANCE

Suppose a choreographer composes a piece that consists in its entirety of the following:

> The curtain rises on three dancers standing immobile on the stage. The dancers remain immobile for exactly four and a half minutes. The lights play over them, rising and dimming, changing color slightly so that there are variations in shadows and in the perceived colors of the bodies and costumes.
> At the end of the specified time period, the curtain falls.[27]

Has this choreographer composed a *dance*? What if even the lights do not move? Does it make a difference whether the performers are actually dancers, or could the stagehands perform this piece just as well? Is this (almost) the same work as John Cage's *4' 33"* in a different medium? Exactly what *is* the medium of each of these works?—M.P.B.

1-19. "I PAINT WHAT I SEE" (see p. 24)

What is the connection between art and the real world? What are the snakes and spiders the artist has painted paintings of? What about the trees? Do artists who "paint what they see" imitate nature as it is, as it should be, as they wish it were, or as their artistic vision presents it to them?—M.M.E.

1-20. AESTHETIC EQUIVALENCE

"I've got it. Exactly. After five years of trying different chords, motifs, and textures, a precise musical equivalent of my favorite Kandinsky watercolor: It's a short fantasy for string trio."

Could this composer be justified in his claim? Suppose a poet were to make a similar claim about the same Kandinsky watercolor: "I've got it. I've finally struck on *just* the right words. My sonnet and that Kandinsky are just the same as artworks." Is there any reason to think this claim is more (or less) justifiable than the composer's? If both claims were justifiable, would that mean that the string trio and the sonnet would in turn be exact equivalents? If these claims were unjustifiable, would there be *any* circumstances under which one artwork might be aesthetically identical to another, might fully substitute for it artistically?—J.L.

1-21. *ERASED DE KOONING*

In 1959, Robert Rauschenberg, a young though not inconsequential artist, asked Willem de Kooning to participate in an art project. De

"I paint what I see, child."

Kooning, who was not only older and much more established than Rauschenberg, but whose works sold for considerable sums of money, agreed to participate and gave Rauschenberg what he considered to be an important drawing. The drawing de Kooning selected was executed in heavy crayon, grease pencil, ink, and graphite. Rauschenberg spent a month on the work, erasing it completely. Then he placed the de Kooning drawing in a gold leaf frame and hand-lettered the date and title on the drawing: *Erased de Kooning Drawing*, 1953. Rauschenberg had not only erased de Kooning's work, but he had also exhibited the "erasure" as his work of art.

Had Rauschenberg created a work of art, or destroyed one, or perhaps both?—H.R.

1-22. SCULPTURE SOUND

Webster's defines "sculpture" as (1) "the action or art of processing (as by carving, modeling or welding) plastic or hard materials into works of art"; (2) "work produced by sculpture"; (3) "a three-dimensional work of art (as a statue)?"[29]

Michael Brewster, a well-recognized and frequently commissioned artist, has created a series of works that he, and those who commission and review him, consider sculpture. These works typically consist of two or more speakers that emit tones designed to interact so as to produce different sounds in different parts of the space in which they are installed. For example, one such installation produces sounds heard as a uniform, unbroken hum from some positions, and as a series of discrete beeps from others. Although both Brewster and his students say the important thing about such works is how they sound, the works are never presented as music, for example, in a concert. Some have been commissioned in connection with music festivals, but they are exhibited in galleries, not included in the festivals' musical events.

Is *Webster's* wrong? Or have Brewster and his patrons been making a mistake? And what does this tell us about the nature of sculpture or the nature of music? How important is it to differentiate between the different arts?—J.B.

1-23. SUPPRESSING ART

Imagine a tyrant who controls the land in which there lives a very skilled, famous painter. The tyrant is extremely cruel. He also hates art. His cruelty is focused on the painter, among others, because he believes that the painter once caricatured him in a portrait. Thus he wishes to torture the painter in the most vicious ways he can imagine—not stooping to ordinary physical torture but interfering more subtly with the painter's art.

The tyrant is considering two plans. First, he might order the painter never to paint again and have this order enforced by his ruthlessly efficient secret police. Or, second, he might supply the painter with canvas, paints, and a well-lit studio but require that every single canvas the painter paints be brought to him (by the ruthlessly efficient secret police) and destroyed immediately, before any critic or lover of art ever sees it.

Which method of torture would be worse for the artist? Which for the artworld? Can these answers be different? Would the ontological furniture of the world be different if artworks were created that were never seen or if they were never created at all? Would the artworld gain anything from having these works created, even if no one could ever appreciate them? Or if the tyrant decided to prevent the painter from painting altogether, would the paintings that the painter forms "in his mind's eye" be equivalent to paintings that he actually painted but that no one but him ever saw?—s.g.

1-24. THE CASE OF THE ZEALOUS BOOKBURNERS

Suppose that in a wave of new moralism, zealous bookburners attempt to rid the country—indeed, the world—of pernicious literary works. Libraries are purged, private collections are searched, and bounties are offered for individual copies. A couple of copies survive here and there for most of the works on the list, but every single copy of J. D. Salinger's *Catcher in the Rye* is destroyed.

Has *Catcher in the Rye* itself been destroyed? There are still a few old people around who can remember reading it, although they no longer have copies of the text. Will the work die when these old people do? Or will the work continue to exist, even though there are no longer any copies of it and no one will ever be able to read it again?—R.D.

NOTES

1. This comparison is suggested by George Dickie in *Art and the Aesthetic: An Institutional Analysis* (Ithaca, N.Y.: Cornell University Press, 1974), pp. 45–46.
2. Preston McClanaham, "To Prove the Fact of Existence," *Arts Magazine*, 45 (Summer 1971), 37.
3. Clive Bell, *Art*, 4th ed. (London: Chatto & Windus, 1920), pp. 7–8.
4. Leo Tolstoy, *What is Art?*, trans. A. Maude (Indianapolis: Bobbs-Merrill, 1960), p. 139.
5. DeWitt Parker, "The Nature of Art," *Revue Internationale De Philosophie*, 1, no. 4 (1939), 688.
6. Ludwig Wittgenstein, *Philosophical Investigations*, 3rd ed., trans. G.E.M. Anscombe (New York: Macmillan, 1968), p. 32e.
7. Paul Ziff, "The Task of Defining a Work of Art," *Philosophical Review*, 62 (1953), 532.
8. Morris Weitz, "The Role of Theory in Aesthetics," *Journal of Aesthetics & Art Criticism*, 15 (1956), 31.
9. Dickie, *Art and the Aesthetic*, p. 34.
10. George Dickie, *The Art Circle: A Theory of Art* (New York: Haven Publications, 1984), pp. 80–82.
11. William Carlos Williams, *Collected Poems 1909–1939*, vol. 1. Copyright 1938 by New Directions Publishing Corporation. Reprinted by permission of New Directions.
12. See Robert B. Semple, Jr., "Tate Gallery Buys Pile of Bricks—Or Is It Art?" *New York*

Times, February 20, 1976, p. 31, cited in W. E. Kennick, *Art and Philosophy: Readings in Aesthetics* (New York: St. Martin's Press, 1979), p. 116.

13. Tom Stoppard, *Travesties* (New York: Grove Press, 1975), pp. 84–85.
14. Based on a story in the *St. Paul Pioneer Press*, Thursday, October 6, 1983.
15. Richard Wollheim, "Minimal Art," in *Minimal Art*, ed. Gregory Battcock (New York: Dutton, 1968), p. 388.
16. Wollheim, "Minimal Art," p. 388.
17. *Marcel Duchamp* (Museum of Modern Art, New York, and Philadelphia Museum of Art, 1973), pp. 16, 283.
18. Wladyslaw Tatarkiewicz, "What Is Art? The Problem of Definition Today," *British Journal of Aesthetics*, 1 (1971), 34ff.
19. Grace Glueck, "Art Notes: Auction Where the Action Is," *New York Times*, November 15, 1970, p. D26.
20. Mark Rosenthal, "Some Attitudes of Earth Art: From Competition to Adoration," in *Art in the Land: A Critical Anthology of Environmental Art*, ed. Alan Sonfist (New York: Dutton, 1983), p. 68.
21. Jonathan Carpenter, "Alan Sonfist's Public Sculptures," in *Art in the Land*, p. 151.
22. Arthur Danto, *Transfiguration of the Commonplace* (Cambridge, Mass.: Harvard University Press, 1981), p. 102.
23. Alfred Frankenstein, "Christo's 'Fence,' Beauty or Betrayal?" *Art in America*, 64 (1976), 58.
24. D. Crawford, "Nature and Art: Some Dialectical Relationships," *Journal of Aesthetics and Art Criticism*, 42 (1983), 56.
25. Shakespeare, *Hamlet*, act 2, sc. 2, lines 191–192.
26. Norman N. Holland, *5 Readers Reading* (New Haven, Conn.: Yale University Press, 1975), p. 12.
27. Based on a case by Paul Ziff, *Antiaesthetics: An Appreciation of the Cow with the Subtile Nose* (Dordrecht, Netherlands: D. Reidel, 1984), pp. 84–85.
28. See John Elderfield, *The Drawings of Matisse* (New York: Museum of Modern Art, 1984), illustration 79, p. 194.
29. *Webster's Ninth New Dictionary*, s.v. "Sculpture."

CHAPTER 2

BEAUTY, UGLINESS, and AESTHETIC EXPERIENCE

A BEAUTIFUL MOUNTAIN VIEW?

Suppose that for centuries, the residents of a rugged alpine kingdom uniformly regarded the surrounding mountains with anxiety and foreboding. Looking to these towering, craggy peaks, they saw hazards to communication, impediments to commerce, harsh weather, and avalanches, but never did they see beauty, sublimity, or majesty. One day, however, some vacationing Romantic poets visited the kingdom, were much taken with the mountains, and declared them to be beautiful, sublime, majestic, and so on. Soon they had the residents of the kingdom speaking as they did and, indeed, *seeing* the mountains as they did.

Were the mountains beautiful all along, or did they become so only after the poets had effected their "conversion"? Is beauty in the eye of the beholder, or can things be beautiful even when no one sees them this way?[1]

How should one decide whether the mountains are beautiful at any given historical moment? Should it be a matter of whether certain people think or say they are? If so, which people? Or should it be a matter of how people experience them? If so, what sorts of experience guarantee that something is beautiful? Is the experience of beauty unique and irreducible? Or does it share something with other experiences? Imagine mountains so remote they may never have been seen by anyone—and perhaps never will be. Could these mountains be beautiful? Is the beauty of an object a function of the way we see it or a function of the way it really is?

LOSING THE BEAUTY CONTEST

Imagine that the runner-up in a beauty contest is suing the organizers and judges. She alleges that only because the judges failed to adhere to their written instructions was she not selected as the winner. The judges' arbitrary and capricious behavior, she claims, has caused her humiliation, loss of reputation, and loss of commercial opportunities.

The crucial passage in the judges' instructions states: "This is purely a *beauty* contest; you are not to take account of talent, congeniality, personality, or anything other than beauty in reaching your determinations." In support of her claim that she should have won, the plaintiff offers material evidence, including the following: (1) a detailed statistical report showing that in every pertinent physical dimension, from toe size to eyebrow thickness, the plaintiff's features are more like those of other admitted beauties (including the prior winners of this annual contest) than are those of any other contestant, and (2) computer analysis and expert testimony supporting the reliability of this report.

If the jury accepts item 2 above as accurate, and agrees with the plaintiff's selection of "admitted beauties" in item 1, should the plaintiff win the case?

Is beauty simply a matter of individual whim and fancy, or may one appeal to objective standards in deciding what is beautiful? In judging whether A is more beautiful than B, should someone have in mind a set of ideal qualities, or configurations of qualities, that A more nearly approximates? How much weight should be given to past judgments of beauty in reaching present judgments? How much weight should be given to the declared views of large numbers of people on this point? Could most people be wrong about what is beautiful? Could everyone be wrong? The evidence the plaintiff presents is available to her partly because of recent advances in the technology of measurement and in the integration of statistical information. Do such advances make our judgments of beauty more accurate than those of our forebears, who merely "eyeballed" the objects they judged?

REMAINS OF THE INCA PALACE

Four hikers in a remote mountainous region of Peru come upon the nearly intact ruins of a breathtaking Inca palace. Covered with fanciful carvings, and encrusted with jade and gold ornaments, it is a dazzling sight in the high morning sunshine.

"Beautiful," whispers the first, "simply beautiful!"

"I can't agree," says the second; "It's a wonderful discovery, of course. But it's one of those ancient extravagances that were designed simply to be stared at; it lacks the warmth and functional humanity that makes things beautiful."

"Right," says the third, "It doesn't do a thing for me, either; but as you know I don't care for much of anything but . . ."

"Restaurants and bars!" his companions chime in, laughing.

The fourth shakes his head gravely and thoughtfully. "No," he says, "it's magnificent, grand, and awe-inspiring, all right; but, knowing that it was built with the sweat, pain, and broken lives of slaves for the glorification of a ruling elite, I just cannot find it beautiful."

The four fall silent; but in a short while the first hiker speaks up again: "I understand and agree with much of what you've all said. Yet I'm still convinced that this ruined palace is beautiful. You see, I don't think its beauty has much to do with who made it, or how, or for what. Indeed, it would be just as beautiful if it turned out we were all hallucinating right now, and the thing didn't exist at all. What makes it beautiful is what happens in *me* as I contemplate it. And I am inwardly sure beyond the slightest shade of doubt that that ruin is beautiful."[2]

Is the first hiker right to insist that beauty judgments may be detached from the reality of things judged beautiful? More generally, can judgments of aesthetic beauty be insulated from other forms of value judgments, including moral, political, and religious judgments, and perhaps also judgments of nonaesthetic "taste"? If we recognize something as morally ugly, should we be inclined to see it as aesthetically ugly as well? What is the role of aesthetic experience in shaping and determining aesthetic values?

CRITICAL AND UNCRITICAL USES OF "BEAUTY" AND "UGLINESS"

Any parents can tell you that there is ample evidence, based on the widest reports, that their babies are beautiful. It would seem to follow from this that all babies are beautiful, provided the reports can be trusted. Can they be trusted? Are all babies beautiful? Or is there more to the question of whether all babies are beautiful than the validity of reports? Parents know that people often mistake the gender of their babies; why shouldn't they expect that people are equally likely to misjudge their beauty? Is it harder to make mistakes about beauty? Or is beauty simply not the kind of thing about which one can be mistaken?

It is perhaps no less remarkable that people should rest secure in their aesthetic judgments than that they should have such an ample repertoire of them in the first place. People who hesitate to express geographical, political, theological, and even arithmetic judgments will often be quite tenacious in their views about what is beautiful and what is ugly. Even though they are often at a loss to explain why they hold these views, they are generally loath to give them up and cannot be talked into narrowing their scope. *De gustibus non est disputandum*, we are fond of saying: matters of taste are not a subject for (rational) disputation.

Why might this be? Perhaps it is because there is an affinity between saying that something is beautiful and saying that one *likes* it, and, by the same token, between saying that something is ugly and saying that one *dislikes* it. People in general have an enormous inventory of likes and dislikes they are prepared to declare and about which they regard themselves the only reliable experts. But an affinity is not an identity. Although deeming something beautiful may imply liking it, and deeming something ugly may imply disliking it, there certainly appears to be more to a thing's being beautiful or ugly than *merely* being liked or disliked. Most people will readily concede that there are lots of things they like that they will not call beautiful and lots of things they dislike that are not ugly. I may like boxing matches but I wouldn't be tempted to call them beautiful; I dislike salted potatoes but wouldn't say they're ugly. So it appears that liking or disliking a thing may be a *necessary* condition of its being judged to be beautiful or ugly, but it is not a *sufficient* condition.

Suppose that, as we review the way we and others ascribe beauty and ugliness to things, we find that wherever something is said to be attractive people are prepared to assent to its beauty, and wherever something is thought repulsive they are prepared to assent to its ugliness. Inquiring further, we find that people explain their willingness to call things attractive or repulsive by saying that they are so *because* they're beautiful or ugly in certain ways. Yet we find that not all things called beautiful are ones we found to be attractive and not all things called ugly are found to be repulsive. Attractiveness and repulsiveness, then, are at best *sufficient* though not *necessary* conditions of beauty and ugliness.

When people disagree, as they do almost endlessly, about matters of beauty, ugliness, and other aesthetic values, they may be differing with one another on two fronts. First, they may differ as to what it means to call a thing beautiful, ugly, and so on. Second, they may differ as to which things are to be counted beautiful, which ugly, and so on, even if they agree on the first issue. How should these disputes be resolved?

Appeal to majority opinion may be inappropriate here, because opinions on these issues can be vague, incomplete, inconsistent, and changeable. Moreover, many people insist that their own judgments on aesthetic matters are not subject to supervenience by those of others. A theory of aesthetic value—for instance, a theory of beauty—is based on a set of reasoned arguments delineating criteria, credentials, or defining features of that value. Some theories claim to identify features that, taken together, are both necessary and sufficient grounds for a thing's having a given value; other theories do not, either because necessary and sufficient conditions cannot be identified, or because these empirical details are held to be inappropriate means of guiding usage and resolving aesthetic disputes. Every theory, however, advances reasons for accepting one or another ascriptive policy or standard of use; that is, every theory argues for one or another resolution to the first kind of dispute mentioned above. The prevailing assumption is that once it is clear what it means to say that something is beautiful, differences about what is beautiful will disappear. If they do not, reason can go no farther, and the differences will simply remain, subject to modification only by new information about the things observed and about the process of observation.

A view of aesthetic value for which no theoretical basis or principled defense is proposed is an *uncritical* view. Philosophical aesthetics provides critical views of beauty and other values, presenting a wide variety of theories in the forums of public discussion and published debate, where rival theories and proposals for modification and rejection of their components compete openly.

GENERAL AND PARTICULAR BEAUTY

Historically, beauty has been the subject of far more, and more interesting, discussion than any other aesthetic value. Yet the first question that must be faced in the construction of a theory of beauty is: How much of the field of aesthetic value does this concept occupy?

If beauty is taken to be a particularly commodious concept, it may follow that whatever has any trace of positive aesthetic value at all is, to that extent, beautiful. According to one such view, pleasure is the key to aesthetic value in general. As John Ruskin put it, "[A]ny material object which can give us pleasure in the contemplation of its outward qualities without any direct and definite exertion of the intellect, [is] in some way or in some degree beautiful."[3]

This certainly appears to be an exaggerated claim, for it is easy to contemplate qualities of material objects (e.g., unfavorable press notices about our rivals) that do cause us pleasure but do not, or should not, count as beautiful. Perhaps it might be argued that all ignoble pleasures involve some exertion of the intellect or attach themselves to meanings rather than to material objects per se. But, no matter how it is interpreted, Ruskin's is an extremely generous view of beauty. In his opinion, beauty subsumes the sublime, the elegant, the comical, the delightful, the dainty, the picturesque, and a vast array of other subconcepts ordinarily distinguished from it. Would it make better sense to regard beauty as one positive aesthetic attribute among the rest, rather than a dominant genus under which most, if not all, other positive aesthetic attributes are presented as species?

Some theorists have been inclined to take a broad view of one sort of beauty and a narrower view of others. R. G. Collingwood, for instance, insists that

> the highest beauty somehow contains within itself subordinate and contributory elements, both the sublime and the comic, and indeed all other forms of beauty; so that these forms appear as parts of a whole, the whole being beauty.... Between these two poles of sublimity and comedy lies the whole of that experience which is the contemplation of perfect beauty.[4]

Others have taken a much more restricted view, insisting that beauty is one, but just one, high aesthetic value. In deciding whether something should be called beautiful, then, it will obviously be important to make clear whether beauty is being attributed to its object in the wider, generic sense, or in some narrower, specific sense. If something is deemed "pretty," say, that may count decisively toward qualifying it as beautiful in the former, but not in the latter, sense.

SUBJECTIVE AND OBJECTIVE BEAUTY

The most frequently asked (and possibly the most misleading) question about beauty is whether it is objective or subjective. The chief reason this question is potentially misleading is that people are, for the most part, quite unclear as to what they mean by "objective" and "subjective" in this context. It is an ancient muddle and one about which philosophers of art from Plato forward have had much to say. E. F. Carritt once posed the question in a way that looks helpful: "Is beauty ... objective or subjective? Is it a property of things independently of us, like the weight of a sovereign, or rather, like the coin's value, a property lent them by the human mind?"[5]

What a coin weighs does not (in any obvious sense) depend on what you or I think, argue, or hope. What it is worth, however, depends in some measure on some or all of these. But it would be rash to suppose that the coin's objective qualities are as utterly independent of us as Carritt's dichotomy suggests. In the wake of a nuclear holocaust destroying all life on this planet, how much would a sovereign weigh? Would it have weight without there being someone to weigh it? Would it have color if there were no eyes to see it? Would its inscription be English words if there were no one to read them? Perhaps we would want to say that under such conditions it is not a sovereign at all, but merely a lump of metal.

But there are difficulties with a thoroughgoing subjectivist view such as Carritt's. When we speak of a coin's value as being "lent it by the human mind," it seems rash to suppose that the coin is a purely neutral object to which *any* value whatever might be assigned. As the objectivist points out, the coin's value does not seem to depend *wholly* on mental fiat; surely the way the world *is* imposes some limitation on the capacity of the mind to lend values, and part of the reason a coin can have the value it does in commercial transactions has to do with its durability, portability, and so on. If I decide to think of a pile of gravel as more beautiful than a butterfly's wing, does my mere thinking make it so?

The objectivist insistence that beauty is a real quality, not a matter of subjective imposition of value on a neutral object, is stated with particular force by C. E. M. Joad:

> Beauty is an independent, self-sufficient object. . . . [A]s such it is a real and unique factor in the universe, and . . . it does not depend for being what it is upon any of the other factors in the universe. . . . When I say that a picture or a piece of music is beautiful, I am not making a statement about any feeling that I or any other person or body of persons may have or have had in regard to it, or about a relation subsisting between my mind and the picture or piece of music in question, but . . . about a quality or property possessed by the picture or piece of music itself.[6]

In starkest contrast, perhaps the most extreme form of the subjectivist tendency is to be found in the works of George Santayana, who defined beauty simply as "pleasure regarded as the quality of a thing.'"[7] In a contemporary version, Virgil Aldrich's subjectivist theory of beauty does not detach beauty from its objects and identify it entirely with a feeling in the subject, but it does stress the primacy of feeling:

> The airy radiance of a thing of beauty is very much akin to, if not identical with, the feeling of him whom it enthralls. That is why it is a joy forever. To him it seems as if he consummates his emotional self in the beautiful object. He swathes it with his own feelings, and thereby lends to it a good part of its appeal.[8]

If Santayana and Aldrich are right, the mountains of the remote alpine kingdom cannot have been beautiful before they were seen as beautiful, because the requisite quality of feeling was, up to that point, missing. If Joad is right, they were beautiful all along; people just failed to recognize this.

Efforts to reconcile objectivist and subjectivist tendencies have moved aesthetic theory in the direction of recognizing some necessary contribution on both sides. There must, on the one hand, be something in the composition, configuration, or setting of the object that invites the attribution of beauty; and there must, on the other, be something in the constitution of the mind that is susceptible to the special impact such an object can have on it. Collingwood put the point this way:

> [R]eal beauty is neither "objective" nor "subjective" in any sense that excludes the other. It is an experience in which the mind finds itself in the object, the mind rising to the level of the object and the object being, as it were, preadapted to evoke the fullest expression of the mind's powers.[9]

THE STANDARD OF BEAUTY

Frequently, theories of beauty propose *standards* that are meant to support some beauty claims and discredit others, or that are meant to provide a measure of relative degrees of beauty within a group of objects. In the case of the beauty contest runner-up, a claim is made that one contestant is conclusively more beautiful than the others because, as she maintains, she comes closer than any other contestant to fulfilling criteria that constitute the standard of correct judgment. As it happens, the standard to which she appeals is *implicit*; it has not been stated openly, but is instead revealed (she maintains) in a series of past judgments and presumably may be educed from them. Many theories of beauty attempt to make *explicit* standards that are implicit in what we say and do. To prevail, the contestant may find it helpful, and perhaps even unavoidable, to rely upon one such theory. There are, of course, many reasons why she might still fail. She might have struck upon one good standard, but not the one the judges were in fact required to apply; she might have been right about the standard, but wrong about their application of it; and, worst of all, there might be no true standard after all, but only a discouraging welter of approbations, disapprobations, preferences, feelings, and gestures.

The last of these positions—a form of value-skepticism—is not without its recent philosophical supporters. Ludwig Wittgenstein, for instance, once remarked:

> We think we have to talk about aesthetic judgments like 'This is beautiful', but we find that if we have to talk about aesthetic judgments we don't find these words at all, but a word used something like a gesture, accompanying a complicated activity. . . . A characteristic thing about our language is that a large number of words used under these circumstances are adjectives—'fine,' 'lovely,' etc. But you see that this is by no means necessary. . . . Would it matter if instead of saying "This is lovely," I just said "Ah!" and smiled, or just rubbed my stomach?[10]

Wittgenstein seems to have meant that the search for a standard of beauty is futile because claiming that something is beautiful is not asserting that it possesses certain identifiable qualities or meets some test; rather, it is making a *gesture* of approval, perhaps in a way that invites others to join in the approval. But what should be the grounds for joining in? Under what conditions is the gesture apt? Can we learn anything from the smiles, sighs, and belly-rubbings of others; and can we inform them with ours?

Historically, few aestheticians have accepted this skeptical view. Most have maintained that standards of beauty can be stated and have undertaken to state them. It is true that the record of attempts to state them is marked by unremitting diversity and controversy. But disagreement has, for the most part, centered on the issue of what the criteria of beauty are, and not on whether beauty has any criteria. Indeed, attempts to identify the criteria of beauty began with the ancient Greeks. For instance, Aristotle said that the "chief forms of beauty are order and symmetry and definiteness."[11] And he went on to explain that, "to be beautiful, a living creature, and every whole made up of parts, must not only present a certain order in its arrangement of parts, but also must be of a certain definite magnitude. Beauty is a matter of size and order."[12]

Here we have the beginnings, at least, of a program for determining the beauty of things that might be of use to the irate beauty contestant. Aristotle provided explicit instructions for the judges: look for order, symmetry, definiteness. His various successors have supplied amendments, refinements, and clarifications. St. Thomas Aquinas, for example, identified the elements of order requisite for beauty as integrity or perfection, due proportion or harmony, and brightness or clarity.[13]

Aristotle's and Thomas's are "objectivist" views, early efforts in a continuing tradition of attempts to state a standard of beauty. In contrast, subjectivist views shift attention away from the properties of beautiful objects to the mental processes involved in appreciation of them. David Hume's essay, "Of The Standard Of Taste," does not aspire to identify features of beauty so much as it aims to identify mental characteristics conducive to judging that it is present:

> Strong sense, united to delicate sentiment, improved by practice, perfected by comparison, and cleared of all prejudice, can alone entitle critics to this valuable character [i.e., sound aesthetic judgment]; and the joint verdict of such, wherever they are to be found, is the true standard of taste and beauty.[14]

Immanuel Kant, too, analyzed beauty chiefly by characterizing its inward effects rather than its outward causes (see note 2 at the end of this chapter). He suggested that we can know when we are rightly judging a thing to be beautiful by noticing that our mental faculties are being stimulated in such a way that the imagination enters into a kind of free play with the cognitive powers, producing a variety of pleasure completely independent of interest or of concern over whether the thing taken to be beautiful actually exists. But although he analyzed beauty by its inward effects, Kant did not hold that it was simply a "matter of taste, not to be disputed" in which there were no grounds for agreement or the resolution for disagreement. Rather, he argued that judgments of beauty are subjectively universal; in other words, they ought to be held valid for everyone in that they have no features that would tie them to any particular person's interest.[15]

If questions of beauty are to be resolved by referring objects (e.g., beauty contest contestants) to standards, the judgment process will inevitably turn on two different questions of detail: First, the standard itself will have to be defended successfully against objections and counterclaims in the course of aesthetic controversy. Second, it will have to be shown that a given object meets the qualifications presented in the standard (or that it does so more nearly than do its rivals). This is true whether the standards are objectively or subjectively stated. Philosophical aesthetics aims to provide assistance in defending standards but can be of no help in determining whether an object actually meets them.

BEAUTY AND OTHER AESTHETIC VALUES

Beauty is, of course, but one aesthetic value among others, albeit a particularly prominent one; however, as we mentioned earlier, many theorists regard beauty as comprehending most other positive aesthetic values. Aesthetic values typically come into play when we are making judgments about artworks or other aesthetic objects (or considering and assessing the judgments of others). In the course of these practices, we are more likely to rely on a wide range of value concepts than on beauty alone. As we observed, we will speak of objects as elegant, sublime, horrible, comical, dainty, picturesque, dumpy, dreary, and so on, and perhaps only rarely speak of them as beautiful or ugly. The discussion of beauty we have just pursued may throw some light on these other concepts—but how much, and how directly? It may be, for instance, that the objective/subjective distinction we observed in relation to judgments of beauty will pertain to all other values as well. But it is likely that there are features distinctive to each value that veer away from our analysis of beauty and require independent treatment. And it is equally likely that these values will interact in a highly complex manner, sometimes complementing one another, sometimes conflicting, and often working together in subtle and unpredictable ways.

As we shall see again in Chapter 6, all of this makes the enterprise of aesthetic judgment a highly complicated business. Clearly, we cannot in this limited space begin to present a perspicuous account of general aesthetic value or its role in aesthetic judgment. It will, however, be useful to consider one other value, namely, *ugliness*. In a sense, this will clarify and extend our discussion of beauty; for just as in coming to know who we are we must take stock of who we are not, we may best understand beauty by considering it together with its tandem opposite. Equally important, even a brief discussion of ugliness will serve to expose the controversial status of relations between aesthetic values. For, although beauty and ugliness may at first seem unproblematically related as antonyms, a closer inspection reveals that their connection and opposition may be understood in several ways, each with different consequences for aesthetic judgment.

THE RELATION OF BEAUTY TO UGLINESS

In many respects, the aesthetic analysis of ugliness is similar to that of beauty. Questions of definability, objectivity or subjectivity, generality or particularity, skepticism, and so on arise for the one as readily as for the other. This is not to say, however, that the concepts are parallel or paired in any strict sense. Although there is undeniably an opposition between beauty and ugliness, aesthetic theorists have long disagreed over how to characterize that opposition. Is it contradiction, contrariety, polar repulsion, or some more complicated or subtle relation? Is everything ugly necessarily not beautiful, and vice versa? Or are there some beautiful ugly things and some things that are ugly despite their beauty?

In the case about the hikers, the fourth hiker concluded that the Inca palace *could not* be beautiful, despite appearances, because it was (morally) ugly. The underlying assumption must be that the ugliness of a thing does not merely militate against its beauty, it cancels it. And lurking behind this assumption seems to be another—that the incompatibility of these concepts follows from their opposing uses as markers of value; what is highly valued, either morally or aesthetically, cannot be at the same time disvalued in either domain. This idea, that one principle governs both judgments of beauty and ugliness as well as judgments of good and evil, may be traced to Plotinus in the third century A.D.:

> All shapelessness whose kind admits of pattern and of form, as long as it remains outside of Reason and Idea, has not been entirely mastered by Reason, the matter not yielding at all points and in all respects to Ideal Form, is ugly by that very isolation from the Divine Thought. But where the Ideal Form has entered, it has grouped and coordinated what from a diversity of parts was to become a unity; it has rallied confusion into cooperation. . . . And on what has thus been compacted to unity, Beauty enthrones itself, giving itself to the parts as to the sum. This, then, is how the material thing becomes beautiful—by communicating in the thought that flows from the Divine.[16]

Even if beauty and ugliness lie at opposite ends of the same scale, however, it does not follow that what is ugly cannot be in some measure beautiful (and vice versa). For there are at least two senses in which the claim that they are "on the same scale" might be taken. On the one hand, we might think of the scale itself representing units of aesthetic value, of which the highest is called beautiful, the lowest ugly, and the gradations in between lesser degrees of both values, which meet in the middle at neutrality. Perhaps this is pretty much the picture Plotinus had in mind; in any event it would make clear why the ugly cannot be beautiful and vice versa. On the other hand, we might think of the scale as representing units of beauty, of which the highest is pure, or ideal, beauty and the lowest is beauty reduced to its absolute minimum, which we may choose to call ugliness. St. Augustine appears to have held such a view; he thought that what we humans are disposed to call ugly is always only a lesser degree of beauty, the unbeautiful aspect, which reveals the imperfection of the observer rather than the observed. In this view, it is clear, the ugly is not only compatible with the beautiful but must partake of it, though to a vanishingly small degree. Thus, Augustine held, ugliness does not really exist; it is simply the occasion on which we fail to see beauty, just as we experience no positive evil, but only the absence of good. Many religious mystics hold similar views, as do some artists and art theorists. John Constable, for example, is reported to have said: "No, madam, there is nothing ugly; I never saw an ugly thing in my life: for let the form of an object be what it may,—light, shade, and perspective will always make it beautiful."[17]

Some theorists have argued that beauty and ugliness are asymmetrical; they do not fall on the same scale at all. For instance, Benedetto Croce conceived of beauty as "successful expression," a status that does not admit of degrees. Ugliness, in contrast, does admit of degrees, since there are infinite gradations of inadequate or incomplete expression. Furthermore, some writers, particularly the Romantics, have found a hidden affinity between ugliness and beauty. The two may, for instance, be seen to cooperate as influences heightening our sensibilities as we make progress toward some important metaphysical objective. Or they may serve as foils for each other, much as the goodness of certain characters in a play is made the more striking by the villainy of others. In some instances, proponents of such views maintain, the ugly can be converted to beauty in the process. Samuel Alexander observed: "Ugliness . . . is an ingredient in aesthetic beauty, as the discords in music or the horrors of the tragedy. When it becomes ugly as a kind of beauty it has been transmuted. Such ugliness is difficult beauty."[18] Alexander's notion of difficult beauty is itself difficult to understand and accept. But it hints at the positive role ugliness may play in art, a role for which its negative nature may seem to have left it unprepared.

THE "PROBLEM OF THE UGLY" IN ART

How can art that portrays, dwells on, or even glorifies ugliness have positive aesthetic value? Why do grotesques, *danses macabres*, and graphic pictures of sordid subjects sometimes strike us as great art, even as beautiful? Some artists, for example, Francis Bacon, seem to revel in deliberate and shocking ugliness. In the *Poetics*, Aristotle points both to the purgative value of representations of untoward events and to the admiration we have for the accuracy of such representations; both teach us important lessons about the powers and limitations of mankind. Similarly, Plutarch said:

> In essence, the ugly cannot become beautiful; but the imitation is admired if it is a likeness. The picture of an ugly thing cannot be a beautiful picture; if it were, it could not be suitable to or consistent with its original. . . . The reason why we admire such representations in art . . . is [that] the artist's cunning has an affinity for our intelligence.[19]

If this view were sound, however, the positive value (the beauty?) of artistic portrayals of ugliness might be thought to reside in our admiration of the artist, as revealed in his or her work, rather than in the work or its subject. But is the value of ugliness in art restricted to revealing beauty in the skill of its representation? Both artists and aestheticians have argued that it is not. In *The Flowers of Evil* Charles Baudelaire revels in his discovery that a wide variety of truly ugly objects have properties that, under certain conditions, can be seen as beautiful. Though we may admire Baudelaire's skill, imagination, and ingenuity in describing these things, it is ultimately the ugliness of the things themselves that the reader finds engaging. In *The Aesthetic of Ugliness* Karl Rosenkranz argues that artistic rendition of ugly objects is an indispensable element in the full and honest presentation of the world requisite for man's spiritual edification:

> If art is not to represent the idea in a merely one-sided way it cannot dispense with the ugly. . . . If mind and nature are to be admitted to presentation in their full dramatic depth, then the ugly of nature, and the evil and diabolic, must not be omitted.[20]

If this last view is correct, however, then those who condemn works that portray ugliness (as, for example, the fourth hiker, who

Francis Bacon, *Painting*, 1946. Oil and tempera on canvas, 6'5⅞" x 52".
The Museum of Modern Art, New York.
Purchase.

declines to call beautiful that which is morally ugly) are missing a bet, for such a portrayal may be a valuable heuristic aid to our moral development. Similarly, an art form with an ugly and immoral subject matter may serve a profoundly moral end. Cockfights, for instance, are widely regarded as inherently ugly spectacles—aesthetically as well as morally. Yet the anthropologist Clifford Geertz has argued that, in certain cultures, cockfights are an edifying artform.

> Like any art form . . . the cockfight renders ordinary, everyday experience comprehensible by presenting it in terms of acts and objects which have had their practical consequences removed and been reduced (or, if you prefer, raised) to the level of sheer appearances, where their meaning can be more powerfully articulated and more exactly perceived. . . . An image, fiction, a model, a metaphor, the cockfight is a means of expression; its function is neither to assuage social passions nor to heighten them (though in its playing-with-fire way it does a bit of both), but, in a medium of feathers, blood, crowds, and money, to display them. . . . The slaughter in the cock ring is not a depiction of how things literally are among men, but, what is almost worse, of how, from a particular angle, they imaginatively are.[21]

Of course, Geertz does not use the terms "beautiful" and "ugly" in this striking passage; his remarks conjure up the tensions between beauty and ugliness and between moral and aesthetic value without mentioning them. As he sees it, the implicit values at issue are fully submerged in the aesthetic experience of the cockfight. These values, and perhaps a host of others, mingle, compete, and come to have force and meaning purely as a function of the peculiarly intense experience the audience has in viewing this violent event. Perhaps it would be possible to tease apart all these values and reach a complex judgment of the event by weighing them all and comparing their priorities. But in doing so it would be easy to lose sight of the primacy of the *experience* itself. The claim being made here is that the cockfight fuses values together in the crucible of a rare and distinctive kind of experience, precisely the kind that not only makes art but makes it worthwhile.

AESTHETIC EXPERIENCE

What, however, is "aesthetic experience"? Is it possible to demarcate this from the vast array of other kinds of experience? And if we can, is it possible to identify just what it is in experiences of the aesthetic kind that lends them their (allegedly) unique value?

It is not easy to be very clear about these matters, partly because writers who have considered them have said widely disparate things and have often compounded the confusion with vagueness and obscurity. It is easy to say that the cockfight spectator Geertz describes is, if undistracted and fully engaged in the event, having an aesthetic experience. Likewise, the first hiker, who found the Inca palace beautiful, seemed to be having one. But it is less easy to say just what it is they are having. Sometimes the concept "aesthetic experience" is used to refer to psychological phenomena of a specific, recognizable type—a special variety of thrills and tingles we prize for their own sake. Sometimes, however, it is used to refer to *whatever* mental states we undergo when we perceive things in a certain frame of mind, the so-called aesthetic attitude, for example. And sometimes it is used to refer to all mental aspects of our acquaintance with whatever objects we take to be aesthetic objects. Unfortunately, many discussions fail to make clear which of these uses are in play.

This much is clear, however. There is all the difference in the world between what happens to us when we look at the mountains of the remote alpine kingdom with our heads full of meteorology or forestry or real estate, and what happens when we simply savor their lines and shadows, their angularities and smoothnesses, their dazzle and blush in the waning daylight. It may well be that your savoring differs from mine in various respects, and even that my savoring differs in some ways from one moment to the next. But there is a familiar, undeniable satisfaction here that does seem, before reflection, to stand apart from other experiences—something we prize in a way all its own. This plain, stubborn perception is the inspiration behind a tremendous variety of "theories of the aesthetic" and the root of endless controversies about the right way to account for it.

Once again, the ancients had a good many useful things to say on the subject. Plato, for example, was highly suspicious of the "ecstatic" state of mind artists claimed to enjoy, chiefly because of the false knowledge it seemed to engender. But the first real heyday of philosophical speculation about aesthetic experience took place in England and Germany in the eighteenth and early nineteenth centuries. This was the period during which theories of "taste" blossomed and flourished. First Joseph Addison, Francis Hutcheson, Edmund Burke, and David Hume, then Immanuel Kant, Friedrich von Schiller, and Arthur Schopenhauer all undertook to explain the workings of those faculties and powers through which we are able to enjoy distinctively aesthetic phenomena. In addition, they sometimes sought to identify the sorts of things to which the faculties of taste best responded. Predictably, they reached different conclusions (in part because they often asked different questions); but this proved no obstacle to the popularity of their views with a wider public concerned chiefly to *cultivate* taste rather than understand it.

At the end of the nineteenth century, inspired in part by developments in the nascent science of psychology, a rather different account of aesthetic experience took hold. This was the "aesthetic attitude" theory, which maintains that a certain way of looking at things is an all-important precondition of aesthetic experience. The key element in the standard formulation of this theory is *distance*, the idea that, in order for aesthetic experience to take hold, ordinary, practical experience must be put out of reach. Its foremost proponent, Edward Bullough, explained this idea by describing the differences between nonaesthetic and aesthetic experience of a sea fog:

> Imagine a fog at sea; for most people it is an experience of acute unpleasantness. Apart from the physical annoyance and remoter forms of discomfort such as delays, it is apt to produce feelings of peculiar anxiety, fears of invisible dangers, strains of watching and listening for distant and unlocalised signals. . . . Nevertheless, a fog at sea can be a source of intense relish and enjoyment. Abstract from the experience of the sea fog, for the moment, its danger and practical unpleasantness, . . . direct the attention to the features "objectively" constituting the phenomenon—the veil surrounding you with an opaqueness as of transparent milk, blurring the outline of things and distorting their shapes into weird grotesqueness; observe the carrying-power of the air, . . . note the curious creamy smoothness of the water, . . . and, above all, the strange solitude and remoteness from the world . . . and the experience may acquire . . . a flavour of such concentrated poignancy and delight as to contrast sharply with the blind and distempered anxiety of its other aspects.
>
> . . . In the fog, the transformation by Distance is produced . . . by putting the phenomenon, so to speak, out of gear with our practical, actual self.[22]

This vivid depiction strikes a familiar chord in most of us. Perhaps we have suffered through concerts or art exhibits during which practical concerns so interfered with our attention that we did not enjoy them at all. Perhaps we have experienced—on a roller coaster, say—an unexpected reversal of attitude similar to the one described above and have felt exhilaration where first we felt blind fear. Bullough and the other aesthetic attitude theorists would have us believe that experiences such as these afford us direct personal contact with that which sets the aesthetic off from the nonaesthetic and makes it valuable. What gives aesthetic experience, so conceived, its special worth is that in moving us away from our everyday practical concerns it conduces to the perception of the "objective," that is, the impersonally observable, qualities of things.

Some recent writers—for instance, Jerome Stolnitz—have tried to improve on Bullough's account by clarifying the way in which "distance" and similar features of the aesthetic attitude affect the way we see the world. Among other features they have taken to be essential to aesthetic attitude are disinterest (an absence of concern for any ulterior purpose), sympathy (an acceptance of objects on their own terms), and contemplation (an appreciation of objects that does not involve analysis or asking questions about them). However, other writers, for instance, George Dickie, have attacked Bullough's view and its successors by denying that there is any one thing that we can identify as *the* aesthetic attitude and by attempting to show that when we regard things in appropriate and rewarding ways our attention frequently does not exhibit the features the aesthetic attitude theorists say it should. They insist that there needn't be any conflict between practical concerns and aesthetic appreciation, and point to instances in which we observe, say, movies, critically and unsympathetically and yet seem to get the most out of them.

If, as these critics allege, the aesthetic attitude is a myth, it might seem to follow that aesthetic experience is also a myth. But this is true only if we take aesthetic experience to mean that which we enjoy when, and only when, we take the aesthetic attitude. Several recent theorists have proposed accounts of aesthetic experience that are independent of traditional claims about the aesthetic attitude. Virgil Aldrich's account stresses the peculiar ways in which aesthetic perceptiveness allows us to see one object as a series of interchangeable "aspects." We may, for example, see the object below alternatively as (1) a square suspended in a frame, (2) a lampshade seen from above, (3) a lampshade seen from below, (4) a tunnel seen head on, or (5) an aerial view of a truncated pyramid.[23] What makes experience aesthetic, Aldrich thinks, is fundamentally that it begins with "aspection"—the trained, and sometimes highly refined, ability to see the several aspects of things. In a rather different vein, Monroe Beardsley has suggested that the key to aesthetic experience is the way we tie mental activity to the form and qualities of certain objects to render that activity unified, intense, complex, and pleasurable.[24]

Aldrich, Beardsley, and other contemporary writers have sought to explain the cherished phenomena of aesthetic experience as richly

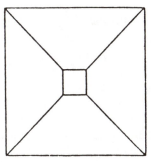

Virgil C. Aldrich, *Philosophy of Art* © 1963, p. 20. Reprinted by permission of Prentice-Hall, Inc., Englewood Cliffs, N.J.

diverse rather than narrowly centered on a criterion of taste or a few
fixed aspects of aesthetic attitude. Nevertheless, their theories, like
those of their predecessors, have been criticized as missing the mark,
either by failing to recognize essential conditions of aesthetic experience, or by wrongly supposing that aesthetic experience is a concept
coherent enough to have necessary and sufficient conditions. Like the
theoretical issues discussed previously, aesthetic experience remains a
topic of lively and unremitting debate.

An important companion issue is the question of how aesthetic
experience (however conceived) is related to aesthetic value. According
to some views, the experience is the important thing, and once one has
it the value terms one chooses to describe or promote it are more or
less optional and perhaps interchangeable. According to others, our
appreciation of aesthetic values leads us into aesthetic experience,
helps us re-identify experiences of a given kind, and makes plain why
we prize them. Thus we are left with a question: Is it our sense of
beauty and ugliness that makes our experience of certain objects so
worthwhile, or is it our wordless delight or disgust in the experience
itself that creates these values? Are concepts like "beautiful," "ugly,"
"sublime," and all the rest just feeble and often ineffectual reminders
of what counts, or are *they* what counts, and our fleeting aesthetic
experiences simply their erratic and fragmentary revelations? These
questions, like those we have raised earlier about beauty, ugliness, and
aesthetic experience, remain importantly, and intriguingly, open.

CASES

Beauty and Other Aesthetic Values

2-1. TWO WORLDS

Imagine two worlds, said G. E. Moore, one beautiful, one ugly. Imagine
the beautiful world as having "mountains, rivers, the sea; trees, and
sunsets, stars and moon . . . all combined in the most exquisite
proportions," and the ugly world as "one heap of filth, containing
everything that is most disgusting to us . . . without one redeeming
feature."[25] But also imagine that neither world will ever be experienced
by any human being—no one will ever live in either one, or even see
it. If only one world could exist, which should it be?

Moore thought that it would be better to have the beautiful one
exist than the ugly one, even if there were *no* possibility of human
experience of either world. Is Moore right? What *reason* could be given

for preferring the beautiful world to the ugly one when neither world would ever be lived in or even seen by human beings? Or does any reason ultimately make covert appeal to human experience? Does beauty have intrinsic value, or not?[26]—M.P.B.

2-2. BEAUTIFUL PLUMAGE

In many species of birds, the male has brilliant plumage, which attracts females of the same species: think of the peacock, the China pheasant, the many varieties of parrot, and so on.

Is it correct to say that the male plumage is *beautiful* or that the female birds *find the plumage beautiful?* Can birds appreciate beauty? How would we go about trying to answer this question, if the only observation we can make is that the females are indeed attracted by the plumage? Is there human beauty versus bird beauty? If so, should all our references to beauty be of the form, beautiful to whom? Or are only human beings able to appreciate beauty, and if so, what is it about human beings that gives them this distinction?—M.P.B.

2-3. MARTIAN MARSKS

Let us suppose that we discover on Mars remnants of a culture that died long ago. Most of the things we find are completely alien to us; we cannot even guess how they were used. We have not deciphered the Martian language and we know nothing about the physical appearance of the Martians, whose bodies must have completely disintegrated millions of years ago. One set of objects, however, is strikingly familiar to us: we find numerous items that look exactly like African masks. We name them Marsks. Again, we have no idea how these objects were made by the Martians, and for what purpose.

Are the Marsks works of art? Are they beautiful? Are they meaningful? If yes, how? If not, are African masks works of art? Are they beautiful? Are they meaningful to us? After all, we know very little of the culture that produced them.—E.M.Z.

2-4. A MAN-MADE GRAND CANYON

Defending a secular view of nature, Frederick Turner wrote:

> Suppose the Grand Canyon were man-made. It could have been formed (though it wasn't) by agricultural or industrial erosion; the results of poor farming methods can look very similar—artificial badlands—if on a smaller scale. Would this hideous scar on the fair face of the earth still be a national park? Would anyone visit it other than groups of awed schoolchildren studying Environmental Destruction, absorbing the

dreadful lesson of what can happen to a desert raped by human exploit-
ers? Strip mining can produce spectacular and dramatic landscapes.
W. H. Auden loved the lead-mining landscapes of Cornwall above all
others; the evocative and aromatic hillsides of the Mediterranean, with
their olives, sages, thyme, and dwarf conifers, are a result of centuries of
deforestation, goat herding, and the building of roads and cities.[27]

If aesthetic appreciation is of the appearance of things, must a
man-made Grand Canyon be a "hideous scar on the fair face of the
earth"? Cannot it be, rather, as beautiful and as inspiring as the
original? If not, must "the evocative and aromatic hillsides of the
Mediterranean" be seen as somewhat less beautiful when understood
in light of their origins in human exploitation?—A.C.

2-5. THE PICTURESQUE

In 1840, Nathaniel Willis wrote of the upstate New York landscape
around Lake George:

> The mountains on the shore of this exquisite lake consist of two great
> ranges.... Both these ranges alternately approach the lake, so as to
> constitute a considerable part of its shores, and recede from it again to
> the distance sometimes of two or three miles. The summits of these
> mountains are of almost every figure, from the arch, to the bold, bluff,
> and sharp cone.... There is every variety of chasm, crag, promontory,
> and peak, which a painter would require for the noblest composition of
> mountain scenery.[28]

Willis seems to suggest, in appealing to the later-eighteenth- and
early-nineteenth-century notion of the "picturesque,"[29] that the
beauty here is such that any painter who faithfully represented the
scenic landscape would create a beautiful picture.

Is the beauty of such scenery due to its resembling or suggesting
a beautiful picture or painting? To call it *picturesque* seems to imply
this, since the term is thought to have been derived from the French
word *pittoresque,* meaning "of or suggesting a picture." But some
writers argue that the true root of the term lies in the Italian word
pittoresco, which means "having to do with a painter." In their view,
picturesque scenes please us not because they remind us of pictures,
but because in viewing them *we* become like painters, exercising our
powers of visual acuity and sensitivity to "compose" the scenery.

Are picturesque scenes, such as might be captured in a photograph
or postcard, beautiful simply because they resemble or remind us of
beautiful pictures? Or is their beauty better described as something
captured by an observer who has creatively framed a scene to be
appreciated? In other words, is the beauty of such a scene something it

has itself? Or does some (or even most) of our satisfaction in looking at it come from the contribution of the viewer, who acts like an artist in actually *composing* a natural scene for viewing? In short, is the French *pittoresque* ("like a picture") or the Italian *pittoresco* ("like a painter") the more plausible root for this type of beauty?—D.W.C.

2-6. THE SUBLIME

After crossing from France to Italy in late October, 1688, via the mountain pass at Mount Cenis in the Savoy Alps, the English critic and dramatist John Dennis described his experience in a letter:

> As soon as we had conquered one half [of the ascent], the unusual height in which we found ourselves, the impending rock that hung over us, the dreadful depth of the precipice, and the torrent that roared at the bottom, gave us such a view as was altogether new and amazing. On the other side of the torrent was a mountain that equalled ours, about the distance of thirty yards from us. Its craggy cliffs, which we half discerned through the misty gloom of the clouds that surrounded them, sometimes gave us a horrid prospect. And sometimes its face appeared smooth and beautiful as the most even and fruitful valleys. So different from themselves were the different parts of it: In the very same place nature was seen severe and wanton. In the meantime we walked upon the very brink, in a literal sense, of destruction; one stumble and both life and carcass [would have] been at once destroyed. The sense of all this produced different emotions in me, *viz.* a delightful horror, a terrible joy, and at the same time that I was infinitely pleased, I trembled.[30]

Was Dennis's experience of nature in crossing the pass an *aesthetic* experience? How can something so frightening simultaneously be pleasing? Do any experiences in the realm of art have this dual character as well, or is this experience of the sublime confined to nature and not possible for art?—D.W.C.

2-7. ENJOYING PORNOGRAPHY

Jim likes pornography—hard-core pornography, that is. In fact, the dirtier the picture, the more Jim enjoys looking at it. Like everyone else, Jim refers to the pictures as "sheer smut," but this does not shorten the time or lessen the pleasure with which he regards them.

One day, in Jim's aesthetics class, the professor explains Aquinas's view (a view shared by many contemporary aestheticians, e.g., J. O. Urmson) that beauty is that whose mere observation is pleasing. Jim wonders whether that implies that he finds pornographic pictures *beautiful.* So far he thought that the pictures were really ugly, quite sordid, but that some ugly things may nevertheless be pleasurable to look at. He wonders whether he was wrong all along; after all, it was the *mere observation* of smut that gave him pleasure.

But was Jim *merely* observing? Are the pictures Jim enjoys *beautiful*? Is Jim's pleasure in the pornographic pictures sufficient to show that Aquinas and Urmson were wrong in their definition of beauty? Or is something else going on here?—E.M.Z.

2-8. VAN GOGH'S UGLIEST PAINTING

Describing his own painting *The Night Cafe*, Van Gogh said:

> The picture is one of the ugliest I have done. . . . I have tried to express the terrible passions of humanity by means of red and green. The room is blood-red and dark yellow with a green billiard table in the middle; there are four citron-yellow lamps with a glow of orange and green. Everywhere there is a clash and contrast of the most disparate reds and greens. . . .[31]

Because Van Gogh himself insisted that the picture is ugly, must we agree with him? Because he asserted that it was "one of the ugliest I have done," must we also regard it as less valuable than his other, more beautiful pictures? Or if as he stated, he was trying to "express the power of darkness," does its ugliness make this painting a better one?—A.S.

Aesthetic Experience

2-9. LIFE ON THE MISSISSIPPI

In *Life on the Mississippi*, Mark Twain wrote:

> The face of the water, in time, became a wonderful book—a book that was a dead language to the uneducated passenger, but which told its mind to me without reserve, delivering its most cherished secrets as clearly as if it uttered them with a voice. . . . In truth, the passenger who could not read this book saw nothing but all manner of pretty pictures in it, painted by the sun and shaded by the clouds, whereas to the trained eye these were not pictures at all, but the grimmest and most dead-earnest of reading matter.
>
> Now when I had mastered the language of this water and had come to know every trifling feature that bordered the great river as familiarly as I knew the letters of the alphabet, I had made a valuable acquisition. But I had lost something, too. I had lost something which could never be restored to me while I lived. All the grace, the beauty, the poetry had gone out of the majestic river: I still keep in mind a certain wonderful

sunset which I witnessed when steamboating was new to me. A broad expanse of the river was turned to blood; in the middle distance the red hue brightened into gold, through which a solitary log came floating, black and conspicuous; in one place a long, slanting mark lay sparkling upon the water; in another the surface was broken by boiling, tumbling rings, that were as many-tinted as an opal; where the ruddy flush was faintest, was a smooth spot that was covered with graceful circles and radiating lines, ever so delicately traced; the shore on our left was densely wooded, and the sombre shadow that fell from this forest was broken in one place by a long, ruffled trail that shone like silver; and high above the forest wall a clean-stemmed dead tree waved a single leafy bough that glowed like a flame in the unobstructed splendor that was flowing from the sun. There were graceful curves, reflected images, woody heights, soft distances; and over the whole scene, far and near, the dissolving lights drifted steadily, enriching it, every passing moment, with new marvels of coloring.

I stood like one bewitched. I drank it in, in a speechless rapture. . . . But as I have said, a day came when . . . if that sunset scene had been repeated, I should have looked upon it without rapture, and should have commented upon it, inwardly, after this fashion: The sun means that we are going to have wind to-morrow; that floating log means that the river is rising, small thanks to it; that slanting mark on the water refers to a bluff reef which is going to kill somebody's steamboat one of these nights, if it keeps on stretching out like that; those tumbling "boils" show a dissolving bar and a changing channel there; . . . that tall dead tree, with a single living branch, is not going to last long, and then how is a body ever going to get through this blind place at night without the friendly old landmark?

No, the romance and the beauty were all gone from the river. . . . Since those days, I have pitied doctors from my heart. What does the lovely flush in a beauty's cheek mean to a doctor but a "break" that ripples above some deadly disease? . . . Does he ever see her beauty at all, or doesn't he simply comment upon her unwholesome condition all to himself? And doesn't he sometimes wonder whether he has gained most or lost most by learning his trade?[32]

Are understanding something and appreciating it aesthetically, as Twain suggests, mutually exclusive? Is Twain "interested" or "disinterested" in the river when he appreciates it most fully? Has Twain, like the doctor, "gained most" or "lost most" by mastering the language of the river?—A.C.

2-10.   NATURE AND ARTIFICE

How important is it that what we take to be nature actually *be* nature in order for us to appreciate it aesthetically? Consider the following example discussed by Immanuel Kant:

The song of birds proclaims their joyfulness and contentment with existence. At least we so interpret nature, whether or not it has this purpose. But this interest which we here take in beauty requires that it is the beauty of nature; it vanishes completely as soon as we realize we have been deceived and that it is only art—it vanishes so completely that taste can no longer find it beautiful or sight find it charming. What is more highly praised by poets than the bewitching and beautiful song of the nightingale in a lonely thicket on a still summer evening by the soft light of the moon? And yet we have instances where no such songster is to be found, but where a jovial host has played tricks on guests visiting him to enjoy the country air, and to their great satisfaction, by hiding in a bush a mischievous boy who knows how to produce this song exactly like nature (by means of a reed or a pipe in his mouth). But as soon as we are aware that it is a fraud, no one will remain long listening to this song which before was regarded so charming. And it is the same with the songs of all other birds. It must be nature, or must be regarded by us as nature, in order for us to take an immediate interest in the beautiful as such, and still more is this the case if we are to require that others should take an interest in it too.[33]

Is Kant right about cases like this? Does the discovery that the bird's song is not nature but a human imitation of nature significantly interfere with or change our appreciation of the song?—D.W.C.

2-11. CHARLES AND THE SLIME

Charles is watching a horror movie about a terrible green slime. He cringes in his seat as the slime oozes slowly but relentlessly over the earth destroying everything in its path. Soon a greasy head emerges from the undulating mass, and two beady eyes roll around, finally fixing on the camera. The slime, picking up speed, oozes on a new course straight toward the viewers. Charles emits a shriek and clutches desperately at his chair. Afterwards, still shaken, Charles confesses that he was "terrified" of the slime.[34]

Was Charles really afraid of the slime? His heart raced, his muscles tensed, his breath was short. But he didn't rush out to warn his family or call the police. It didn't even occur to him to look for a phone, or even to flee the theater. He knew the slime wasn't real and that he was in no danger. He did *say* that he was terrified of the slime, however. Must we take his word for it? Did he mean it? Could he be mistaken about what he felt? In general, what is the nature of the emotions evoked by works of fiction? Do we respond emotionally to fictional people and events in the ways we do to real ones?—K.W.

2-12. THE ILLUSION OF REALITY

Peter Ustinov was once asked on television why he made the film *Billy Budd* in black and white rather than in color.

"So that it would seem real," he explained.

"This was a strange reply," Ivor Montagu wrote later. "But it was stranger still that nobody seemed to find anything strange in it."[35]

Should the members of the audience have found Ustinov's comment strange? Most of us see real things in color, not in black and white, so why would we find more real those pictures of them that don't show colors than those that do? Or is there nothing strange about the illusion of reality that Ustinov sought to achieve?—F.L.

2-13. DARWIN'S EAR

Charles Darwin, the famous English naturalist and author, apparently had a poor musical ear. It is reported that he could neither hold nor easily recognize a tune, and a close friend spoke of his "want of musical memory." And yet Darwin was extremely fond of music. Darwin's friend described the intensity of feeling and great delight Darwin derived from the music of Handel, Mozart, and Beethoven, and Darwin is known to have often gone out of his way to listen to musical performances, especially the choir singing at King's College Chapel in Cambridge.

Darwin himself was aware of this curious state of affairs. He reported that his pleasure at hearing the choir at King's College Chapel was so intense "that my backbone would sometimes shiver." But he also remarked, "I am so utterly destitute of an ear, that I cannot perceive a discord, or keep time and hum a tune correctly; and it is a mystery how I could possibly have derived pleasure from music."[36]

Was Darwin deriving pleasure from music? Was he deriving pleasure from the *sound* of the music, or from something else? What sort of musical pleasure could it have been, if, as Darwin claimed, he could not have perceived even a discord? Was Darwin's pleasure of a "lower" sort than that of other, more sensitive listeners? Is this situation as mysterious as Darwin thought?—P.A.

2-14. SYNTHESIZING FILM

Suppose there were a method of making films by *directly* encoding tape or compact discs with information that would generate images. The images would be indiscernible from those produced by filming real objects with a motion picture camera: you would appear to see a street ("Hey, it's Broadway and 49th!"), cars passing, dogs barking, and people interacting who might even resemble well-known actors and actresses. However, at no stage of the production of this "film" would any camera or sound recorder have been involved; at no point would any lens have been trained on any real street or house or prop or actor. Rather, all would have been the product of sophisticated computer

simulation/encoding technology, produced by the film analogue of the
electronic music synthesizer.

Assuming you were told about the difference between one of
these constructions and an ordinary film, how would this knowledge
affect your experience or appreciation of what you were seeing and
hearing, if at all? Would you still thrill with the chases, weep at the
broken romances, fall in love with the heroes and heroines? Do you
think all films should eventually be produced by synthesizer, if the
process turns out to be cheaper and more efficient?—J.L.

2-15.   OWNING AND VIEWING ART

In John Galsworthy's *The Forsyte Saga*, Soames Forsyte is an avid
collector of paintings and takes obvious pride in them whenever he
shows them to friends. To all appearances his main interest in them
derives from the fact of his ownership of them and the pride he takes
in this ownership. Is this incompatible with viewing them aesthetically? Does it show that he is not a discriminating collector and
sensitive appreciator of paintings?[37]—J.H.

2-16.   *POWERFUL FEELINGS*

COMPOSED ON WESTMINSTER BRIDGE, SEPTEMBER 3, 1802:

Earth has not anything to show more fair:
Dull would he be of soul who could pass by
A sight so touching in its majesty:
This City now doth, like a garment, wear
The beauty of the morning; silent, bare,
Ships, towers, domes, theatres, and temples lie
Open unto the fields, and to the sky;
All bright and glittering in the smokeless air.
Never did sun more beautifully steep
In his first splendour, valley, rock, or hill;
Ne'er saw I, never felt, a calm so deep!
The river glideth at his own sweet will:
Dear God! the very houses seem asleep;
And all that mighty heart is lying still!

—WILLIAM WORDSWORTH

According to Wordsworth's definition, poetry is "a spontaneous over-
flow of powerful feelings." Does this poem show whether he had had
powerful feelings? Whether he was having them at the time he
composed the poem? If he did have powerful feelings, is it possible to

tell what feelings they were? Does the poem produce powerful feelings in the reader and, if so, are they the same feelings that Wordsworth appears to have had?[38]—J.H.

2-17. LEAVING ONE COLD

A student in the film department of a university had just completed a paper for her film theory class. She decided to celebrate by going out to a movie.

"How was it?" asked a classmate the next day.

"It was wonderful," she replied. "I had no emotional response to it whatsoever."

"Oh, you mean it left you cold? It can't have been a very good film, then."

"On the contrary, it did just what a successful film should do—it made me think about its meaning. It provided a completely intellectual experience. If I had let the film touch my emotions, I couldn't have understood it—I would have just been allowing the film to manipulate me."

Could the student have understood the film if it had engaged her emotions? What is the role of emotion in the appreciation of art?—F.L.

2-18. FORCED CHOICE

Imagine terrorists of a rather perverse stripe who take over a small museum and threaten to blow it up unless their demands for a plane and a million dollars in cash are met. In addition, out of spite they are going to destroy one of two designated paintings in the museum's collection, call them X and Y. X is a difficult, unusual work that gives intense pleasure to a small elite; Y is an open, accessible work that gives moderate pleasure to a far greater number. The decision is left to the museum's curator—she must tell them which painting to destroy, and if she does not decide, both will be destroyed.

What should she tell the terrorists? Is there anything else she should know about X and Y before making this choice? Should she refuse to make the choice at all, knowing that both would be destroyed?—J.L.

2-19. ANCIENT GLASS

Recent research has established that the iridescence characteristic of much ancient glass—for instance, that originating in Syria between the seventh and third centuries B.C.—is not, as had been thought, the product of a now-lost coloration technique but rather the product of the chemical leaching of the glass. The original glass was clear or slightly greenish in color; the leaching process, called "layering," occurs when glass is buried for long periods. Thus, the beautiful iridescent colors that have been highly prized by collectors result not from artistic efforts, but accidental natural processes.

As curator of your museum's classical antiquities section, should you display your collection of early Syrian glass "as found"—with its iridescence—or should you attempt to remove this leached surface layer in order to display the clear original glass as the early Syrians saw it?—M.P.B.

2-20. CÉZANNE'S MOUNTAINS

During his later years, Cézanne painted numerous canvases of Mont-Sainte-Victoire. The 1978 show "Cézanne: The Late Work" at the Museum of Modern Art, in New York City, included a very large number of these. One artist, Darby Bannard, commented:

> For me, seeing a wall full of Mont-Sainte-Victoires was like tasting a dozen vintages of Chateau Latour. Really elitist, I suppose, but comparison is everything in art.[39]

Another artist, Rackstraw Downes, said:

> Pictures for exhibition should be chosen and hung so they are free to be themselves . . . they should not tire, and they should not make a point. Twenty-four mountains all in a row did both. They made Cézanne into a serialist, or a groper. But Cézanne did not paint those pictures for the sake of the interest created between them, nor was he groping after something he did not attain.[40]

In deciding how to show multiple works of a single artist, ought one give primary weight to the artist's original intentions and aims, to the audience's experience, to the historical record, to the commercial success of the show, or to something else? How many Cézannes should one hang in a row?—M.P.B.

2-21. ART AS PSYCHOTHERAPY

Gladys is a college sophomore suffering from the despondency and various dissatisfactions, tensions, listlessness, and so on that many sophomores share. She goes to see her college counselor, who, after listening to her litany of complaints for an hour and consulting Monroe Beardsley's well-known works on aesthetics, arrives at a prescription:

I recommend that you take in some art. You know, music, poetry, drama, dance; that sort of thing. It's good medicine. Experiencing art relieves tensions and quiets destructive impulses; it resolves conflicts (at least lesser conflicts) within the self, and helps to create a harmony, an integration, in the personality; it refines perception and discrimination; it develops the imagination, and along with it the ability to put oneself in the place of others; it fosters mutual sympathy and understanding, and, indeed, offers an ideal for human life.[41]

Is the counselor right that art would improve Gladys's condition?
—R.M.M.

NOTES

1. Although the details of this example are invented, it reflects a real historical transformation in western aesthetic responses to nature. See Marjorie Hope Nicholson, *Mountain Gloom and Mountain Glory: The Development of the Aesthetics of the Infinite* (Ithaca: Cornell University Press, 1959).
2. This case is based on Immanuel Kant's discussion in the *Critique of Judgment* (1790) (trans. J. H. Bernard [1790; New York: Hafner, 1951], pp. 38–39). Kant's text is as follows:

   If anyone asks me if I find that palace beautiful which I see before me, I may answer: I do not like things of that kind which are made merely to be stared at. Or I can answer like that Iroquois Sachem, who was pleased in Paris by nothing more than by the cook shops. Or again, after the manner of Rousseau, I may rebuke the vanity of the great who waste the sweat of the people on such superfluous things. In fine, I could easily convince myself that if I found myself on an uninhabited island without the hope of ever again coming among men, and could conjure up just such a splendid building by my mere wish, I should not even give myself the trouble if I had a sufficiently comfortable hut. This all may be admitted and approved, but ... in saying it is *beautiful* and in showing that I have taste, I am concerned, not with that in which I depend on the existence of the object, but with that which I make out of this representation in myself.

3. John Ruskin, *Modern Painters*, vol. 1, 3rd ed. (New York: Thomas Crowell, 1906), p. 101.
4. R. G. Collingwood, *Essays in the Philosophy of Art*, ed. Alan Donagan (Bloomington: Indiana University Press, 1964), pp. 75, 85–86.
5. E. F. Carritt, *The Theory of Beauty*, 4th ed. (London: Methuen, 1941), p. 19.
6. C. E. M. Joad, *Matter, Life, and Value* (London: Oxford University Press, 1929), pp. 266–267.
7. George Santayana, *The Sense of Beauty* (New York: Charles Scribner's Sons, 1896), p. 48.
8. Virgil Aldrich, "Beauty as a Feeling," *Kenyon Review*, 1 (1939), 300.
9. Collingwood, *Philosophy of Art*, p. 87.
10. Ludwig Wittgenstein, *Lectures and Conversations on Aesthetics, Psychology, and*

Religious Beliefs, ed. C. Barrett (Oxford: Blackwell, 1966), paragraphs 35, 7, respectively.

11. Aristotle *Metaphysics* 1078a, in *The Basic Works of Aristotle*, ed. Richard McKeon (New York: Random House, 1941).

12. Aristotle *Poetics* 1450b–1451a.

13. Thomas Aquinas *Summa Theologica* Q. 39, Art. 8, in *Basic Writings of St. Thomas Aquinas*, vol. 1, ed. Anton Pegis (New York: Random House, 1945).

14. David Hume, *Essays, Moral, Political and Literary*, vol. 1, ed. T. H. Green and T. H. Grose (1777; London: Longmans, Green, 1875), pp. 278–279.

15. Kant, *Critique of Judgment*, pp. 196–200.

16. Plotinus *Ennead* I, vi, 2, in *The Essence of Plotinus*, ed. G. H. Turnbull, trans. Stephen Mackenna (New York: Oxford University Press, 1934).

17. C. R. Leslie, *Memoirs of the Life of John Constable* (1843), cited in Monroe Beardsley, *Aesthetics from Classical Greece to the Present* (New York: Macmillan, 1966), p. 296.

18. Samuel Alexander, *Beauty and Other Forms of Value* (New York: Thomas Crowell, 1968), p. 164.

19. Plutarch *De Audiendis Poetis*, sec. 3, cited in Bosanquet, *History of Aesthetic*, 2nd ed. (London: Allen & Unwin, 1904), p. 107.

20. Karl Rosenkranz, *The Aesthetic of Ugliness* (1853), cited in Bosanquet, *History of Aesthetic*, p. 404.

21. Clifford Geertz, *The Interpretation of Cultures* (New York: Basic Books, 1973), pp. 443, 446.

22. Edward Bullough, " 'Psychical Distance' as a Factor in Art and an Aesthetic Principle," *British Journal of Psychology*, 5 (1912), 88.

23. Virgil Aldrich, *The Philosophy of Art* (Englewood Cliffs, N.J.: Prentice-Hall, 1963), p. 20.

24. Monroe Beardsley, "Aesthetic Experience Regained," *Journal of Aesthetics and Art Criticism*, Fall 1969, 5.

25. G. E. Moore, *Principia Ethica* (Cambridge, England: Cambridge University Press, 1971), pp. 83–84.

26. Also see Monroe Beardsley's discussion of Moore's example in *Aesthetics: Problems in the Philosophy of Criticism* (New York: Harcourt, Brace & World, 1958), pp. 511–512.

27. Frederick Turner, "Cultivating the American Garden: Toward a Secular View of Nature," *Harper's*, August 1985, pp. 45–52.

28. Nathaniel Willis, *Black Mountain—Lake George* (1840), in *The American Landscape: A Critical Anthology of Prose and Poetry*, ed. John Conron (New York: Oxford University Press, 1973), pp. 181–182.

29. W. Gilpin first defined the picturesque as "that peculiar kind of beauty which is agreeable in a picture" (*An Essay on Prints*, London: J. Robson, 1768, p. 2).

30. John Dennis, *Critical Works*, vol. 2 (Baltimore: Johns Hopkins University Press, 1939–1943), p. 380.

31. Albert J. Lubin, *Stranger on the Earth: A Psychological Biography of Vincent Van Gogh* (New York: Holt, Rinehart and Winston, 1972), p. 143.

32. Mark Twain, *Life on the Mississippi* (New York: Penguin, 1984), pp. 94–96.

33. Immanuel Kant, *Critique of Judgment*, sec. 42, translation by Donald W. Crawford.

34. Kendall W. Walton, "Fearing Fictions," *Journal of Philosophy*, 75 (January 1978), 5.

35. Jurij Lotman, "The Illusion of Reality," in *Film Theory and Criticism*, 2nd ed., ed. Gerard Mast and Marshall Cohen (New York: Oxford University Press, 1979), p. 65.

36. Peter Brent, *Charles Darwin* (New York: Harper & Row, 1981), pp. 79–80, 87, 237, 505.

37. John Hospers, *Understanding the Arts* (Englewood Cliffs, N.J.: Prentice-Hall, 1982), p. 361.
38. Hospers, *Understanding the Arts*, pp. 227–228.
39. "The Late Cézanne: A Symposium," *Art in America*, March–April 1978, p. 83.
40. "The Late Cézanne," p. 85.
41. See Monroe Beardsley, *Aesthetics: Problems in the Philosophy of Criticism* (New York: Harcourt, Brace & World, 1958), pp. 571–576.

CHAPTER 3

MEANING
and
INTERPRETATION

WHO LEARNS FROM ART?

Suppose that the faculty of a large state polytechnic university is revising the institution's general education requirements to ensure that all students receive a sound education that will be useful to them in their later lives. Until 1974, all students had to study the same traditional great works of literature, music, and visual art. Since 1974, they have been permitted to take any course about anything now thought of as art, whether it be a course on Shakespeare's plays, Chaplin's films, Bach's music, rock and roll, Renaissance painting, or American textiles and quilts.

The Dean of the School of Agriculture insists that even the more recent requirement be dropped:

> Agriculture majors are serious students who come to this university to learn, and nothing much can be learned from art. Before 1974, our students were required to study so-called great poetry and plays and paintings and music. These seem meaningless to me, but, even if they do mean something, students could never learn what they mean because the experts disagree about it.
>
> The requirement we've had since 1974 is not much use, but at least our agriculture majors can fulfill it by taking a course specially designed for them by the Art History Department.

This course is relevant for future farmers. It focuses on agricultural art, like paintings of fruit by Caravaggio, Chardin, and Cézanne; orchards painted by Van Gogh; pictures of barnyard animals and fowl by Cuyp, Stubbs, Audubon, and Hicks; flower pictures by Redon; and even pictures of processed food, like Vassallo's *The Larder*. Even so, learning from art is not efficient because artistic representations of agriculture, whether in painting or in such literature as William Langland's *Vision Concerning Piers the Plowman*, Edward Thomas's "Haymaking," or H.D.'s "Orchard," are not as instructive as, and are harder to understand than, standard agricultural science textbooks.

Is the Dean right that nothing much, or perhaps nothing at all, can be learned from art, and that, consequently, art should have no place in a university's core curriculum?

Should we value art because we learn from it and use it to enhance our understanding of some aspects of the world in which we live? If art does have value for cognition, what sorts of things can be learned from it? Do art objects acquire cognitive value by teaching us about mundane matters of the world, such as facts about farming? Suppose that those things could also be learned from other sources, would it not be more efficient to acquire knowledge from textbooks, for example, than from the less straightforward process of interpreting works of art? Why should the study of art be thought of as an appropriate university-level subject?

Some people believe that artworks can instruct us about certain matters more effectively than standardized teaching methods. For instance, some think of art as an effective vehicle for moral education. Others think that art teaches us how to recognize and deal with emotional states. But those who hold such views should be prepared to explain how words or pictures or sounds, when organized into poems or paintings or music, acquire a special capacity to teach morality or to give us insight into the nature of our emotions. Moreover, anyone who thinks that art objects are capable of teaching should also offer criteria for determining whether what an artwork appears to teach is true.

Our usual tests for truth and falsehood are designed to apply to statements of theory or fact. Do these tests have any application to a medium, such as poetry, in which metaphors and other modes of figurative language are given a larger role than straightforward statements? Can the standard tests for truth be extended to apply to pictures, including nonrealistic pictures and pictures that are so abstract as not to be representational at all? What about music? Can music be used to convey truth? If art has cognitive value, how can we learn to learn from it? In order to understand different works, must we learn special symbol systems or the iconographies of different cultures and stylistic periods in the histories of the different arts? Or does understanding a work of art require reference to what the artist intended the work to mean? Perhaps art's value for cognition differs so much from our usual methods of learning that we confuse ourselves by invoking such familiar cognitive concepts as "understanding," "meaning," and "truth"?

PICASSO'S PORTRAITS

It is said that Pablo Picasso, in response to complaints that his portrait of the writer Gertrude Stein did not look like her, replied, "Everybody thinks she is not at all like her portrait, but never mind, in the end she will manage to look just like it." Roland Penrose, who reported this remark, added that in later years the portrait was acclaimed by all as an admirable likeness.[1]

Describing the painting that eventually became known as *La Femme-Fleur*, Françoise Gilot reported that Picasso originally began a fairly realistic portrait of her—indeed, the underpainting of that form is still visible beneath the final version. But, according to Gilot, after working a while on the painting Picasso said: "No, . . . a realistic portrait would not represent you at all." Gilot relates:

> Suddenly he remembered that Matisse had spoken of doing my portrait with green hair and he fell in with that suggestion. "Matisse isn't the only one who can paint you with green hair," he said. From that point the hair developed into a leaf form, and once he had done that the portrait resolved itself in a symbolic floral pattern. . . . The face had remained quite realistic all during these phases. . . . He studied it for a moment. "I have to bring in the face on the basis of another idea," he said. . . . "Even though you have a fairly long oval face, what I need, in order to show its light and its expression, is to make it a wide oval. I'll compensate for the length by making it a cold color—blue. It will be like a little blue moon."
>
> He painted a sheet of paper sky-blue and began to cut out oval shapes corresponding in varying degrees to this concept of my head. . . . Then he pinned them on the canvas, one after another, moving each one a little to the left or right, up or down, as it suited him. None seemed appropriate until he reached the last one. . . . He stuck it to the damp canvas, stood aside, and said, "Now, it's your portrait."[2]

If we want to acquaint ourselves with the looks of Gertrude Stein and Françoise Gilot, will we learn more from Picasso's

(left) Françoise Gilot.
Photo: Robert Doisneau/Rapho/Photo Researchers.
(right) Françoise Gilot, *La Femme-Fleur* by Pablo Picasso.
Photo: Robert Doisneau/Rapho/Photo Researchers.

portraits of them or from photographs of them? Will the
portraits or the photographs be better representations?

How do we determine what the subject of a picture is? At first
glance, the answer in at least some cases seems simple and clear. A
picture's subject is what the picture looks like. A photograph is a
picture of you, not just because you were what the camera captured on
film, but because it looks like you. You are the subject of your portrait
because your portrait imitates your looks. However, when Gertrude

Stein's friends complained about the discrepancies between her features and Picasso's picture, would they have been justified in using the lack of resemblance to conclude that the painting was not a picture of Stein? Picasso used a blue moon-shaped oval as Gilot's face. Why is his picture a picture of Gilot rather than a picture of a little blue moon? Do the leaf forms he used to represent her hair picture leaves, or do they picture hair? What could Picasso be showing or teaching us by picturing Gilot's hair as green rather than black?

PICTURING HISTORY

One of John Heartfield's photomontages shows Hitler giving the Nazi salute and receiving in his raised hand some money from a German capitalist. Heartfield obviously tampered with the actual photographic image, but it often is said that, by doing so, he created a truthful statement about a source of Hitler's power.

Edouard Manet was not present when the Emperor Maximilian was executed in Mexico in 1867. Manet based his historical painting *Execution of Maximilian* on eyewitness reports printed in European newspapers and portrait photographs of Maximilian and his generals. Although Manet's painting is not literally a "true" account of what took place,

Edouard Manet, *The Execution of Maximilian*, third version, 1867–68.
Städische Kunsthalle, Mannheim.

it has been said to reveal the "true" synthesis of the impersonal forces that resulted in Maximilian's death with the personal sympathy and admiration he elicited in France.[3]

What can we learn from a picture whose creator does not or cannot picture what actually occurred? Would the cognitive value of Manet's painting diminish if the newspaper reports that informed him were false? Suppose you encounter Manet's painting in a museum but you cannot find out its title, or have never heard the story of Maximilian. If all you see is a picture of three people being shot by a firing squad, can you fully appreciate the painting and benefit from its cognitive value? And what if you do not recognize Hitler in Heartfield's photomontage, so that all you see is a photograph of a man with a mustache who is being handed some money? How much historical knowledge is needed to understand works of art? Are we unable to grasp their meanings or appreciate them if we do not know the historical contexts in which they were created or to which they refer? And what if a picture's subject is mythological or fictional, such as Botticelli's *Birth of Venus*, which depicts Venus stepping out of a giant seashell? Can this be a picture of Venus's *birth*, since Venus is a mythological entity who never existed and thus never was born? Given the nonexistence of the event of Venus's birth, can we learn or understand anything from Botticelli's painting?

"DARK SATANIC MILLS"

"AND DID THOSE FEET IN ANCIENT TIME"

From Preface to MILTON by William Blake

And did those feet in ancient time
Walk upon England's mountains green?
And was the holy Lamb of God
On England's pleasant pastures seen?

And did the Countenance Divine
Shine forth upon our clouded hills?
And was Jerusalem builded here
Among these dark Satanic Mills?

Bring me my bow of burning gold!
Bring me my arrows of desire!
Bring me my spear! O clouds, unfold!
Bring me my chariot of fire!

I will not cease from mental fight,
Nor shall my sword sleep in my hand,
Till we have built Jerusalem
In England's green and pleasant land.

—WILLIAM BLAKE

The interpretation of the phrase "dark Satanic mills" in this poem occasioned a vehement argument between critics John Wain and F. W. Bateson. Bateson charged that Wain's attempt to make the poem relevant to modern readers resulted in an anachronistic interpretation:

> To Mr. Wain ... Blake's mills are a nineteenth-century textile-factory: "dark" with the soot from its steam-engines, "Satanic" because of capitalism's indifference to human suffering. Aesthetically this interpretation may perhaps be preferable to Blake's ... There can be no question of Blake or his original readers giving "dark Satanic mills" ... the sense that Mr. Wain prefers. There were no grim steam-driven textile factories when Blake wrote, ... nor apparently did capitalism, as a coherent economic theory, ever penetrate his consciousness. To substitute for the Old Testament hand-mills (a civic institution) the steam-driven mills of the nineteenth-century (the children of the capitalist *entrepreneur*) is ... to re-write Blake's poem. And, in the last analysis, this is what Mr. Wain is really encouraging the modern reader to do.[4]

Wain takes the modern interpretation of "dark Satanic Mills" as an aesthetic improvement on what the words meant to Blake. Does that make it the right meaning? If the modern meaning is right, was Blake's meaning wrong? Could both meanings be right, even though they differ and may not be compatible?

Does the fact that Blake cannot have been referring to the textile factories of the industrial revolution mean that the poem ought not be read as if he had? Or does the fact that readers in later historical periods are familiar with these factories justify Wain's assigning a transformed meaning to Blake's poem? Should we establish the meaning or interpretation of an artwork by reference to the artist's intentions or by trying to discover how the artist's contemporaries understood the work? Do the meanings of artworks remain the same throughout history, or does the meaning of each work change to reflect the changing experience and interests of audiences in different historical periods? Should we talk as if artworks possess meaning, thereby suggesting that art is analogous to language and that its primary purpose is as a means of communication, or is it misleading to conceive of art in this way?

IMITATION AND REALITY

Although both Plato and Aristotle held the imitation theory of art, taking artworks to present likenesses of things, they drew different conclusions about whether art could contribute to knowledge. Plato thought one acquired knowledge only by directly encountering the Forms or Ideas that, in his philosophy, constitute true reality and make it possible to understand ordinary physical objects. Thus, since artworks are merely imitations of ordinary physical objects, which themselves participate only derivatively in the Forms, they are, as he said in Book 10 of the *Republic*, "at the third remove" from reality and cannot provide us with knowledge. Indeed, artworks are distractions that divert us from learning about true reality, the Forms. Thus, art for Plato was not a source of knowledge or even of reliable opinion. Plato also believed that, because an artist cannot possess expertise about all the many different kinds of things imitated in art, artworks cannot even provide reliable practical knowledge. For instance, a painting may portray animals, plants, rock, sky, sea and sun, but it is implausible that the painter could be an expert in husbandry, botany, geology, meteorology, oceanography, and astronomy. Similarly, a drama may depict military strategy, shipbuilding, civic life, domestic organization, or death, but one would scarcely expect the playwright to be an expert general, shipwright, statesman, domestic authority, and doctor too. Because Plato found it impossible to believe that either painter or playwright had the knowledge to render accurate imitations, he concluded that art could provide neither intellectual nor practical knowledge.

Like Plato, Aristotle also held that artworks were imitations, but he claimed that it is natural and beneficial for humans to learn by imitating and also to learn from imitations that are artistically made. In circumstances where it is impractical or unilluminating to try to learn about real things directly, imitations can teach us. Exploring these matters in the *Poetics*, Aristotle pointed out that tragic poetry, unlike history, tends to express general truths, that is, not just the facts of what has actually happened as history does, but the kind of thing that is likely or certain to happen.[5] History, he said, describes individual, often coincidental, events that have actually taken place, whereas poetry discovers generalizable truths about the sorts of things that "probably or necessarily" occur. These truths govern what happens to us in reality. But when we are living in the midst of events that accord with these general truths, it may be difficult to understand them in their entirety, to discover their patterns, and to draw lessons from them.

So, Aristotle suggested, by composing an imitation of an action to be acted out on stage, the tragedian can exhibit the same truth as is displayed by real action, but in circumstances conducive to learning. Whereas a real action, replete with real death and real destruction, might distract us from the opportunity to learn, a suitably idealized replica of the action—for instance, Sophocles' *Oedipus Rex*—permits us to comprehend those principles of probability or necessity that govern human activity. It is somewhat as studying a plastic laboratory model of a human heart might facilitate learning about the typical structure of the heart more effectively than dissecting the heart of a randomly selected, perhaps diseased, corpse. In such a case, the model reproduces and emphasizes the heart's essential structure and general features but eliminates both the idiosyncrasies and distracting repulsion of an actual specimen.

Viewing classical thought from the perspective of postmodern art, Arthur Danto suggested that the Greek tradition established that art's essential character resided in its difference from real things, and that this contrast between imitation and reality continues to influence our concept of art.[6] Indeed, according to Danto, not only classical Greek sculpture and tragedy but later artworks as diverse as the religious paintings of Raphael, the plays of Shakespeare, the portraits of Joshua Reynolds, the novels of Émile Zola, and the painting of Renoir all can be seen as unabashedly imitative in the sense that they seek to represent the real world without posing any danger of being mistaken for real things. If you go to a production of Shakespeare's *Othello*, for instance, and during the crucial scene in which Othello strangles Desdemona someone jumps up on the stage shouting, "Call the police! Save that lady!" you would be astonished that anyone would mistake the acting in a play for the real act of murder. So, it seems reasonable to hold that one element crucial to understanding art is realizing that art objects must be different from "real" things.

According to Danto, however, postmodern artists try to reduce the distance between art and real things. For instance, as we noted in Chapter 1, Marcel Duchamp used a real shovel as the artwork *In Advance of the Broken Arm*. However, if you needed to dig your car out of the snow and used *In Advance of the Broken Arm* to do it, your using an artwork as a real thing would not be the same sort of mistake as interfering with the actor playing Othello when he imitates strangling the actress playing Desdemona. The cases are different because *In Advance of the Broken Arm* is a real shovel, whereas the actor merely imitates strangulation. According to Danto, postmodern artists characteristically create objects that are, ambiguously, both art and real things. For instance, Robert Indiana paints pictures of bull's-eye targets that are imitations of targets and, at the same time, real targets (since the concentric circles of the paintings are indiscernible from the concentric circles of a target). Such cases raise interesting questions. For instance, if a Robert Indiana painting and a target made for archery practice were to hang next to each other in a museum, would it be appropriate for the museum director to object to your shooting arrows into the Indiana painting? Could he or she reasonably urge you to restrict your shooting to the target, when the painting and the target look exactly alike?

Not only is it traditional in Western thought to believe that art tells or shows us about reality by imitating real things, but it is commonsensical to think this way. It may seem that the simplest explanation of why we know that a portrait is a picture of its sitter, or that *Gone with the Wind* is about the American Civil War, is that the portrait imitates in paint the facial shape and features of the person portrayed, and the novel imitates in words how someone who was there would describe the clothing and houses and social and military events of the Civil War. But there are problems in thinking that whenever anyone understands what a work of art is about, he or she is learning from the work as from a model or imitation of a real thing.

First, some artistic media, such as music and textiles, are difficult to conceive of as imitative, that is, they do not lend themselves to resembling other kinds of things. Even in music like Tchaikovsky's *Peter and the Wolf*, where an instrumental theme is assigned to represent each character in the narrative, it is implausible to say that the sound of each theme imitates the sound of the animal it represents. (The duck theme comes closest, but even here Tchaikovsky sacrificed faithful imitation of a duck's quacking to musicality.) Meaning in music seldom is achieved through direct imitation (one rare exception is Tchaikovsky's use of drums to imitate the sound of the hunters shooting the wolf). But even in these cases the imitative sounds are typically a very small part of the musical composition.

There is another difficulty in analyzing one's understanding of an artwork in terms of one's recognition of it as an imitation. If artworks functioned by imitating, then accuracy would seem to be the appropriate standard for judging a work's success. The more accurate the imitation, the more we might expect to learn from a work, and the easier it might be to do so. Yet in cases like the Picasso portraits of Gertrude Stein and Françoise Gilot, representation does not seem to be a matter of accurate imitation. Indeed, on Picasso's own testimony, part of the Gilot portrait imitates a moon, but the picture does not represent or mean or teach us about anything having to do with moons. The picture is a portrait of Gilot, but not by virtue of being an accurate copy of her.

ICONS, SYMBOLS, FIGURATIVE MODES

Since the imitation theory appears not to provide a sufficiently general explanation to cover all or even most cases of understanding works of art, philosophers and other theorists have attempted to develop more illuminating approaches. One proposal is that artworks are a means of communication, roughly analogous to languages, codes, or the pictorial symbols used internationally. An example of the last category is the red circle with a line through it: when the line is drawn through a picture of a cigarette, it is easily understood to mean No Smoking; when the line is drawn through a picture of a car, it means No Automobile Traffic. In fact, this symbol is so widely understood that its meaning is transparent even when adapted to new or bizarre uses. Are artworks symbols, and, if so, how do we learn what the symbols mean?

Some people think there are natural symbols whose meanings we understand without learning any rules or conventions. Imitations might be considered natural symbols because the resemblance between imitation and imitated object is obvious and need not be learned. However, the evidence about whether people naturally see resemblances, or whether they need training to do so, is inconclusive. For instance, there is some anthropological research to show that people who have never seen a photograph cannot recognize clear photographs of the most familiar objects—even humans. But there is also evidence that the objects become recognizable when compensation is made for such features as the distractingly shiny surface of photographic paper. Other examples of natural symbolic relations are the use of a picture of fire or the color red to symbolize heat. In these cases, it is claimed, people naturally associate fire with heat, and red with fire, so no one needs to teach them the meaning of the symbols. But even if this were true, natural symbols are likely to have meaning only for those who have had the opportunity to learn to make the associations. If people were no longer to use matches, gas stoves, and fireplaces, or, indeed, ever to see a fire burning, a picture of a fire would likely be ineffective in getting them to think about heat.

Clearly, some learning is needed to understand the symbolic dimensions of many artworks. John Milton's poetry, for instance, is full of references to biblical texts, and readers will fail to apprehend the full impact of his work if they do not understand these references. For instance, in Milton's famous sonnet on his blindness, "When I consider how my light is spent," the line "And that one talent which is death to hide" refers not only to Milton's despair at failing to exercise his own talent for writing, but also to the parable of the talents in Matthew 25, in which the third servant buries the gold coins that his master had entrusted to him. By grasping both references, the reader understands

Milton to be drawing attention to similarities between the spiritual emptiness occasioned by being unable to use one's creative talent and the spiritual emptiness occasioned by denying Christ.

Similarly, in much Western painting, Christian divinity is symbolized conventionally by the halo. A viewer who had not learned this convention would not understand that the gold rings around the heads of certain figures in Renaissance paintings signify that the figures represent holy persons. Nor would someone completely unfamiliar with Renaissance painting conventions be likely to recognize that the figures with wings on their shoulders are not freaks or hybrid human birds, but angels, spirits, or divine beings.

Sometimes, learning a special fact about a particular work, rather than the conventions of the style or cultural period in which the work was made, helps us understand it. In Bach's secular cantata "Lasst uns Sorgen, Lasst uns Wachen: Hercules auf dem Scheidewege," the words "for the snakes which tried to seize me with their lullaby" are accompanied by rising and falling music in the bass. The winding figures of the bass are often described as representing snakes, yet what "winds" is not the sound of the music but the appearance of the notation in the music's score. A somewhat similar case is that of the fifteenth-century French song "Belle Bon Sage" by Baude Cordier. Someone who does not understand the words or the notation can nevertheless understand that it is a love song—the score is written in the shape of a heart. In both cases, the meaning of the music is enhanced for those who have seen, even if they cannot read, the musical score. These cases, and many others, illustrate how understanding the conventions of a stylistic or cultural period, or knowing enough historical information to decipher allusions, helps us to grasp the symbolic meaning of artworks or to comprehend what certain works are about.

Some contemporary philosophers, such as Nelson Goodman, believe that representation and description in art are completely conventional. According to Goodman, nonlinguistic systems differ from languages, depiction from description, the representational from the verbal, and paintings from poems primarily with respect to certain properties of the symbol schemes. Goodman writes in *Languages of Art*:

> A picture in one system may be a description in another; and whether a denoting symbol is representational depends not upon whether it resembles what it denotes but upon its own relationships to other symbols in a given system. . . . A symbol is a representation only if it belongs to a [symbol scheme which has certain structural properties].[7]

If Goodman is right, to understand artworks is to understand which symbol systems are relevant and how they work.

Some of the ways in which artists convey their meaning undoubtedly rely on our understanding of nonartistic symbol systems, such as the conventions of ordinary language. Figurative language, for example, metaphor and simile, seems to work this way. From Aristotle on, almost all theories about metaphorical language (and about pictorial metaphor as well) have presumed that figurative expressions gain force by operating in contrast to standard or literal expression. Thus, we understand the figure of speech "He fought with the heart of a lion" not as literally asserting that "He had a lion's heart transplant" or "He used a lion's heart as a weapon," or even "He and a lion's heart battled against each other," but rather as metaphorically attributing courage to the way the subject fought. It appears that we first must understand the usages of literal assertion in ordinary contexts to recognize when these conventional usages are being employed figuratively. What else has to be understood to understand metaphor and other types of figurative expression is best revealed by careful analysis of a great variety of cases.

EXPRESSION

In response to those who, like the Dean of the School of Agriculture in the beginning of this chapter, complain that art objects are not very efficient vehicles for communicating knowledge, some theorists, particularly in the nineteenth and twentieth centuries, have proposed that art is expressive of human feelings, and some insist that what art teaches us about emotions cannot be learned in any other way.

What does it mean to say that an artwork "expresses emotion"? Among expression theorists, Leo Tolstoy and R. G. Collingwood held very different views, but both said that artworks communicate because artists make objects that express their feelings, which in turn are experienced by those who appreciate the works. But whether we can appreciate artworks only if we actually feel the emotions they express is problematic. On the one hand, if someone in the audience laughs heartily throughout a production of *Oedipus Rex*, particularly during the part in which Oedipus first discovers that he is the murderer of his father and then hears that his wife has killed herself, the laughter is evidence of an emotional response so inappropriate to the situation that we may think the person does not understand the play. So it seems as if experiencing the appropriate feelings is relevant to comprehending at least some art.

On the other hand, the requirement that one must have certain feelings to fully grasp the meaning of a work may be too strict. If you have seen and read *Oedipus Rex* many times, and you are seeing it once again to prepare for a literature test, you may not feel the emotions you experienced when you were just appreciating the play rather than making notes and memorizing the plot. In this case, even if you do not feel *any* emotion, it is hardly fair to say that you do not understand the play.

Some expression theorists do not believe that audiences need feel the feelings of the artist, or any particular feelings at all, for artworks to express emotions. These theorists typically observe that we most commonly assume that emotions are being expressed when outer behavior shows what is felt. Art, they say, is believed to express feelings when it has features that are characteristic of human beings expressing emotional states. Thus, if a piece of music is slow and hushed, it exhibits the same observable features as humans do when they are sad. By virtue of these features, we perceive the music as expressing sadness, even if we do not actually *feel* sad. Similarly, horizontal lines appear restful, and vertical and jagged lines do not, because humans typically assume a horizontal position when they relax or sleep.

Undoubtedly, much great (and minor) art concerns human emotion. The emotion to be understood is conveyed by a complex set of factors, which may vary from artwork to artwork. Indeed, in some instances, the emotional expression we attribute to a work may be affected by other artworks we have perceived. The following case, cited by Eduard Hanslick in *On the Musically Beautiful*, illustrates this point:

> How many works by Mozart were declared in his time to be the most passionate, ardent, and audacious within the reach of musical mood-painting. At that time, people contrasted the tranquillity and wholesomeness of Haydn's symphonies with the outbursts of vehement passion, bitter struggle, and piercing agony of Mozart's. Twenty or thirty years later, they made exactly the same comparison between Mozart and Beethoven. Mozart's position as representative of violent, inspired passion was taken over by Beethoven, and Mozart was promoted to Haydn's Olympian classicism.[8]

MEANING, INTERPRETATION, AND TRUTH

How can anyone who experiences an artwork be assured that he or she understands its real meaning? In some cases, we comprehend what a work is about in a direct, immediate revelation that occurs during appreciation of the work. In other cases, a work's meaning is pieced together only after we notice how various features of the object all contribute to that meaning. Interpretive critics differ in the methodologies they employ to construct accounts of the meanings of artworks. Some concentrate on the text, visual surface, or sounds that constitute the work—that is, on the art object itself—and draw attention to perceived patterns. Others investigate the social context in which the work was created, or examine biographical facts about the artist. Quite often interpretive critics using different methodologies arrive at quite different accounts of what a work means.

As mentioned earlier in this chapter, John Wain found a pattern in Blake's poem known as "And Did Those Feet in Ancient Time" that makes it particularly meaningful to modern readers. He saw the poem as showing, among other things, how England's green countryside had been blighted by the factories of the industrial revolution. This interpretation of the phrase "dark Satanic Mills" can make the other things Blake says in the poem especially poignant to the modern reader concerned with the undesirable effects of industrialization. Bateson objected to this reading, however, because his own method of interpretation emphasizes historical fidelity, not the concerns of modern readers. Even though Wain's account enriches the poem by providing an additional level of meaning, Bateson said, Blake and his intended audience could not have understood the poem as a criticism of pollution from factories because they lived before England's industrial revolution. Are there cases in which the meaning of art should be determined by artists' intentions? If so, must the work's meaning in these cases be *limited* to what the artist intended? How do we establish what artists intend? Are there cases in which learning about the artist and his or her society contributes to our understanding? Or would historical or biographical evidence distract us from attending to the timeless significance of the work itself?

Henry James's novella *The Turn of the Screw* is about a young governess who comes to an isolated house to take care of two children. Some strange events occur. According to one interpretation, fully compatible with the text, James related a story in which certain strange events are caused by the ghosts of wrongdoers. If this is the case, the lesson of the story may be construed to be a moral one about the nature of good and evil. According to another interpretation, also fully compatible with the text, the strange events occur only in the mind of the governess as she experiences a nervous breakdown. If this is the case, the lesson of the story may have nothing to do with good and evil, but instead concerns how a person can develop psychological problems. Must we choose between these two interpretations? If so, what kind of evidence would be relevant? Would any evidence be decisive?

Some contemporary theorists would resolve cases in which more than one interpretation of an artwork is proposed by insisting that each interpretation creates a new and different work of art. We need not worry about interpretations being incompatible with each other, with the text, or with the visual surface or score, in such a theory, because each interpretation creates another aesthetic object. But there would be in principle no limit to the number of works thus created, and *The Turn of the Screw* would not be a single artwork, but as many different artworks as there were critics and readers providing interpretations of it.

In the case with which this chapter begins, the Dean is concerned about whether we can learn from works of art. Some theorists believe that we can do so only if artworks are capable of being true or false. Of course, in at least some of the artistic media, an art object clearly can have elements or aspects that are capable of being true or false. If the real Mona Lisa, the Renaissance woman who posed for the painting called the *Mona Lisa*, had been a curly-haired blonde, then there would be a sense in which Leonardo's portrait falsely depicts her with straight dark hair. If the recently advanced theory that the painting is a disguised self-portrait of Leonardo is true, the painting can be said to depict Leonardo falsely as a woman. Similarly, we can say that the many Gilbert Stuart portraits of George Washington are true in presenting Washington without a mustache, crossed eyes, or a harelip, and that Dickens's novels contain true descriptions of nineteenth-century English social practices.

Does it make sense, though, to speak of an entire art object as capable of truth or falsity? Is Shakespeare's *Hamlet* true in addition to being profound, enlightening, or revealing? What kinds of reasons would be appropriate for demonstrating that *Hamlet* is true or false? In *Art and Illusion* Ernst Gombrich makes the following point: "a picture . . . can no more be true or false than a statement can be blue or green."[9] Just as the kind of thing statements are logically precludes their having colored surfaces, the kind of thing pictures are logically precludes their being true or false. But even if art objects are not true and false in the way that the propositions of science are true and false, there remain cases in which we desire to raise questions about the truth or correctness of what an art object conveys. John Berger, for instance, denounces the whole tradition of Western representations of women, both in painting and photography, on the grounds that all the images imply a standard of femininity that is false.[10] In making this charge, Berger is claiming not that Western pictures are false because they contain inaccurate images, but rather that the images they contain both result from, and contribute to, an inappropriate standard to measure women.

Some theorists maintain that art can lead us to truths even though artworks cannot contain or convey directly what is true or false. The philosopher Martin Heidegger, for instance, believed that the cognitive value of art lay in its capacity to stimulate thoughts that led far beyond what was depicted or portrayed. Heidegger claimed that art revealed an object's truth of being—that is, art "disclosed" an object's being as being, let it "emerge into the unconcealedness of its being." For instance, Van Gogh's painting of a pair of peasant shoes may depict nothing but two empty shoes, yet

> [f]rom the dark opening of the worn insides of the shoes the toilsome tread of the worker stares forth. In the stiffly rugged heaviness of the shoes there is the accumulated tenacity of [the peasant woman's] slow trudge through the far-spreading and ever-uniform furrows of the field swept by a raw wind. On the leather lie the dampness and richness of the soil. Under the soles slides the loneliness of the field-path as evening falls. In the shoes vibrates the silent call of the earth, its quiet gift of the ripening grain and its unexplained self-refusal in the fallow desolation of the wintry field. . . . This equipment belongs to the *earth*, and it is protected in the *world* of the peasant woman.[11]

Thus, Heidegger said, Van Gogh's painting lets us discover the "equipmental quality" of equipment—it lets us know what shoes are in truth. But it does not do so, he claimed, by means of propositions or descriptions.

Are there good educational reasons to support the proposal to make courses about art part of a university's general core requirements? Answering this question depends, to some extent, on whether we maintain that everything that is valuable to learn can be expressed propositionally—in other words, by using statements that can be proven to be true. We may be more inclined to include art in the university's curriculum if we believe nonpropositional modes of learning exist for which truth and falsity are not appropriate criteria. But if art is a nonpropositional mode of learning, can it function effectively in organized educational settings? Are there ways of testing whether people have been successful in learning from art? Could someone convey what he or she had learned from artworks to other people without their actually experiencing the same artworks? If learning from art requires direct experience of the artistic vehicle through which the information is conveyed, what role does a teacher play, and what are the teacher's contributions to learning from art? We may note how much easier it would be to answer these questions if we were addressing some part of the curriculum other than art. But despite the complexities of understanding how art is related to cognition, many people believe that an education is impoverished if art is omitted from it.

CASES ▬▬▬▬▬▬▬▬▬▬▬

Meaning and Interpretation

3-1. SOCRATES: PORTRAIT OR PHOTOGRAPH?

Which would we rather have, a portrait of Socrates by Rembrandt or a photograph of Socrates? What would the Rembrandt portrait be likely to reveal? What would the photograph be likely to reveal? Suppose the photograph were by Alfred Stieglitz. Would this make us more or less likely to want it than the Rembrandt portrait? Is our wanting to have known Socrates a relevant criterion for choosing between the photograph and the portrait?—M.L.

3-2. VENUS'S TRUE BIRTH

The proposition "Handel composed the oratorio *Messiah*" is generally held to be true just in case there was someone, namely, Handel and there was something, namely, the oratorio *Messiah* and that someone composed that something. So the proposition in question is true. Now consider the proposition "Alexander the Great slew the Minotaur." Because the Minotaur is a mythical beast, that is, one that never existed, the real Alexander, who did exist, cannot have slain it. So "Alexander slew the Minotaur" is either false, as some philosophers would have it, or neither true nor false, as others would have it, but it cannot be true, because there was no Minotaur for Alexander to slay.

   Is the proposition "Botticelli's *Birth of Venus* depicts the birth of Venus" true, false, or neither true nor false? If we assume that there never was such an event as the actual birth of Venus (as we safely can), then this proposition would appear to be analogous to "Alexander slew the Minotaur." But this proposition is true: Botticelli's *Birth of Venus* does depict the birth of Venus.

   In what ways are the propositions "Alexander slew the Minotaur" and "Botticelli's *Birth of Venus* depicts the birth of Venus" alike? Is the only difference that one of them is about an artwork, and the other is not? If so, why should that matter?—W.E.K.

3-3. HE DREAMS SHE DREAMS OF HIM

How do you know that this is a picture of him dreaming of her dreaming of him? Does it look like a dream? Must one have seen a drawing like this before to understand it? If this is a conventional way

Drawing by Sempé; © 1985
The New Yorker Magazine, Inc.

of representing dreams in pictures, why this convention rather than some other one?—D.E.C.

3-4. STOUT CORTEZ

ON FIRST LOOKING INTO CHAPMAN'S HOMER

Much have I travell'd in the realms of gold,
   And many goodly states and kingdoms seen;
   Round many western islands have I been
Which bards in fealty to Apollo hold.
Oft of one wide expanse had I been told
   That deep-brow'd Homer ruled as his demesne;
   Yet did I never breathe its pure serene
Till I heard Chapman speak out loud and bold:
Then felt I like some watcher of the skies
   When a new planet swims into his ken;
Or like stout Cortez when with eagle eyes
   He star'd at the Pacific—and all his men
Look'd at each other with a wild surmise—
   Silent, upon a peak in Darien.[12]

This sonnet is among the most famous of the works of John Keats. However, as a fact of history, it was Balboa, not "stout Cortez" (line

11), who reached Darien (the former name of the Isthmus of Panama), and who discovered the Pacific.

Would Keats's poem be a still better one if the historical facts were correct? (Incidentally, none of Keats's contemporaries recognized this mistake.)—B.H.

3-5. UNTRUE CONFESSIONS

William Styron's 1967 novel *Confessions of Nat Turner* portrays the black hero as torn by indecision, recoiling from violence, and lusting for the white woman he murdered. Historians charged Styron with distortion, pointing out that the real Nat Turner had a wife on a nearby plantation. Styron appeared undecided about how to defend himself. At one point, he insisted that Turner's halfhearted, indecisive tactics implied inner doubts and conflicts. In other words, he defended his novel as a plausible interpretation of historical fact. Later, however, he denied the relevance of historical fact, saying that his artistic objective was "imaginative truth, which transcends what the historian can give you."[13]

Why use real historical figures and events as the characters and narrative elements of a novel if the novel is not meant to provide a plausible historical account? Can the *Confessions of Nat Turner* be "imaginatively true" if it is not true to the historical facts?—A.S.

3-6. JOAN OF ARC

In Schiller's play *Jungfrau von Orleans*, Joan of Arc is portrayed as dying on the battlefield rather than at the stake, an historical inaccuracy which is also followed in Verdi's early opera *Giovanna d'Arco*. Do these historical inaccuracies, in your view, lessen the value of the works of art in which these inaccurate portrayals occur? If they disturb you, in what way do they disturb you?[14]—J.H.

3-7. MILTON'S COSMOS

Milton was aware of the new Copernican astronomy, but deliberately chose to make his cosmos in *Paradise Lost* Ptolemaic.[15]

Is knowing this fact important in reading *Paradise Lost*? Would we read *Paradise Lost* differently if we knew that Milton wasn't aware of the Copernican astronomy? Does knowing Milton's choice concerning the character of his cosmos cast any light on his characterizations of Adam, Eve, Satan, or God?—J.H.

3-8. BABBAGE'S ACCURACY

Shortly after Alfred, Lord Tennyson, published "The Vision of Sin," he received the following letter from Charles Babbage, English mathematician *extraordinaire* (and inventor of both the cowcatcher and an important early calculating machine):

> Sir,
>
> In your otherwise beautiful poem there is one verse which reads
>
>> Every moment dies a man,
>> Every moment one is born.
>
> It must be manifest that if this were true, the population of the world would be at a standstill. In truth the rate of birth is slightly in excess of death. I would suggest that in the next edition of your poem you have it read
>
>> Every moment dies a man,
>> Every moment one and one-sixteenth is born.
>
> Strictly speaking this is not correct, the actual figure is so long that I cannot get it into a line, but I believe the figure one and one-sixteenth will be sufficiently accurate for poetry.
>
> I am, Sir, yours, etc.[16]

Should Tennyson have accepted Babbage's point? Since he did not, and since his poem has not been revised as the birth rate has changed, is "The Vision of Sin" a misleading or false poem? Just how accurate is "sufficiently accurate for poetry"?—R.M.M.

3-9.   RAPHAEL'S REALISM

In his *Fourth Discourse on Art*, Sir Joshua Reynolds insisted that we can find realistic art meaningful even when we know it is not accurate. He said of Raphael's painting:

> In all of the pictures in which Raphael has represented the apostles, he has drawn them with great nobleness; he has given them as much dignity as the human figure is capable of receiving; yet we are expressly told in scripture they had no such respectable appearance; and of Saint Paul in particular we are told by himself, that his *bodily* presence was *mean*.[17]

Are Raphael's depictions of the apostles, and particularly of St. Paul, true? False? Informative? Misleading? When Reynolds said that inaccurate realistic art can be "meaningful," what could he possibly have had in mind?—A.S.

3-10.   CAN MUSIC REPRESENT THINGS?

Some philosophers have claimed that music can represent objects and events in the world by sharing a structure with them. Demonstrating a shared structure is a matter of establishing an isomorphism between the music and the object/event, and that, in turn, involves analyzing the music, on the one hand, and the object/event, on the other, as a system of elements and relations between those elements. Finally, one must show that, given a correspondence between the elements of the music and those of the object/event, there is a relation between musical elements that corresponds to every relation between object/event elements. For example, a melody that rises can represent a rising object because each note in the melody corresponds to a time-slice of a rising object (these are the elements); the relation later-in-time-than between notes corresponds to that same relation between time-slices; and the relation higher-in-pitch-than between notes corresponds to the relation higher-off-the-ground-than between time-slices.

Other philosophers have attempted to cast doubt on this claim by pointing out that, according to this scheme, it would be possible for a falling melody to represent a rising object: simply change the second correspondence between relations to a correspondence between higher-in-pitch-than and closer-to-the-ground-than. The isomorphism, and so, presumably, the sameness of structure, is still there, but now the falling melody represents a rising object.

Consider this example. The first line of the U.S. Air Force song ("The Wild Blue Yonder") generally rises, but the last prepositional phrase, "into the sun," falls. Does this spoil the representational quality of these lines, or can a falling melody represent a rising object? Is it wrong to suppose that an isomorphism of this type shows sameness of structure? Or if music *can* represent by sharing a structure with what it represents, is it the case that a piece of music *does* represent whatever it shares a structure with? Does music

The U.S. Air Force ("The Wild Blue Yonder") by Robert Crawford. Copyright © 1939, 1942, 1951 by Carl Fischer, Inc., New York. Copyrights renewed. All Rights Reserved. Used by Permission.

ever represent anything anyway, and if so, how does it accomplish this?—B.V.

3-11. MUSICAL PICTURES: TEASPOONS AND LOCOMOTIVES

Richard Strauss once maintained that he could portray a teaspoon musically and that he did so in *Domestic Symphony*. Honegger, similarly, once said, "I portray the visual impression, not merely the sound of the locomotive, in *Pacific 231*."

Suppose that someone—a skilled music listener—attends performances of *Domestic Symphony* and *Pacific 231*, but that neither images of teaspoons nor of locomotives come to mind.

Does this show that the listener has not, after all, really *heard* these pieces? That he has not heard them correctly? That he has heard them, but could not see them? Or that his hearing and response refute the claims of Strauss and Honegger?—R.M.M.

3-12. HANDEL'S *MESSIAH*

Handel's *Messiah* is widely praised as a musical composition of great devotional power and religious appeal. Its libretto is basically scriptural, comprising various meditations on Christian themes, especially the idea of redemption. One choral section, for example, is based on the passage from Isaiah (9:6): "For unto us a Child is born, unto us a Son is given, and the government shall be upon His shoulder."

However, as a matter of fact, the melody from the chorus "For unto us a Child is born" was originally composed by Handel for an erotic love duet. The words for this passage of the duet are "No, I don't want to trust you, blind love, cruel Beauty! You are too flattering a deity!" The music that accompanies the words "And the government shall be upon His shoulder" in the *Messiah* was taken from a passage in the erotic duet in which a lover is accused of fickleness.[18]

Is Handel guilty of sacrilege? Of blasphemy? Of musical misjudgment? How could the same music serve to convey such different meanings?—P.A.

3-13. *ADORATION OF THE LAMB*—OR THE FOUNTAIN?

The Van Eyck altarpiece in Ghent, commonly known as the *Adoration of the Lamb*, has had a preeminent place among works of its kind. Millions of visitors have admired it as an honest and sincere work, a fitting altarpiece for a Roman Catholic cathedral. But it is an odd

Jan Van Eyck, *Adoration of the Lamb* (panel from the altarpiece), Cathedral of St. Baron, Ghent, Belgium.
Giraudon/Art Resource, N.Y.

composition, and some viewers have wondered about the prominence of the fountain in the work, which is surely at least as much a focal point as the lamb. Indeed, an ingenious scholar has followed the gazes of the figures in the painting and discovered that more people seem to be looking at the fountain than at the lamb.[19]

The *Adoration of the Lamb* was painted at the time of the Anabaptists. Does its composition provide evidence for thinking that it is a subtle attack on the Roman Catholic church? If so, what sort of confirming evidence would we need? Would similar subtle characteristics of other Van Eyck paintings be sufficient evidence, or is some kind of external evidence or verbal statement required?—J.F.

3-14. MERCE CUNNINGHAM'S *WINTERBRANCH*

The dancer and choreographer Merce Cunningham describes the reactions of different audiences to his piece *Winterbranch:*

> "We did the piece . . . some years ago in many different countries. In Sweden they said it was about race riots, in Germany they thought of concentration camps, in London they spoke of bombed cities, in Tokyo they said it was the atom bomb. A lady with us took care of the two children who were on the trip. She was the wife of a sea captain and said it looked like a shipwreck to her. Of course, it's about all of those and not about any of them, because I didn't have any of those experiences, but everybody was drawing on his experience, whereas I had simply made a piece which was involved with *falls,* the idea of bodies falling."[20]

Is *Winterbranch* about race riots, concentration camps, bombed cities, shipwrecks, and the other human catastrophes in terms of which people see it? Is it only about falls? Or is it not *about* anything? Is Cunningham's intention when he made the piece relevant to legitimate interpretation of the piece?—A.B.

3-15. READING A GARDEN

Eighteenth-century English gardens differed from those of the present day in many respects, most notably in their lack of flowers and in their profusion of temples, follies, and grottoes. These gardens performed other functions beyond that of pleasing the senses. In particular, they conveyed sophisticated messages to those who wandered through them. Thus eighteenth-century writers as well as present-day commentators and historians used the phrase *"reading a garden"* to describe the viewer's experience of these landscapes.

One of the most famous of all such gardens was designed by William Kent at Stowe, in Buckinghamshire. One section of that garden, known as the Elysian Fields, contained an architectural complex consisting of three temples. The first was the Temple of Ancient Virtue, a round classical structure based on the Temple of Vesta at Tivoli. Inside were statues of Homer, Socrates, Lycurgus, and Epaminondas, representing the greatest poet, philosopher, lawgiver, and general, respectively, of the ancient world. Nearby was the Temple of Modern Virtue. This was in the less refined Gothic style and was, moreover, built as a ruin. Downhill from these two temples, across a small stream, lay the Temple of British Worthies. This semicircular structure had sixteen niches, each containing a bust of a British notable. The statues "looked uphill" to their ancient predecessors.

The significance of architectural style and topographical placement of this ensemble was further enhanced by Kent's choice (and alteration) of inscription. A quotation from Virgil appears without a crucial line praising the priesthood. Queen Anne is not among the British Worthies. Eighteenth-century viewers would have noticed these omissions—and grasped their anti-Catholic, anti-Stuart message.[21]

When we "read" Stowe's Elysian Fields, do we unpack its message any differently than we would that of a literary text or a painting? Is reading a garden like reading a book? What sorts of gardens can be "read"? Are there limits to the kinds of messages a garden or a landscape can convey?—S.R.

3-16. THE TRUTH ABOUT THE MAYANS

Only recently have scholars deciphered Mayan hieroglyphics and learned that the Mayans, previously seen as benevolent and peaceful, actually engaged in violent blood sacrifices. The reluctance of scholars to accept this view when they were unable to read Mayan texts is startling because they already possessed many examples of Mayan relief sculpture showing scenes of ritual self-mutiliation. In these scenes, rulers were shown letting their own blood by perforating earlobes or genitals, and sacrificing high-ranking captives to provide blood offerings to the gods.

Are pictures unaccompanied by (deciphered) words unreliable, incomprehensible, or otherwise unacceptable as primary historical sources? What basis could the historians have had for determining whether the sculptured reliefs were either fictional scenes based on myths, stories, or artists' imaginings or depictions of real life?—A.S.

3-17. CÉZANNE CONFUSES HIS FRAMES

In his memoirs, Ambroise Vollard, the nineteenth-century art dealer, tells of putting a Cézanne painting of female nudes in an old frame for an exhibit, but forgetting to remove the title of the former canvas, *Diana and Actaeon*. The press described the work as *Diana Bathing* and praised the picture of the goddess surrounded by her virgins.

Shortly thereafter, Vollard agreed to loan Cézanne's *Temptation of St. Anthony* to another exhibition. To his horror, he discovered that he had already sold the *St. Anthony*, so he sent the *Diana and Actaeon* instead. However, the title *Temptation of St. Anthony* had already been entered in the catalogue. The press, which had previously praised the noble qualities of Diana and her virgins, now praised the "sly, beguiling smile" in one of the daughters of Satan.

Did the press make a mistake? Did Vollard? Are titles a help or a hindrance in interpreting art?

Postscript: Vollard told the story to Cézanne, who was quite indifferent, saying that he had no particular subject in mind at all and was just trying to render certain kinds of movements.

Was he right in his unconcern?—J.F.

3-18. *THE DEER HUNTER*

In the film *The Deer Hunter* there are set in Vietnam scenes in which characters are playing a game of Russian roulette with each other. There is no evidence that such games were played during the American involvement in Vietnam. The director, Michael Cimino, said that the roulette game was a symbol of the uncertainty of each man's fate in wartime. Do you agree that the device should be called a symbol? Why?[22]—J.H.

3-19.   IBN GABIROL'S POEM

The Spanish poet and philosopher Shlomo Ibn Gabirol (1022–1058), who wrote in Hebrew, began his poem *Avey Shhakim* by describing winter clouds as a herd of bulls, bellowing and stampeding across the sky. This beautiful metaphor is dropped later on, and we find a nonmetaphorical description of the rain on the mountain. However, the poem's penultimate line coincidentally picks up the metaphor. It says that after the rain, *bull* is returning to the mountain. Of course, Ibn Gabirol did not know English. *Bull* is the Hebrew word for "crop." Yet reading *bull* as if it were an English word enhances the poem's unity and overall beauty, since it echoes the opening simile. The translation, "crop," makes the line, and the whole poem, a lot weaker. Indeed, the poem is far superior if we take the word to refer to what *we* mean by *bull*, not to its literal translation.

Are we allowed to interpret the poem in this way? Why or why not?—E.M.Z.

3-20.   FUNCTIONAL ART

During the summer of 1986, the Center for African Art in New York City mounted an exhibition of objects which included a bat-eared mask from the Boki region of Nigeria. Looking at the mask, one was immediately aware of the gigantic leather ears, the painted wooden head and the scattered cowrie shells. Also in the exhibition was an Ivory Coast mask bearing, high above the head, the figure of a weaverbird. The catalogue, *African Aesthetics: The Carlo Monzini Collection*, explained that both masks had practical functions. The former was like a judge's gavel and robes; government officials used it to enforce correct behavior by intimidation. The latter was used to enforce correct behavior by example, because the weaverbird was prized for its industriousness and exemplary social behavior.

Is it preferable to view the objects first without knowing their functions, so as to perceive them "purely," and then to read the catalogue so as to view them a second time with knowledge of their functions? Or should the first viewing be an informed one, so one is sure to understand the objects fully?—A.S.

3-21.   THE GREAT EASTERN TEMPLE

To help American viewers appreciate its 1986 exhibition of Japanese Buddhist art from Tōdaiji, the Chicago Art Institute produced a catalogue called *The Great Eastern Temple*, which explained the religious views of the period. Could someone ignorant of Buddhism understand these works without the catalogue? Could someone who knows that a sculpture is entitled *Amida Meditating Through Five Kalpas* understand the work without knowing the significance of meditation in Buddhist doctrine? Could one be fully aware of the realism of the thirteenth-century sculpture of the monk Dōgen if one were ignorant of the fact that the sculpture depicts a thirteenth-century monk who supervised the rebuilding of Tōdaiji?—A.S.

3-22. A LADYLIKE HAND

Art historians sometimes discover, or decide, that a work thought to be by one artist should instead be attributed to another. In 1893, the Louvre purchased a painting praised as one of Frans Hals's finest. However, a signature was discovered: that of the painter Judith Leyster. Critical treatment of the painting rapidly changed, and it was soon considered far inferior to the work of Hals.[23] According to one critic, the painting exhibited "the weakness of the feminine hand"; this critic insisted that it was an unsuccessful attempt to copy Hals's style, for "the vigorous brush strokes of the master were beyond their [women's] capability."[24]

The Leyster case is not an isolated one. In 1922, the Metropolitan Museum of Art spent $200,000 on a painting that was believed to be by Jacques-Louis David. However, around 1951, it was decided that the work was very probably attributable to Constance Charpentier, a student of David who exhibited in the salons and won prizes in the late eighteenth and early nineteenth centuries. After the painting, *Portrait of Mademoiselle Charlotte du Val d'Ognes* (see p. 88), was attributed to Charpentier instead of David, a critic wrote: "Its poetry, literary rather than plastic, its very evident charms, and its cleverly concealed weaknesses, . . . all seem to reveal the feminine spirit."[25]

How do you account for the fact that one painting was not seen as expressing lack of vigor and the other painting was not seen as revealing the feminine spirit until each was attributed to a woman painter? Do you think the critics in these cases noticed properties that previously went unrecognized, or did their beliefs about the gender of the artist determine their perception of the work? Are there stylistic characteristics, expressive properties, and/or special subjects that constitute evidence that a painting should be attributed to a woman rather than to a man? Are there some kinds of weaknesses or mistakes that are clues to the gender of the artist? Can we read from the properties of paintings to such characteristics as the artist's social condition or religious convictions or emotional state? The Metropolitan Museum of Art now lists the *Portrait of Mademoiselle Charlotte du Val d'Ognes* as "by an unknown artist." Does such indeterminacy about the identity of the painter affect how we see the painting?—P.Z.B.

French painter, unknown, *Portrait of a Young Woman, Called Mlle. Charlotte du Val d'Ognes.*
Metropolitan Museum of Art. Bequest of Isaac D. Fletcher, 1917. Mr. and Mrs. Isaac D. Fletcher Collection.

3-23. THE *LAKE PLACID* MÉNAGE

You are probably familiar with pictures that can be seen under two completely different aspects, such as the Necker Cube, the Duck-Rabbit, or the Old Woman–Young Woman. Some artists (Salvador Dali for one) are famous for such double-aspect paintings. Suppose, however, that J. Smith is not among them. All he ever paints are pastoral landscapes. But years after Smith's *Lake Placid* is bought and exhibited by a very conservative museum, an art critic discovers that by tilting the painting 90 degrees, it can be seen as a painting of a devil embracing two nudes. The critic calls this aspect *Ménage.* The enraged artist protests that he had never intended to paint the lewd picture, that his painting is a realistic representation of Lake Placid and nothing more, and that the critic's interpretation is illegitimate.

Is *Ménage* a work of art? If so, is it a work by Smith? Can *Ménage* be a better painting than *Lake Placid* (or vice versa)? Or is this painting neither *Lake Placid* nor *Ménage*? Would you, as the conservative curator, remove the painting? Should Smith be considered a mannerist (since the mannerists are known for their double-aspect paintings) or a lyrical realist?

Now change the above story in the following way. One cannot see *Ménage* just by tilting *Lake Placid*. The art critic had to look at *Lake Placid* through a portable light polarizer to see *Ménage*. How would you answer the previous questions in this case? Suppose that *all* Smith's paintings are discovered, under polarized light, to reveal similar unintended fiendish aspects. Would this strengthen or weaken the critic's interpretation?—E.M.Z.

3-24. SMOKE

In *On Moral Fiction*, John Gardner writes:

> There is a game—in the 1950s it used to be played by members of the Iowa Writers' Workshop—called "Smoke." It works as follows. The player who is "it" chooses some famous person with whom everyone playing is surely acquainted (Harry Truman, Marlon Brando, Chairman Mao, Charles DeGaulle, for instance) and tells the other players, "I am a dead American," "I am a living American," "I am a dead Asian," "I am a dead European"; and then each of the other players in turn asks one question of the person who is "it," such as, "What kind of smoke are you?" (cigarette, pipe, cigar—or, more specifically, L&M, Dunhill, White Owl) or "What kind of weather are you?" "What kind of insect are you?" or "What kind of transportation?" The person who is "it" answers not in terms of what kind of smoke his character would *like*, if any, but what kind of smoke he would *be* if, instead of being human, he were a smoke, or what kind of weather, insect, transportation, and so forth, he would be if reincarnated as one of those. Thus, for example, Kate Smith if an insect would be a turquoise beetle; Marlon Brando, if weather, would be sultry and uncertain, with storm warnings out; and as a vehicle of transportation Harry Truman would be (whatever he may in fact have driven) a Model T Ford. What invariably happens when this game is played by fairly sensitive people is that the whole crowd of questioners builds a stronger and stronger feeling of the character, by unconscious association, until finally someone says the right name—"Kate Smith!" or "Chairman Mao!"—and everyone in the room feels instantly that that's right. There is obviously no way to play this game with the reasoning faculty, since it depends on unconscious associations or intuition; and what the game proves conclusively for everyone playing is that our associations are remarkably similar. When one of the players falls into some mistake, for instance, saying that Mr. Brezhnev of the U.S.S.R. is a beaver instead of, more properly, a crafty old woodchuck, all the players at the end of the game are sure to protest, "You misled us when you said 'beaver.'" The game proves more dramatically than any argument can suggest the mysterious rightness of a good metaphor—the one requisite for the poet, Aristotle says, that cannot be taught.[26]

Does this game indeed demonstrate the Aristotelian claim that metaphor cannot be taught? Could such a game be played only by "fairly sensitive people," as Gardner puts it?—J.T.

3-25. LOWELL'S TRANSLATIONS

A young Classics instructor is teaching a course on Greek drama in translation for undergraduates. He is about to be disciplined by the Classics Department because he is using Robert Lowell's texts of some of the plays. The Classics Department insists that these are "renderings," not literal translations. The instructor defends himself by saying that the Lowell versions may not be faithful translations but they bring out the spirit of Greek drama for the contemporary reader better than any literal version. Besides, he argues, we do not have a sufficiently adequate conception of synonymy to make the idea of a literal translation conceptually respectable and practically workable.

Has the instructor violated the approved description of the course by failing to teach Greek drama? Or is he teaching it better than his colleagues in the Classics Department?—J.M.

3-26. PARAPHRASING POEMS

In "The Heresy of Paraphrase" the critic Cleanth Brooks raises the following question:

> Is it not possible to frame a proposition, a statement, which will adequately represent the total meaning of the poem [any poem]; that is, is it not possible to elaborate a summarizing proposition which will "say," briefly and in the form of a proposition, what the poem "says" as a poem, a proposition which will say it fully and will say it exactly, no more and no less? Could not the poet, if he had chosen, have framed such a proposition?[27]

These are rhetorical questions for Brooks: the answer to all of them is, apparently, no. In a footnote he says:

> We may, it is true, be able to adumbrate what the poem says if we allow ourselves enough words, and if we make enough reservations and qualifications, thus attempting to come nearer to the meaning of the poem by successive approximations and refinements, gradually encompassing the meaning and pointing to the area in which it lies rather than realizing it. . . . But such adumbrations . . . will be at best crude approximations of the poem.[28]

Does paraphrasing a poem present different problems from paraphrasing a prose statement? If I paraphrase a poem (i.e., if I say in a "proposition" what it means), then, no matter how excellent my paraphrase may be, will it at best be merely an "adumbration" of what the poem means or says, a "crude approximation of the poem"? Is this just to say that a prose paraphrase of a poem is not a poem just as a statue of man is not a man? Suppose I paraphrase a *prose* statement, for example, a passage from Hume or Ruskin or Cleanth Brooks. Is the same true that I can produce only an "adumbration" of what the passage says?—W.E.K.

3-27. CARAVAGGIO'S *CONVERSION OF ST. PAUL*

Commenting on Caravaggio's *Conversion of St. Paul*, the nineteenth-century critic Jacob Burckhardt wrote: "How coarsely Caravaggio could compose and feel . . . *The Conversion of St. Paul* . . . shows, where the horse nearly fills the whole of the picture."[29] (See p. 92.)

The art connoisseur Bernard Berenson described the picture thus: "We are to interpret this charade as the conversion of Paul. Nothing more incongruous than the importance given to horse over rider, to dumb beast over saint. . . . No trace of a miraculous occurrence of supreme import."[30]

Writing a few years later, the art historian Rudolf Wittkower asserted:

> In his *Conversion of St. Paul* he rendered vision solely on the level of inner illumination. . . . [Like the Counter-Reformation religious] reformers, Caravaggio pleaded through his pictures for man's direct gnosis of the Divine. Like them, he regarded illumination by God as a tangible experience on a purely human level.[31]

If Wittkower is right, Burckhardt and Berenson have completely misinterpreted the work by making too much of the horse. If Burckhardt and Berenson were right, Wittkower is wrong, and the horse cannot be ignored. How do we decide which of these great writers is right?—D.E.C.

3-28. MACHIAVELLI'S JOKE?

The term "Machiavellian" is widely taken to be synonymous with deceit and treachery in political life, as vividly depicted in Niccolò Machiavelli's treatise *The Prince*. Historian Garrett Mattingly, however, has argued that *The Prince* was written as a satire. Some of his evidence for this interpretation includes the following:

1. The manuscript was dedicated to a Medici long dead.
2. The manuscript was circulated *only* among close friends; the Medici never read it.

Michelangelo da Caravaggio, *Conversion
of St. Paul*. Rome, Sta. Maria del Popola.
Alinari/Art Resource.

3.   In its dedication Machiavelli presents the manuscript as a gift
and requests a job in return—in spite of the fact that he had just been
imprisoned, tortured, and exiled by the Medici.

4.   Machiavelli uses ironic language to extol the "success" of
rulers like Pope Alexander VI, Cesare Borgia, and the Medici notorious
for their tyrannical rule.

5.   Machiavelli wrote other forms of satire and was well known
for playing practical jokes on his friends.

6.   No other manuscript of Machiavelli's praises a monarchy; all
of his other writings heartily endorse republican rule.[32]

Is there any way one can tell, by looking at *The Prince* itself,
whether Machiavelli intended it as a satire? Are our problems in
determining whether it is a satire or a serious treatise of any importance in evaluating the (im)moral code of ethics *The Prince* presents?
—P.Z.B.

3-29.   THE PARABLE OF THE DARNEL IN THE FIELD

In Matthew 13:24–42 Jesus relates the Parable of the Darnel, darnel
being a poisonous weed resembling rye, sometimes called rye grass.

"The kingdom of Heaven is like this," he says.

> A man sowed his field with good seed; but while everyone was asleep his enemy came, sowed darnel among the wheat, and made off. When the corn [grain] sprouted and began to fill out, the darnel could be seen among it. The farmer's men went to their master and said, "Sir, was it not good seed that you sowed in your field? Then where had the darnel come from?" "This is an enemy's doing," he replied. "Well, then," they said, "shall we go and gather the darnel?" "No," he answered; "in gathering it you might pull up the wheat at the same time. Let them both grow together till harvest; and at harvest-time I will tell the reapers, 'Gather the darnel first, and tie it in bundles for burning; then collect the wheat into my barn.' "

Jesus's disciples come to him and ask him to explain the parable to them. Jesus replies:

> The sower of the good seed is the Son of Man. The field is the world; the good seed stands for the children of the kingdom, the darnel for the children of the evil one. The enemy sowed the darnel is the devil. The harvest is the end of time. The reapers are angels. As the darnel, then, is gathered up and burnt, so at the end of time the Son of Man will send out his angels, who will gather out of his kingdom everything that causes offence, and all whose deeds are evil, and these will be thrown into the blazing furnace, the place of wailing and grinding of teeth.

When Jesus answers the disciples, are his words an *interpretation* of the parable? If the very same words were uttered by one of the disciples to answer another's request for explanation, would they be an interpretation of the parable? How could the same words both be and not be an interpretation?

Now think of a poet who is asked to explain one of her poems. Theological considerations aside, would the poet's explanation of her poem be analogous to Jesus' explanation of his parable, or to one of the disciples' explanation, or neither? In answering this question, consider the following among possible sources of asymmetry between the two cases: Assuming Jesus' sincerity, it would have been quite inappropriate for one of the disciples (and not simply because he was a *disciple*) to doubt or to challenge Jesus' explanation, that is, to suppose that he might have been wrong. Would it always be similarly inappropriate to doubt or to challenge the poet's explanation, to suppose that she could have been wrong, even assuming her sincerity? Must a poem mean whatever the poet sincerely says it means? Or must the poet mean whatever she sincerely says she means? And if your answer to these questions is in the negative, would it follow that whatever a poet sincerely says she or her poem means is an interpretation of the poem?

To complicate matters further, think of someone relating a dream he has had. You ask him what it means, and he tells you. Is he interpreting his own dream? If so, how? If not, why? After all, are we not the "authors" of our dreams?—W.E.K.

3-30. *PINCHER MARTIN*

William Golding's third novel, *Pincher Martin*, provoked considerable critical confusion. Initially, critics seem to have had trouble figuring out just what was going on in the novel. But even after the initial difficulties in reading are resolved, two competing and incompatible readings remained. One reads the novel as an extended development of the device used by Ambrose Bierce in his short story "Occurrence at Owl Creek Bridge." According to this reading, the events of the story are an expanded hallucination that in real time takes only the few moments during which Pincher Martin drowns. The alternative reading treats the events of the novel as a literal purgatory—an extended period of time after the first death of Pincher Martin and before his second death. This requires that one accept a more overtly religious cosmology for the novel.

The critical disagreement can be supported on both sides. However, the issue was further complicated when the author entered the fray and in interviews provided overt statements of his intent. These were incorporated into the American edition of the novel as a title change when the novel became *The Two Deaths of Christopher Martin*. The following material is from the novel's opening:

> He was struggling in every direction, he was the centre of the writhing and kicking knot of his own body. There was no up or down, no light and no air. He felt his mouth open of itself and the shrieked word burst out.
> "Help!"
> When the air had gone with the shriek, water came in to fill its place—burning water, hard in the throat and mouth as stones that hurt. He hutched his body towards the place where air had been but now it was gone and there was nothing but black, choking welter. His body let loose its panic and his mouth strained open till the hinges of his jaw hurt. Water thrust in, down, without mercy. Air came with it for a moment so that he fought in what might have been the right direction. But the water reclaimed him and spun so that knowledge of where the air might be was erased completely. Turbines were screaming in his ears and green sparks flew out from the centre like tracer. There was a piston engine too, racing out of gear and making the whole universe shake. Then for a moment there was air like a cold mask against his face and he bit into it. Air and water mixed, dragged down into his body like gravel. Muscles, nerves and blood, struggling lungs, a machine in the head, they worked for one moment in an ancient pattern. The lumps of hard water jerked in the

gullet, the lips came together and parted, the tongue arched, the brain lit a neon track.

"Moth—" . . .

Of course. My lifebelt.

It was bound by the tapes under that arm and that. The tapes went over the shoulders—and now he could even feel them—went round the chest and were fastened in front under the oilskin and duffle. It was almost deflated as recommended by the authorities because a tightly blown-up belt might burst when you hit the water. Swim away from the ship then blow up your belt.

With the realization of the lifebelt a flood of connected images came back—the varnished board on which the instructions were displayed, pictures of the lifebelt itself with the tube and metal tit threaded through the tapes. Suddenly he knew who he was and where he was. He was lying suspended in the water like the glass figure; he was not struggling but limp. A swell was washing regularly over his head.

His mouth slopped full and he choked. Flashes of tracer cut the darkness. He felt a weight pulling him down. The snarl came back with a picture of heavy seaboots and he began to move his legs. He got one toe over the other and shoved but the boot would not come off. He gathered himself and there were his hands far off but serviceable. He shut his mouth and performed a grim acrobatic in the water while the tracer flashed. He felt his heart thumping and for a while it was the only point of reference in the formless darkness. He got his right leg across his left thigh and heaved with sodden hands. The seaboot slipped down his calf and he kicked it free. Once the rubber top had left his toes he felt it touch him once and then it was gone utterly. He forced his left leg up, wrestled with the second boot and got it free. Both boots had left him. He let his body uncoil and lie limply. . . .

"Help! Is there anybody there? Help! Survivor!"

He lay shaking for a while and listened for an answer. . . .

From the novel's closing:

Mr. Campbell took his eyes away from the stretcher.

"They are wicked things, those lifebelts. They give a man hope when there is no longer any call for it. They are cruel. You do not have to thank me, Mr. Davidson."

He looked at Davidson in the gloom, carefully, eye to eye. Davidson nodded. . . .

"The harvest. The sad harvest. You know nothing of my—shall I say—official beliefs, Mr. Davidson; but living for all these days next to that poor derelict—Mr. Davidson. Would you say there was any—surviving? Or is that all? Like the lean-to?"

"If you're worried about Martin—whether he suffered or not—"

They paused for a while. Beyond the drifter the sun sank like a burning ship, went down, left nothing for a reminder but clouds like smoke.

Mr. Campbell sighed.

"Aye," he said, "I meant just that."

"Then don't worry about him. You saw the body. He didn't even have time to kick off his seaboots."[33]

Here is an array of comments from critics:

The Surface pattern of *Pincher Martin* is the most turbulent of any of his [Golding's] books. Raw sensation is succeeded by hallucination, which is again succeeded by what seems to be metaphysical fantasy and mystical vision, all shot through with bolts of horror and fear, greed and wonder. The surface story of the book is resolved in the last section, in a manner of speaking, with the device that Ambrose Bierce employed in "An Occurrence at Owl Creek Bridge." . . . That the entire tale of the mariner stranded on a bare rock in the middle of the North Atlantic is a hallucination does not invalidate it as a vision of reality. The images that flash through the dying mind of Christopher Martin are dreadfully characteristic of him and, through him, of the personality of mankind in general.[34]

(E. L. Epstein)

Pincher Martin is a wartime naval officer (in the Royal Navy certain surnames take invariable nicknames—Nobby Clark, Spud Murphy, Pincher Martin) torpedoed, and washed up on Rockall. Here he survives miserably for a few days, sick and hallucinated, eating algae and sea anemones. Then he dies. . . .

The ending of *Pincher Martin* is a major puzzle. When Martin is still swimming in the night sea, before he has been cast up on Rockall, he kicks off his seaboots to lighten himself. . . . In the last chapter of the book we are translated to an island in the Outer Hebrides where the official who registers deaths comes to a lonely crofter and they look together at Pincher Martin's body, washed across two hundred miles of ocean. The crofter wonders if he suffered much before drowning, and the official says no: "he didn't even have time to kick off his seaboots." That is the last sentence in the book. What exactly has happened? He has somehow got his seaboots back on again. (And his Mae West.) On the level of sheer physical narrative, this is impossible. It is therefore a symbol of the supernatural. Are the seaboots the grace of god? If so, has the whole spell on Rockall been an allegory of purgatory? It may have, and a fine allegory too. But, and here's the rub, we never knew it, and the *lecteur moyen sensuel* can't take the shock of being suddenly told so at the end. This particular trick ending, the trickiest of them all so far, leaves one with a rather rebellious feeling.[35]

(Wayland Young)

The essential point is that this is a story about a dead man. It is about a consciousness so self-centered and so terrified of the infinite that it creates for itself, even in death, a fantasy existence which, however arduous and painful, nevertheless still permits it the luxury of personal identity. Dead as he is, Martin clings savagely to the idea of survival. . . . When, towards the end, he creates an image of God dressed as a mariner, and defies it—"I have created you and I can create my own heaven"—the figure replies soberly, "You have created it." He has indeed, out of the resources of his own being, but these are so utterly impoverished that it cannot endure. . . . He lapses into the death he has repudiated, the compassion (as Golding expresses it) that is timeless and without mercy.[36]

(John Peter)

In *Pincher Martin*, the tale of a modern sailor whose broken body is washed about the Atlantic rock, who eats limpets, is poisoned by his store of food and who eventually goes mad and dies, the pain is in the fight against physical hurt and loss of consciousness, in the struggle to put his educated will against his terrors. It is also in the Job-like protest against a defeat which wrongs everything he has believed in.[37]

(V. S. Pritchett)

As has been rightly suggested the ending leaves open the question whether we have witnessed a "real" struggle for survival or a hallucinatory extension of such a struggle into a man clinging for existence after death. The ambiguity is clear enough, the sea boots Martin abandons at the beginning of the novel are found on his body in the end, but the question itself is very much like the question whether Gregor was "really" a bug. The ambiguity teases our imagination and brings the hero's struggle for identity against the invasion of solipsism into even sharper relief.[38]

(Ralph Freedman)

Everything from that page on that we have been taking as a literal survival story has happened in fact *after* Martin's death, and must be taken as an account of another kind of attempt at survival, the survival of a soul before God.[39]

(Sam Hynes)

The "gimmick" in *Pincher Martin* occurs in the final chapter. . . . The final scene shows that the whole drama on the rock was but a momentary flash in Martin's mind. The dimension of time has been removed and all the microcosmic metaphor is but an instantaneous, apocalyptic vision. In the ultimate sense this revelation enhances the microcosm, compresses all the issues into a single instant in time. But the revelation, in fact, makes the situation too complete, too contrived, seems to carry the development of the microcosm to the point of parodying itself. One can accept the struggle of forces on the rock as emblematic of a constant human struggle, but, when the dimension of time is removed, when the struggle is distilled to an instantaneous flash, one immediately thinks of parody in which the struggle was not significant at all. Here the "gimmick" extends the technique, but so magnifies and exaggerates the extension that the novel ends by supplying its own parody.[40]

(James Gindin)

Here is Golding's comment:

Christopher Hadley Martin had no belief in anything but the importance of his own life; no love, no god. Because he was created in the image of god he had a freedom of choice which he used to centre the world on himself. He did not believe in purgatory and therefore when he died it was not presented to him in overtly theological terms. The greed for life which had been the mainspring of his nature, forced him to refuse the selfless act of dying. He continued to exist in a world composed of his own murderous nature. His drowned body lies rolling in the Atlantic but the ravenous ego invents a rock for him to endure on. It is the memory of an aching tooth. Ostensibly and rationally he is a survivor from a torpedoed destroyer: but deep down he knows the truth. He is not fighting for bodily survival but for his continuing identity in the face of what will smash it and sweep it away—the black lightening, the compassion of god. For Christopher, the Christ-bearer, has become Pincher Martin who is little but greed. Just to be Pincher is purgatory; to be Pincher for eternity is hell.[41]

Are Golding's own comments just one among many possible readings, or do they have special standing? If so, why? Are other critics' views worthless if they diverge from Golding's? What, exactly, is the relationship of these critical comments to each other?—D.T.

3-31.   "THIS LIVING HAND"

> This living hand, now warm and capable
> Of earnest grasping, would, if it were cold
> And in the icy silence of the tomb,
> So haunt thy days and chill thy dreaming nights
> That thou would wish thine own heart dry of blood.
> So in my veins red life might stream again,
> And thou be conscience-calm'd. See, here it is—
> I hold it towards you.[42]

This apparently is one of the last poems John Keats wrote. It was never published in his lifetime, and we know nothing of the circumstances surrounding its composition except that it was drafted or copied on the reverse side of a page of another poem Keats was working on in late 1819.

As it stands, the poem appears to be addressed directly to its reader: "This living hand. . . . I hold it towards you." Some critics have speculated that it is addressed not to the reader but to Keats's intended, Fanny Brawne; other critics have suggested that the poem represents a fragment of a play Keats was thinking about writing at the time, so that the gesture described in the poem would have been part of an action between two characters.

How should we read the poem, in the absence of any firm evidence about the author's intent or the audience to which it was addressed? Can we read the poem at all?—B.H.

3-32.   CAN HAMLET HAVE AN OEDIPUS COMPLEX?

In his *Interpretation of Dreams,* Sigmund Freud recites the legend of Oedipus, in which Oedipus unknowingly murders his father and marries his mother. According to Freud, this legend reflects those psychic impulses that arise in early childhood and that not only lead to psychoneurosis in some persons but also are to be found, though "less markedly and intensively," in those who remain normal. This is the dream of having sexual intercourse with one's mother, the complement to the dream of killing one's father.

Freud then goes on to apply his theory to Shakespeare's *Hamlet.* Here, he says, the wish-fantasy of the child "remains repressed, and we learn of its existence—as we discover the relevant facts in a neurosis—only through the inhibitory effects which proceed from it." Hamlet hesitates; he cannot bring himself to act against the man who killed his father and has taken his father's place with his mother. Anger that should lead Hamlet to revenge gives way to self-reproach, and he is "sicklied o'er with the pale cast of thought," incapable of action. Freud says of his own interpretation of *Hamlet,* "I have here translated into consciousness what had to remain unconscious in the mind of the hero; if anyone wishes to call Hamlet an hysterical subject I cannot but admit that this is the case."[43]

Can one use psychoanalysis to discuss the motives of fictional characters? Can one use psychoanalysis to discuss Shakespeare's characters, given that Shakespeare himself, although familiar with the Oedipus myth, was not familiar with psychoanalysis or, for that matter, with Freud, who lived some four hundred years later? Psychoanalysis sees the origins of neurosis in "infantile psychology" and the events of early childhood. But can we talk at all about Hamlet's childhood, as Hamlet exists only as a fictional character in a specific stage of life? Does this sort of criticism enhance our understanding of *Hamlet,* or does it distract us from appreciating the author's original intentions?—P.W.

3-33. THE PERPLEXING COMPLEX

Compare the following selections excerpted from works of literary criticism:

> It is quite obvious that [Swift's] excremental vision of the Yahoo is substantially identical with the psychoanalytic doctrine of the extensive role of anal eroticism in the formation of human culture.... Displacement from below upward, conferring on the upper region of the body a symbolic identity with the lower region, is Swift's explanation for the Puritan cult of large ears: the ear is a symbolic penis.[44]

> Here have we, not merely a confirmation of the overcarry from Milne's poetically celebrated bear-phobia to his bear-character Pooh, but also an unmistakable representation of the underlying Pooh's meaning. Freud's *Interpretation of Dreams* shows us unequivocally, that to "wander through dark passages and up steep stairs" can only a coitus-equivalent signify. When further we arrive at the opening of a special cage and the out-trotting of something brown and furry ... the reader may easily imagine, that all doubt ceases to retain validity. The friendly male bear Pooh is meant, the unfriendly terrifying female organ to represent.[45]

One of these passages is a serious interpretation of a literary work; the other is a spoof. It is obvious which is which, but *why* is it obvious? How can we identify interpretive criticism that should be taken seriously?—A.S.

3-34. THE PSYCHO-AUTHENTICATOR

Imagine the following advertisement:

> After twenty-four years of research and development, Psycho-Systems, Inc. is pleased to announce production of the revolutionary new
> PSYCHO-AUTHENTICATOR
> a device that, fed a substantial sample of dust from the grave of a deceased composer and a reliable (preferably holographic) score of a given composition of that composer can, with the assistance of a giant computer in Baltimore, report accurately the artist's exact state of mind while he or she was composing the work. This is obviously a device of enormous promise. For the first time we will be able to tell what X really meant in composing Y. One of the most remarkable features of this new technological achievement is that a present-day listener may now be able to enjoy *directly* the state of mind of the composer while listening to his or her music. We can, for example, now put a given listener in exactly the same mental state Igor Stravinsky had in composing *The*

Firebird, so that the listener will think and feel just what Stravinsky thought and felt.

Critic 1: This is a wonderful technology. It allows us to appreciate the music and its meaning fully for the first time, for now we can know what the composer really did mean in making the music.

Critic 2: This technology makes music obsolete. After all, the point of musical art is to convey accurately from one person to another the special feelings the former has felt. Art heretofore has worked indirectly through "infection." Now at last it can work directly, and the artworks formerly required as media of transmission may be dispensed with.

Critic 3: It's nice to know, as the new technology allows, what composer X meant in composing Y. But this has nothing to do with our understanding of or appreciation of Y; for these things we do on our own terms. Who cares if Stravinsky was worrying about a contract when writing *Firebird*? The music stands on its own.

Are any of these critics right? What would it mean to enjoy somebody else's state of mind? Could a *listener* enjoy a *composer's* state of mind? What, if anything, would development of the Psycho-Authenticator do for (or to) art criticism?—R.M.M.

3-35.   NEVER HAVING LOVED; NEVER HAVING PRAYED

A leading theologian makes the following argument:

Surely, a person who has never loved cannot understand or experience a love poem, and a person who knew no sorrow cannot really understand or experience an elegy. Now the vast majority of European art, including Greek art as well, is religious art. It was conceived and executed by religious people who aspired to express their homage to (a) God. Therefore, a nonbeliever cannot possibly understand or experience the music, the paintings, the poetry, or any artform created by believers.

Is the theologian right about what nonbelievers can understand of religious art? About what nonbelievers can experience of religious art?—E.M.Z

3-36.   CÉZANNE AND MONT-SAINTE-VICTOIRE

For almost all of his career, Cézanne made painting after painting of Mont-Sainte-Victoire, often from exactly the same spot. These paintings exhibit the evolution of Cézanne's style. André Malraux once remarked that Cézanne found it terribly important to paint Mont-Sainte-Victoire because he identified with it and was therefore able to realize himself through his depictions of it. Randall Jarrell responded that, for the very same reasons, Cézanne was necessary to Mont-Sainte-Victoire, because it realized itself through him.

In what way does an artist "realize" him- or herself by painting the same subject again and again? How can a painter identify with a mountain? Would a painter who painted the same human model again and again, as Rembrandt painted Saskia, identify with the subject in the same sense that Cézanne is said to identify with a mountain? Does it make any sense to say that Mont-Sainte-Victoire also realizes itself through Cézanne? Would you expect Mont-Saint-Victoire to look different to persons who were familiar with Cézanne's paintings of it? Could a painter realize himself through a subject, or a subject through a painter, if the painter paints the subject only once?

Suppose Seurat, Renoir, Monet, Van Gogh, and Cézanne each painted Mont-Sainte-Victoire only once? Could Mont-Sainte-Victoire realize itself in a set of paintings if each were painted by a different artist? Do various productions of a play contribute to the play realizing itself? How about if each production embodies a different interpretation or emphasis? Do remakes of a film, like the different versions of *A Star Is Born*, function in a similar way?—M.L.

3-37. *IVAN THE TERRIBLE* AND *SYMPHONIE FANTASTIQUE*

The conductor who performs Berlioz's *Symphonie Fantastique* gives an interpretation of the work. The projectionist who shows Eisenstein's *Ivan the Terrible* does not. Yet different showings of the film can differ greatly and in aesthetically important ways—the theater may be spacious or cramped, the sound turned up or down, the focus sharper or fuzzier. Why don't these differences in showings of *Ivan the Terrible* qualify as differences of interpretation, as even subtle variations of tempo or dynamics in performances of *Symphonie Fantastique* do?[46]—K.W.

NOTES

1. Roland Penrose, *Picasso: His Life and Work*, 3rd ed. (Berkeley and Los Angeles: University of California Press, 1981), p. 118.
2. Francoise Gilot and Carlton Lake, *Life with Picasso* (New York: McGraw-Hill, 1964), p. 117.
3. Mark Roskill and David Carrier in *Truth and Falsehood in Visual Images* (Amherst: University of Massachusetts Press, 1983), pp. 21–22.

4. John Wain, F. W. Bateson, and W. W. Robson, " 'Intention' and Blake's *Jerusalem*," in *Aesthetics and the Philosophy of Criticism*, ed. Marvin Levich (New York: Random House, 1963), pp. 375–383. "And Did Those Feet in Ancient Time," often called "Jerusalem," is from the Preface to Blake's *Milton*, pp. 94–95 in *The Complete Poetry and Prose* by William Blake, ed. David V. Erdman, (Garden City, N.Y.: Anchor Books, 1982).

5. Aristotle, *Poetics* IX, 1451b.

6. Arthur Danto, "Artworks and Real Things," *Theoria*, 39 (1973), 1–17.

7. Nelson Goodman, *Languages of Art* (Indianapolis: Hackett, 1976), p. 226.

8. Eduard Hanslick, *On the Musically Beautiful* (1854), trans. and ed. Geoffrey Payzant (Indianapolis: Hackett, 1986), pp. 6–7.

9. Ernst Gombrich, *Art and Illusion: A Study in the Psychology of Pictorial Representation* (New York: Pantheon, 1960), p. 68.

10. John Berger, *Ways of Seeing* (Harmondsworth, England: Penguin, 1972).

11. Martin Heidegger, *Poetry, Language, Thought*, trans. Albert Hofstadter (New York: Harper & Row, 1975), pp. 32–65.

12. John Keats, *Complete Poems*, ed. Jack Stillinger (Cambridge, Mass.: Belknap Press, 1982), p. 34.

13. *New York Times Book Review*, July 6, 1986, p. 20.

14. John Hospers, *Understanding the Arts* (Englewood Cliffs, N.J.: Prentice-Hall, 1982), p. 271.

15. John Hospers, "Aesthetics," *Encyclopaedia of Philosophy* (New York: Macmillan and The Free Press, 1967), vol. 1, p. 45.

16. Cited in Jeremy Bernstein, *The Analytical Engine* (New York: Random House, 1964).

17. Sir Joshua Reynolds, *Discourses on Art* (1797) (Indianapolis: Bobbs-Merrill, 1965), p. 42; passage is from Discourse 4.

18. David Randolph, *This Is Music* (New York: McGraw-Hill, 1964), p. 66; and Eduard Hanslick, *The Beautiful in Music* (New York: Bobbs-Merrill, 1957), p. 35.

19. Alexis Curvers, "La théologie secrète de la prétendu *Adoration de L'agneau*," pp. 227–247, esp. pp. 242–243.

20. Merce Cunningham, *The Dancer and the Dance: Merce Cunningham in Conversation with Jacqueline Lesschaeve* (New York: M. Boyars, distributed by Scribner's, 1984), p. 105.

21. See John Dixon Hunt, "Emblem and Expression in the Eighteenth-Century Landscape Garden," *Eighteenth-Century Studies*, 4 (1971); and John Dixon Hunt and Peter Willis, eds., *The Genius of the Place: The English Landscape Garden 1620–1820* (London: Elek, 1975).

22. Hospers, *Understanding the Arts*, p. 189.

23. Rozsika Parker and Griselda Pollock, *Old Mistresses: Women, Art and Ideology* (New York: Pantheon, 1981), p. 8.

24. Parker and Pollock, *Old Mistresses*, quoting from James Laver, "Women Painters," *Saturday Book* 24 (1964), 19.

25. Germaine Greer, *The Obstacle Race: The Fortunes of Women Painters and Their Work* (New York: Farrar, Straus & Giroux, 1979), p. 142, quoting Charles Sterling, "A Fine 'David' Reattributed," *Metropolitan Museum of Art Bulletin* 9, no. 5 (1951), 121–132.

26. John Gardner, *On Moral Fiction* (New York: Basic Books, 1978), pp. 118–119.

27. Cleanth Brooks, *The Well Wrought Urn* (New York: Harvest Books, 1947), pp. 205–206.

28. Brooks, *The Well Wrought Urn*, p. 206.

29. Jacob Burkhardt, *The Cicerone: Or, Art Guide to Painting in Italy*, ed. A. Von Zahn and trans. A. H. Clough (London: John Murray, 1873), p. 230.

30. Bernard Berenson, *Caravaggio: His Incongruity and His Fame* (London: Chapman & Hall, 1953), p. 20.
31. Rudolf Wittkower, *Art and Architecture in Italy 1600–1750* (Harmondsworth, England: Penguin, 1973), pp. 55–56.
32. Garrett Mattingly, "Reappraisals: Machiavelli's *Prince*—Political Science or Political Satire?" *American Scholar*, 27 (Fall 1958), 482–491.
33. William Golding, *Pincher Martin* (New York: Capricorn Books, 1956).
34. E. L. Epstein, Afterword to the Capricorn edition of *Pincher Martin*, pp. 187–188.
35. Wayland Young, "Letter from London," *Kenyon Review*, 18 (Summer 1957), 478–482, in *William Golding's Lord of the Flies: A Source Book*, ed. William Nelson (New York: Odyssey Press, 1963), pp. 19–21.
36. John Peter, "The Fables of William Golding," *Kenyon Review*, 19 (Autumn 1957), 577–592.
37. V. S. Pritchett, "Secret Parables," *New Statesman*, August 2, 1958, pp. 146–147.
38. Ralph Freedman "The New Realism: The Fancy of William Golding," *Perspective*, 10 (Summer–Autumn 1985), 118–128.
39. Sam Hynes, "Novels of a Religious Man," *Commonweal*, March 18, 1960, pp. 673–675.
40. James Gindin, *Postwar British Fiction* (Berkeley and Los Angeles: University of California Press, 1962), pp. 196–206.
41. William Golding, "Pincher Martin," *Radio Times*, March 21, 1958, p. 8, quoted by James R. Baker, *William Golding: A Critical Study* (New York: St. Martin's Press, 1965), pp. 35–36.
42. John Keats, *Complete Poems*, ed., Jack Stillinger (Cambridge, Mass.: Belknap Press, 1982), p. 84.
43. All quotations are from Sigmund Freud, "The Interpretation of Dreams," in *Basic Writings of Sigmund Freud*, trans. and ed. A. A. Brill (New York: Modern Library, 1938).
44. Norman O. Brown, "The Excremental Vision," in *20th Century Literary Criticism*, ed. David Lodge (London: Longman Group, 1972), pp. 518–552.
45. Frederick Crews, *The Pooh Perplex* (New York: Dutton, 1965), pp. 129–130.
46. Adapted from Kendall Walton, "Review of Nicholas Wolterstorff's *Works and Worlds of Art*," in *Journal of Philosophy*, 80, no. 3 (March 1983), 179–193; see esp. p. 182.

CHAPTER 4

CREATIVITY and FIDELITY: PERFORMANCE, REPLICATION, and READING

In Chapter 1 we considered whether paintings by Betsy, the chimpanzee at the Baltimore Zoo, could be considered *art*. But even if they are not art, could they still be *creative*, and could this be what gives them their aesthetic value? How much similarity is there between what Betsy was doing in applying paint to paper and what human artists do? Does it make a difference which human artists we have in mind? For instance, could we say that Betsy's creativity is very little like Giotto's but rather a lot like Jackson Pollock's? Should knowing a painting was created by a chimpanzee rather than a human being change the way we look at it, or are questions of the circumstances of a work's creation irrelevant to our judgment?

THE STRANGE CASE OF JOHN SHMARB

"One morning Art Freund opened his newspaper and was astonished to come upon the following headline: "FIND MANUSCRIPT OF BRAHMS'S FIFTH SYMPHONY: LOST WORK UNCOVERED IN VIENNA HOME." The accompanying story reported that a grandson of a former student of Brahms, rummaging through an old family trunk, had unearthed some dusty pages that turned out to be an original Brahms manuscript: a fifth symphony completed just prior to the composer's death in 1897. It had never been performed or published, and, in fact, Brahms seems never to have even mentioned it to anyone. According to the newspaper, members of the illustrious Vienna music circle, having seen the score, enthusiastically agreed that the work was a worthy companion to its four famous predecessors.

But they were no more enthusiastic than Art, who firmly resolved to attend the premiere of the Fifth Symphony in Vienna on May 7, the anniversary of Brahms's birth. Only with great difficulty did Art manage to obtain a ticket, for all the most celebrated members of the music world were to be in attendance on this momentous occasion.

When that great day finally arrived, Art's expectations were fully realized. The music was magnificent and the audience response overwhelming. Critics spoke with impassioned, unqualified admiration for the new masterpiece. The *Times* reported: "The four extended movements of the Symphony are each of the highest order and exemplify many of the composer's finest traits. The intense agitation and propulsion of the opening allegro appassionata, the lilting Viennese charm of the andante, the scherzo's cross-rhythms and explosive climaxes, the all'ongarese melodies of the theme and variations finale all testify to the strong Brahmsian character of the piece. But the special significance of the composition is its unusual tendencies toward a cyclical structure, most apparent in the use of the first-movement theme to link the end of the scherzo with the finale. In addition, the main theme of the second movement returns as a counterpoint to the final variation of the last movement. Interestingly, the work is marked by the use of many more nonfunctional harmonic progressions than one encounters in Brahms's other symphonies. This feature gives the work a forward-moving restlessness and enormous impact."

A story later in the week announced that the first

recording of the Fifth Symphony would be released at the end of the year by the Berlin Philharmonia. And when Art arrived home, he found in his mailbox publicity releases from leading American orchestras advising subscribers that performances of the new masterpiece would be scheduled immediately upon publication of the eagerly-awaited score, already in progress.

But several weeks later Art was shocked by another headline: "BRAHMS'S FIFTH SYMPHONY A FAKE: MUSIC WORLD AGHAST." Incredibly, the Symphony had actually been the handiwork of a young American composer, John Shmarb, who had called a press conference to announce his achievement. He explained that after managing to obtain authentic paper and ink of the nineteenth century, he had forged Brahms's handwriting and arranged to have the manuscript found in the old trunk. When asked why he had concocted such an elaborate hoax, young Shmarb replied: "For the last ten years publishers and critics and musicologists have been dismissing my work as inconsequential: because they claimed all I did was copy nineteenth-century music. Well, I finally got fed up. They weren't being fair to my music. Now that the world has judged my work as it would judge the work of any nineteenth-century composer, my genius has been acknowledged. I am not imitating Brahms. I am simply composing as a contemporary of Brahms might have. I find it natural to write in the Romantic vein and want to continue to do so. A great work is a great work, whether composed by Brahms or by Shmarb."

Response to Shmarb's words was swift and unanimously harsh. One German critic typified the attitude of many by denouncing Shmarb as an unscrupulous fraud. "The outrage of it all! Having us waste our time on such worthless music is criminal. Shmarb has shown himself to be a musical charlatan." A leading American avant-garde composer commented: "Shmarb has always been incapable of utilizing his natural abilities. His output is merely derivative. Another sad case of misdirected and misused talent." Word soon followed that the Berlin Philharmonia had eliminated the Symphony from its recording schedule, that plans to publish the work had been abandoned at considerable cost to the publisher, and that all announced performances had been cancelled."[1]

Clearly, John Shmarb is creative in ways that Betsy the chimpanzee is not; whereas her paintings seem to be merely the product of haphazard splashes of paint, Shmarb's work is deliberately, carefully fashioned. But is Shmarb's work "creative" in any important sense? The critics denounce it as "derivative," "worthless," the product of a "charlatan." But how does it differ from the work of Brahms, except in that it was composed a century later? If, musically, they are so much alike, why does Brahms's work count as creative, whereas Shmarb's work is not even considered worthy of a performance by the Berlin Philharmonia? Nor is the fictional case of John Shmarb an implausible one; the music world has seen many real-life examples: for instance, Fritz Kreisler's "18th century" compositions, which were written for many of the same reasons.

PORTRAYING PORTIA

Alice and Emily are each auditioning for the role of Portia in *Julius Caesar*. Alice gives a straightforward, competent reading of this small but important part; Emily expands the part not only with a series of gestures and movements around the stage, making Portia much more powerful and forceful than she is usually played, but by actually adding new lines. These lines employ perfect Shakespearean diction and meter and they fill in the gaps where Portia's argument is incomplete. Before, Portia's claim that she ought to be privy to Brutus' secrets had seemed only provisionally plausible; now it is wholly convincing. Moreover Brutus' promise to tell his secrets, which he does not keep, becomes more central in understanding his character. The result of Emily's expansion of the part is stupendous: she creates a Portia who is much more substantial, formidable, and important in the development of the play, and who thus also augments the portrayal of Brutus' character.

As director, you must decide between these actresses. Alice's rendition seems small, prosaic, dull; Emily's extraordinarily creative in the most perceptive of ways.

You tell your assistant you prefer Emily's magnificent reading, and intend to select her for the part.

"But it isn't Shakespeare," your assistant protests. You look at the text again, and see that, indeed, she has uttered several entire lines that are simply not there. "You're right," you say, but you wonder whether this is really important in performing Shakespeare and, consequently, in deciding whether to choose Emily for the part.

Should the assertion that "it isn't Shakespeare" be decisive in assessing these performances, and is your assistant simply wrong about the role of creativity in performance? Or is the fact that this is a performance of *Shakespeare* somehow relevant, so that, while your assistant might be wrong here, he might be right about other performance contexts? If creativity is a value-making characteristic in the arts, are there limits to the value creativity can add to specific artistic phenomena? Or is fidelity the more important value here? On what basis do we admire creativity in authors, painters, and composers, but demand fidelity in the performing arts?

READING *PARADISE LOST*

In the eighteenth century, *Paradise Lost* was read in orthodox Christian terms: God and God's creatures, like Adam before the Fall, were good; Satan was the very essence of evil. But with the Romantics, especially Blake and Shelley, Satan came to be seen as a kind of hero—a figure in revolution against authority, who, despite his flaws of envy and ambition, exhibited "courage and majesty and firm and patient opposition to omnipotent force."[2]

Does the Romantic reading misinterpret or distort *Paradise Lost*? Is it wrong? Is it justified by the revolutionary context within which Blake and Shelley found themselves? Or couldn't they have meant this reading entirely seriously? More generally, to what degree does historical change limit or extend the range of plausible readings of this text?

This case may seem to pose questions about meaning and interpretation of the sort already considered in Chapter 3. But those questions themselves depend in fundamental ways on questions about the role of the reader or viewer in responding to works of art or performances of them. Are only the author and perhaps the performer the creators of art, or is the viewer's role essentially creative too? Is Blake and Shelley's reading of *Paradise Lost* erroneous, or simply more "creative" than the usual straightforward interpretations of this text? Isn't art, at least good art, always interactive in this way, and isn't every artwork the *mutual* creation of the author, audience, and, if there is one, the performer?

All of these cases involve issues of creativity, whether or not the term itself is actually used. However, in each the notion of creativity is understood differently, sometimes in overlapping, inconsistent ways. Thus, one might be reluctant to say that Betsy the chimpanzee's paintings are creative, though one acknowledges that in a certain odd sense they are—especially when compared to the accomplishments of other chimpanzees. By the same token, we are reluctant to say that

Shmarb's symphony is creative, since it is just mock Brahms; but on the other hand, it does seem to be creative too. Emily's portrayal of Portia is certainly also creative, though in a very different way, and so too are the Romantic readings of *Paradise Lost*. To see what lies beneath these seeming confusions, we must pry apart and explain the various senses of the verb "create."

AMBIGUITY IN THE TERM "CREATE"

The shifting, overlapping meanings of "create," as we shall see in this chapter, can be disambiguated along two principal lines: "create" can refer to a process or a product, or it can be used in descriptive or normative ways. These usages overlap: a work might be called "creative" in a descriptive way that emphasizes the *process* by which the artwork is produced, whereas another work might be called "creative," in a normative way that focuses on the *product*, or artwork itself. Senses also shift and overlap among the cognates of "create," including "creation," "creative," "creating," and "creator," though the uses of the terms do not all vary in the same ways. Similar variation is also found in such related terms as "originality," "innovativeness," "novelty," and their cognates, though such variation by no means correlates precisely with that of the term "create."

Process versus Product

Sometimes it is the process of composition or construction that is said to be creative; sometimes it is the resulting product. This distinction permits us to see the difference between the Betsy and the John Shmarb cases. When Betsy picks up a paintbrush and stands in front of the paper applying paint, it may look as though she is creating something, but if we look more closely at the *process* involved, we see that this cannot be the case. Betsy does not have the mental apparatus necessary for creation, and particularly not for artistic creation; she is just an animal splashing paint. To be sure, chimpanzees are capable of a certain kind of practical problem-solving—as, for instance, in using a stick to poke a banana out of a hollow log—but they cannot entertain a conception of the finished product of their own efforts, that is, they cannot see something "in their mind's eye" before realizing it in an actual construction.

John Shmarb, on the other hand, *can* do this. By contrasting animal capacities with human ones, the Betsy case encourages us to think of creativity as a kind of psychological process; but the Shmarb case shows us that there is more to creativity. If we hesitate to say that Shmarb's work is creative, or at least as creative as Brahms's, it is because we do not attend to the psychological processes Shmarb went through in composing his work as much as the resulting product.

Rather, we see that the product seems to lack a central feature that would allow us to call it creative—namely, advancement beyond the current musical tradition.

Creation as process.   Where "create" and its cognates are taken to refer to the process of composition, one must consider, first, exactly how this process occurs and, second, how it is related to other kinds of human thought and activity.

For Plato, like other Greek thinkers, artistic activity, at least in poetry, originated in a supernatural process: poetry was the result of "inspiration" or divine intervention. Hesiod, Homer, and Pindar all claimed that the Muses spoke through them or implanted artistic truths that were realized in the poetic product. Even though the Greeks recognized the poet's role in shaping poetry (Aristotle particularly emphasized the poet's craft), they generally thought of the poet largely as a mouthpiece for the gods. During this process of transmission, they believed, the poet was in a state of ecstasy. Indeed, the Greek word *ek-stasis* means literally to stand outside oneself. Plato said, "The poet is a light and winged and holy thing, and there is no invention in him until he has been inspired and is out of his senses, and the mind is no longer with him."[3]

Of course, this model of poetic creativity did not really answer the question of *how* artistic creation occurred, since it did not explain how poetry was created by the Muses before being transmitted through the poets to a human audience. Nor did the medieval conception of artistic creation address this issue directly; for in the Middle Ages, God was considered the sole creator, and the artist was understood to work within a tradition of relatively stable artistic forms and modes. It was not until the late eighteenth and early nineteenth centuries that the creative process was really explored with full force. This was made possible partly by the associationist psychology of John Locke and other philosophers who investigated how the imagination worked, and partly because of the interest among the Romantic poets, especially Wordsworth, Coleridge, and Shelley, in the nature of creativity itself.

The Romantics saw creativity as a means to transcend the limited conditions of ordinary life. The earlier Greek notion of ecstatic transport, or possession by the divine, was rediscovered and reinterpreted. For the Romantics, creativity was essentially self-expressive, not only in the superficial sense of conveying one's personal views, but also in the more profound sense of revealing the depths of human existence and meaning. The unconscious was held to play a particularly powerful role: unconscious associations, memories, drives, and desires were understood to usurp the regulative functions of conscious thought. Eventually, the creative process came to be seen as a kind of psychopathology: genius was close to madness.

The notion that artistic creativity was a kind of productive insanity that plumbed deeper psychic roots and resisted conventional constraints has persisted in much of contemporary thinking, even though the Romantic period has long passed, and has found recent expression in psychoanalytic theories. For Freud, imaginative creation was the product of an individual's suppressed fantasies, much like daydreaming. Jung saw creative work in the arts as arising from unconscious depths in the primordial, collective psyche, so that when the "waywardness of the general outlook" of an historical epoch called these primordial images into play, they were expressed both in the visions of artists and seers as well as in individuals' dreams.[4]

But, as Vincent Tomas pointed out, artists cannot literally be madmen, for the pictures they paint and the poetry they write makes sense, whereas those of the insane do not.[5] Art is not the product of psychosis, because, among other things, it is subject to careful control and corrective criticism as it proceeds. True, the initial moments of inspiration in the creative process, accompanied as they often are by a feeling of extraordinary exaltation, may have been the product of psychological forces beyond conscious control, and perhaps some artworks stop there. But the elaboration of the art object itself typically requires painstaking, reflective, analytical work.

This contention and the reply invite a much more careful description of the process of artistic creation. While recent interest in this issue has been expressed primarily by psychologists, there have been a number of efforts among aestheticians to characterize such a process. Most accounts treat it as a series of interacting stages at both preconscious and conscious levels and assume that it remains relatively similar among different individuals. Douglas Morgan, reviewing a variety of accounts of creativity, prroposed a four-step version:

1. A period of "preparation" during which the creator becomes aware of a problem or difficulty [and] goes through trial-and-error random movement in unsuccessful attempts to resolve a felt conflict . . .
2. A period of "incubation," renunciation or recession, during which the difficulty drops out of consciousness. The attention is totally redirected . . .
3. A period or event of "inspiration" or "insight" . . . the "aha!" phenomenon, characterized by a flood of vivid imagery, an emotional release, a feeling of exultation, adequacy, finality . . .
4. A period of "elaboration" or "verification" during which the "idea" is worked out in detail, fully developed.[6]

In this view, the process of creation is inextricably intertwined with ongoing critical judgment of the work as it is brought into being;

it is a process, as Monroe Beardsley put it, of "interplaying invention and selection."[7] This account at last enables us to show why one might be unwilling to say that Betsy's "paintings" are creative. Chimpanzees, we think, are not capable of the innovative, intuitive leap that marks the move from step 1 to step 3, and they are not capable of the continuous mental work involved in step 4.

As Tomas further observed, however, this stepwise characterization of creativity raises additional questions about the degree to which this process is a directed, purposive one, and in particular about whether the artist must have a conception of the finished work that controls the interplay of invention and selection as it proceeds. It may also lead us to ask whether the process of creation is common to different artistic media or contexts, and indeed whether artistic creativity is essentially similar to creativity in, say, politics, human relations, or the sciences. After all, the four stages just listed, as Jack Glickman has observed, describe the creative process in many nonartistic fields equally well. Moreover, they apply to all sorts of other activities—such as trying to remember a name—which are hardly regarded as *creative* at all.[8]

Most important, however, this stepwise characterization of creativity raises a more fundamental question, central to contemporary thought, about the degree to which its presupposition that there is a "self" can be supported at all. Postmodernism calls into question the notion that there is an interior, deeply private realm of experience in which creativity could be rooted and asks whether what we take to be "creative" and "original" is not instead an individual response to socially and culturally shaping forces, the most powerful of which is language.

Creation as product.   In attempting to see why one might hesitate to call John Shmarb's symphony creative, even though Shmarb surely went through all four of the steps just described in creating it, we pointed out that in Shmarb's case one focuses on the product, not the process. But the product, Shmarb's symphony, seems to lack a central characteristic by virtue of which it could be called "creative," regardless of how it was composed. What it lacks is the right sort of relation to the ongoing tradition within which it arises. While Brahms's work stood at the head of the Romantic movement in music, Shmarb's trails almost a century behind. Consequently, since we are talking about the product, not the process, of creation, we can assert that Brahms's work is creative and that Shmarb's is not without knowing anything about the psychological processes either composer underwent. We need only know something about the relation of these composers both to each other and to the musical tradition within which they worked. Brahms was an innovator, a pioneer; Shmarb a craftsman, a follower, a completer of what had gone before. "Creative" in this sense is a contextual predicate, and to see whether it applies to such figures as Brahms or Shmarb we must be familiar with the context of the work and with other works in the history of culture or art.

We often speak of "novelty" or "originality" *within* a tradition, taking the "creative" work to be the one least anticipated by previous works in the tradition. Claims of creativity in this second sense are always expressible in the form "X is creative relative to Y," though the second term in this expression is often omitted. Yet to determine whether such a claim is true about X one must be able to supply information about Y. Thus, to say whether the *Fifth Symphony* is "creative" we must know whether it is by Brahms or Shmarb, and we must be prepared to say that if it were written by Brahms in the nineteenth century, it would be creative, whereas if the identical piece of music were written by Shmarb in the twentieth, it would not. We must also be prepared to decide whether Shmarb could legitimately claim that he was working "within the Romantic tradition," or even that the Romantic tradition "needed completing" though nearly a century had passed since that historical period had come to a close.

But even the distinction between art judged in and out of the context of a tradition is difficult to maintain when applied to contemporary art. Some postmodern and neo-Romantic artists make use of pastiche, replication, reprinting, rephotographing, and other techniques that employ past content and style in a way that makes the "product" difficult to distinguish from previous works in the tradition. Nevertheless, their works are regarded as creative, and not just in the product sense. For instance, the "image appropriators," such as Sherrie Levine, often replicate or reproduce the work of earlier artists; yet both in the process and in the product sense their work is considered new (see Case 4-17).

Clarifying—at least as much as possible—the various senses in which "create" and its cognates are used may clear up some of the puzzles these terms generate. The two senses of "creative" we have considered so far, creative in terms of process and creative in terms of product, may be applied independently of each other, and we may inquire of any art object whether it is creative in either sense. Shmarb's work is creative in the process sense, but not in the sense of a product related to a historical tradition. Betsy's paintings are neither creative in the process sense, nor is there any tradition of chimpanzee painting within which they could be assessed as creative in the product sense. Of course, we often assume that when a work is creative in the product sense it is because of certain psychological processes on the part of the artist. On the other hand, the occurrence of creative psychological processes is responsible for something's being creative in the sense that it is related to a historical tradition. Nonetheless, the two senses of "creative" remain conceptually distinct, though they are often closely entwined in application.

Descriptive versus Normative Uses

John Shmarb, defending his "uncreative" symphony in the style of Brahms, insisted that "a great work is a great work, whether composed by Brahms or Shmarb." What Shmarb was objecting to is the assumption that creativity relative to a historical tradition is a value-making characteristic; that is, he rejected the assumption that a work that is not creative in this sense has little or no value at all. This claim makes evident a second, related ambiguity in the meaning of "create": the confusion of descriptive and normative uses.

Sometimes, to say that people create something is simply to say that they make or fashion it, as, for instance, one may create a passageway through a hedge by clipping away branches. Sometimes, to create something is to make or fashion something new or previously unknown; in this sense we might say that a designer creates a new shade of lipstick or a chef creates a new soup.[9] But very often the term "create" and its cognates carry with them, in addition to or instead of these earlier senses, a valuational or normative component as well: as Tomas puts it, "creative" becomes an honorific, a success or "achievement" term. To say that a chef has created a new soup is not merely to say that he or she has managed to mix unfamiliar ingredients; it is to say that the recipe deserves culinary recognition. Similarly, to say that Salvador Dali is a particularly creative artist is not to say that he has fashioned a series of novel objects, it is also to attach value— high value—to his doing so.

The valuational import of the term "create" changes with changing historical periods. Throughout most of the history of both Western and Eastern art, creativity, especially in the product sense of the term, has not been particularly valued. For instance, Shakespeare was not considered a lesser artist for having reworked old plots in all but two of his plays. The Romantics were the first to celebrate creativity per se; their elevation of this characteristic above virtually all other features of art continues to influence us. In our current cultural epoch to say that an artist is creative, or that his or her work is creative, is perhaps the ultimate compliment. Despite the challenges of postmodernist thought, creativity is still typically valued more highly than technical skill, expressiveness, conversance with the history of art, or other characteristics artists and their artworks might display.

Not only does the ambiguity between descriptive and normative senses make it often hard to tell whether something is said to be "creative" in a factual or valuational sense, but it makes it hard to tell in any given instance of normative use just how strong the normative import is supposed to be. If we say, for example, that Brahms is a very creative composer, are we praising him weakly, strongly, or very strongly? Is the valuational import of creativity stronger in some areas of the arts than others—stronger, say, in performance art, but less strong in ballet? Is creativity a necessary characteristic for excellence in the arts, at least in our current cultural epoch? Must an artist or a work that is clearly uncreative, though perhaps exhibiting other important properties, in the end be considered comparatively worthless? The normative grammar of the term "creative" is quite complex, and the same problem afflicts many of the alternate terms substituted for it in discussions of art, such as "original," "inventive," "ground-breaking," "avant-garde," and so on. To say that an artwork is creative suggests something good about it, but we are far from clear about how good.

Inspecting the varying meanings and applications of "create" reveals no simple, bivalent ambiguity, but a range of shifting, interactive senses. It is a slippery word. Indeed, the art historian H. W. Janson suggests that it has been "so cheapened by overuse" that "the only thing to do is to leave it alone."[10] But while he may be right in avoiding the term, it is important to see that much of our conceptual confusion arises here.

THE LOCUS OF CREATION

A second major group of problems involving creativity has to do with the locus of creative activity. To be sure, creativity occurs in the mind of the artist—perhaps not in the conscious mind *per se*, or in some deeply private, interior "self," but at least in some feature of the artist's activity. One may ask, however, whether a creative process occurs in the perceiver as well. R. G. Collingwood spoke of audience collaboration, for instance, and Ernst Gombrich spoke of "the beholder's share." Monroe Beardsley argued that a work does not come fully into being until it is perceived: "The true locus of creativity is not the genetic process prior to the work but the work itself as it lives in the experience of the beholder."[11] Beardsley asked what a melody was and observed that as we hear the distinct notes that make up a melody and perceive how regional qualities emerge from the succession, "creation occurs before our very ears."[12] Creation "is in the operation of the work itself," not merely in whatever the painter or composer did.[13] One of many representing still more extreme views, the literary critic Roland Barthes insisted that the reader "rewrites the text."[14] These thinkers do not assume, however, that the perceiver "creates" the artwork in the sense of innovation; the perceiver's contribution may also be heavily conditioned by his or her culture.

This relatively new focus on the beholder of art as the locus of creativity in a community of interpretation has gained prominence in recent years, virtually eclipsing aestheticians' conventional concerns with creativity in the artist. It is most conspicuous in the study of literature, where the new focus is the basis of reader-response theory, German *Rezeptionstheorie,* and several other contemporary schools of literary criticism. In these areas, the older terminology has not survived, and such terms as "creativity," "inspiration," "originality," and "genius" are found largely in more traditional discussions that emphasize the artist's creative role. Nevertheless, the new concern with the way the reader or perceiver participates in or constitutes the work preserves many of the traditional issues.

Of course, awareness that the perceiver contributes to the creation of the work carries some disturbing consequences. Jean-Paul Sartre, for instance, argued in *What Is Literature?* that a novelist can never read his own novel, since

> the essence of reading is the free movement of the mind in the face of a story that unfolds in a way that on first reading is unforeseen and even on re-reading represents a sheer factuality that the reader did not devise and cannot control.[15]

The author cannot come innocently to his own work and hence cannot *confront* it. Of course, Sartre acknowledges that time and distance begin to intervene between the artist and his or her creation once it is complete, and that eventually the work becomes part of past reality, as alien to the artist as to any other perceiver; but this is hardly a satisfactory resolution of the problem. In the very act of creation, the artist's authority over his or her work is lost.

Furthermore, the greater the emphasis on the perceiver's role in constituting the work, the more the role of the artist seems to dwindle. The students of the literary critic Stanley Fish wonder "Is there a text in this class?" even though they are able to find it at the bookstore, since continuing emphasis on the constitutive role of the reader raises the question of whether it is ever possible to read a text at all.[16] The text becomes an event or a transaction, no longer an objectively identifiable thing.

FIDELITY, CREATIVITY, AND THE ARTIST'S INTENTION

The complaint of the director's assistant that Emily's reading of the Portia role "isn't Shakespeare" raises further issues of creativity, this time as it is contrasted with fidelity in performance. Alice's performance was faithful, if pedestrian, and Emily's was not. Or was it the other way around? Was Emily actually more faithful to Shakespeare's intent than the unimaginative Alice, even though she deliberately departed from the text?

The issue may be put in this way. If creativity is a value-making characteristic in the original author of a work, is it also value-making in the performer too? How closely ought a pianist performing a Mendelssohn piano concerto conform to Mendelssohn's intentions, as recorded in the score or known from other sources? Do we value innovation and creativity in performance as well? When we take fidelity to be a value, we admire the performer who succeeds in being so "close to the work" as to seem to divine the artist's inmost thoughts and aims. If so, the truest performer will be the one who manages to recreate the work with utmost loyalty to the original, with as little imposition and intrusion of foreign elements as possible. We probably would not as a rule admire a pianist who took huge liberties with the score of a Beethoven sonata and who seemed to ignore Beethoven's intentions, simply improvising as he pleased. But Liszt was just this sort of pianist, and we do admire him. Doesn't Liszt's playing represent a triumph of performance? By parity of reasoning, then, would we not celebrate Emily's performance of Shakespeare? Or was Liszt not really a performing pianist but a composer in disguise, and Emily not really an actress but a meddling playwright? But then what about the uninspired performer who seems only to slavishly reproduce what sits on the page? Is this not just what unimaginative Alice did? Must the good performer always be in some way creative? If so, in what way, and to what degree? At what point does the performer become so "creative" that he is no longer performing someone else's work? Did Emily reach that point?

We can clear up such muddles a bit by identifying the referents of creativity and fidelity in contexts of artistic performance. Fidelity to what? we must ask; creativity vis-à-vis what? We might assert certain minimal conditions. For instance, we might say that in the performance of a play or a concerto or a dance, fidelity to the text or score at the very least involves speaking the words, playing the notes, or making the movements it indicates. To perform *Julius Caesar* one must recite the words "Friends, Romans, countrymen" in the right order and in the right place during the action of the play. But of course there is much more to acting the part of Marc Antony than literal recitation, and renditions of this three-word line by the great Shakespearean actors have been remarkably varied. Each actor would no doubt claim that his rendition was faithful to the play or, perhaps still more accurately, to Shakespeare's intentions in the play. But discerning or reconstructing what these intentions were must always involve creative conjecture. Alternatively, one might maintain that the playwright's intentions are unimportant and in any case inaccessible. If so, one would be more concerned with arriving at an interpretation that is consonant with the text of the play, but creative in respects not stipulated by the text. So, for instance, the script of *Julius Caesar* underdetermines the features of performance: it does not specify how slowly or quickly the words of Antony's soliloquy are to be spoken, or with what intonation or volume. It does not tell the speaker which direction to face, or what nuances of urgency, irony, desperation, disdain, or other characteristics to express. Perhaps we could appropriately assess creativity with respect to these features of the performance and could praise an actor's portrayal of Antony as "a creative triumph" without in any way suggesting that the actor had been unfaithful to, or had taken unwarranted liberties with, the play. Of course, Emily did more than this. Emily, in a sense, created Shakespeare's play.

To understand the roles of creativity and fidelity in the performing arts, we must also consider whether such an account could succeed in areas besides drama. Musical scores, for instance, specify more precisely how the performance is to occur: the tempo is given by specific metronome markings, the volume is determined by indications such as *pianissimo* or *forte,* and the mood is stipulated by such instructions as *doloroso.* Here, it would seem, the composer announces his or her intentions much more clearly and fully than is customary (or perhaps possible) in drama. Were a horn solo in a Tchaikovsky symphony to be performed with the range characteristic of a Marc Antony soliloquy, differing markedly from the score, and from other horn solos in terms of duration, volume, expression, and so on, such performances might be described as "creative," but the term would be used in a pejorative, derisive way.

Thus, one answer to the question of what constitutes fidelity might be formulated in the following way: fidelity in performance is fidelity to the script or score and to whatever specific instructions it provides. Since these may be assumed to indicate the artist's intentions concerning how the work is to be performed, fidelity is ultimately fidelity to these intentions. We might insist that a genuine performance of a work is always faithful in this sense; Nelson Goodman even argues that nothing qualifies as a musical performance unless it complies exactly with the score.[17] Nevertheless, in cases where the script or score underdetermines the features of performance—and no script or score in any of the arts is exhaustively determinative—a variety of performances may be appropriate. The most conservative approach would be to try to divine the artist's intentions from the score or other relevant material and to provide a performance that is consonant with the conjectural reconstruction of those intentions. Alternatively, one might take the script or score as a set of minimal constraints and attempt to give a reading or performance of the work that expands as broadly and inventively as possible beyond those constraints (as, for instance, in modern-dress or politicized interpretations of classical plays). Here there is no claim that the performance matches the artist's intentions, whatever they may have been, though the performance is not *unfaithful* to the play. In either of these cases, however, we can consider performance as a kind of externalized interpretation, displayed by the musician or actor or dancer for the benefit of an audience; and this, in turn, raises again all the questions of interpretation and meaning we have just considered in Chapter 3. Because the performed work is interpreted first by the performer and again by the viewer, listener, or reader, the issues of interpretation are compounded, not resolved.

We may also note that these issues have important analogues in other fields. For instance, issues regarding artistic performance resemble those concerning constitutional interpretation in law. Strict constructionists, claiming to be faithful to the original framers' intent, vie against more liberal constructionists, who argue that each generation should re-read the Constitution in its own linguistically and culturally conditioned terms, or indeed that each generation can *only* read it this way. The kinds of issues that arise in aesthetics are by no means confined to this field, and the way in which they are approached here may shed a good deal of light on other areas.

Assessment of artistic performance by its fidelity to the author's intent may neglect other potentially valuable factors. Recordings exist of playwrights reading from their own works and of composers performing their own pieces. Should these not be definitive performance models? And should the excellence of any subsequent performance not be measured by fidelity to them? But this standard seems quite wrong. It is not just that some artists are not very skilled performers, but that re-creation of the artist's vision of the work should not be the performer's only objective. Richard Wagner insisted that conformity to the composer's intentions was not at all what he hoped for in opera, that it was merely a point of departure for the performing artist in doing his or her own creative, interpretative work. Wagner said, for instance, that the singer should first learn the music in tempo, but, once that had been done,

> then at last I urge an almost entire abandonment of the rigor of the musical beat, which was up to then a mere mechanical aid to agreement between composer and singer, but which with the complete attainment of that agreement is to be thrown aside . . . From the moment when the singer has taken into his fullest knowledge my intentions for the rendering, let him give the freest play to his natural sensibility, nay, even to the physical necessities of his breath in the more agitated passages; and the more creative he can become, the more he will earn my delighted thanks.[18]

There are of course a great many vigorously disputed practical issues that have their roots in issues about creativity. Prominent among them, for instance, is the issue of integral versus purist restoration: do we replace the damaged parts of an artwork so that the work resembles as nearly as possible its original state, or do we refuse to substitute for the damaged parts something that is not genuine? This is in part the question of whether we *can* re-create an artwork. The issues of forgery, editing, dubbing, and exact copies, raised in the cases to follow, all have a great deal to do with issues of creativity (though in quite different ways) and they can lead to some curious puzzles. Can something be both a forgery and an original work of art? Jan van Meegeren's *Christ and the Disciples at Emmaeus*, for instance, might seem to be so: it was painted as a forgery of Vermeer, yet no Vermeers have religious subjects, and clearly, van Meegeren was quite creative in an enterprise that is more often slavish copying. Improvisation is a central component of jazz. Yet what is it that makes improvisation appropriate and valued in some contexts but not others? Is it the audience's expectation that some passages will be spontaneous but not others? If so, is improvisation actually *creative* when it is anticipated and expected in this way? Similarly, the issue of exact copies raises the problem of whether replicas might not be considered to be as creative as the objects they imitate, at least where the replica is perfect, since it is exactly like the original in all physical respects. All of these issues, of course, involve concepts and principles not confined to creativity alone, including those of beauty, interpretation and meaning, nonartistic values, and critical judgment. But issues about creativity—including whether there really is any such thing and, if so, whether it is to be valued—are implicated in many of these neighboring problems. Indeed, questions about creativity are the source both of a good deal of the confusion in talk about art and of many of art's most interesting practical problems.

CASES

Replication: Restoration, Exact Copies, and Forgery

4-1. CIMABUE'S *CRUCIFIXION*

The *Crucifixion* by the thirteenth-century Florentine painter Giovanni Cimabue was horribly damaged in the 1966 Florence flood. Large portions of the figure, including the right eye and the nose, had been simply washed away, and the remaining portions were flaking. As the painting dried out, the friction caused by the different rates at which the painting and its wooden support dried did further damage.

A team of art conservators first removed the canvas of the painting from its wooden support and then cleaned the painting of a series of varnish layers. A resin-wax mixture was used to reattach the flaking paint; however, the large gaps in the face could not be repaired. The conservators chose to fill these gaps with tiny flecks of colored paint toned to fit with the surrounding painting but appearing as large, flat, uniform patches in the face.

Objectors to this choice pointed out that photographs of the *Crucifixion* before it was damaged were available, that paint types and tones could have been matched with the remaining areas of the painting, and that the restored painting had lost the remarkable spirituality that characterized it before. The conservators should have attempted to recreate the painting as it was before the flood, they argued, and not merely preserved the surviving wreckage.[19]

Are these objectors right?—M.P.B.

4-2. VAN DYCK'S *SAINT ROSALIE*

Autoradiographic techniques have revealed the existence of a "delicate little self-portrait," in the words of one critic, under Anthony Van Dyck's *Saint Rosalie.*[20] It is clear that the self-portrait is authentic, and apparently it is of very high quality. An assistant curator in your museum proposes that a restorer be employed to remove the upper layers of paint to reveal the underpainting. Attempts could be made to save the *Saint Rosalie,* but they would probably be unsuccessful. Nevertheless, he argues, even if the *Saint Rosalie* were damaged or destroyed, it is already familiar to the art world, and its important features could be preserved by careful photographic and descriptive recording. To make accessible an entirely new work, which the art world does not and cannot now fully know, he claims, would contribute more to the understanding and appreciation of Van Dyck than to preserve a work that is already known.

Should you take the assistant curator's advice?—M.P.B.

4-3. SELECTING "AUTHENTIC" SCORES

The conductor of a large orchestra dedicated to the performance of "authentic" music is selecting a program for the next concert. The program will include Schubert's Symphony no. 8 in B Minor (the so-called Unfinished Symphony) and Stravinsky's *Danses Concertantes,* but in each case the conductor must choose the most appropriate score for his players.

In the case of Schubert's Eighth, written in 1822, there are two choices. The first is an autograph score published in 1923 in facsimile edition, that is, a reproduction of the score in Schubert's own handwriting. Since the score for the Eighth was not published in Schubert's lifetime, nor was the Eighth played while Schubert was alive, the conductor assumes that the autograph score is very close to Schubert's intention. A reasonably accurate printed version of the autograph score has been available since 1967. Oddly enough, however, that version is rarely used by orchestras. What has come to be known and appreciated as Schubert's Eighth is actually based on a set of printed editions that have significant differences from the autograph score. The origin of these differences is not known, but it is clear that a performance based on the autograph will sound surprising and strange to nearly everyone who has heard the work performed.

In the case of Stravinsky's *Danses Concertantes*, only one edition is available. Stravinsky did, however, conduct the pieces before he died, and the performance deviated widely from the score. The performance was recorded on a set of limited fidelity 78 RPM records, which preserve at least the broad outlines of these deviations. The conductor can, if he wishes, try to transcribe the changes incorporated into Stravinsky's performance into musical notation on the basis of what one can hear on the old discs.[21]

Which scores should the conductor make available to his orchestra?—P.A.

4-4. MUSIC LESSONS

Some things just never change. Here we are with a permanent colony on Uranus, ongoing negotiations about opening an embassy in the Alpha Centauri System, undersea communities, an implantable synthetic cortex . . . and some people still play the guitar! And I'm not talking about the Compuguitar or the Synthestring. They'll go just as the Moog went. Remember those old acrylic things with pickups? And then there was the whole laser fad, and all variety of piddling with energy fields, and who can forget those disastrous instruments run on Thorium 228 decay. They tried everything. Never quite stamped out those old rosewood boxes with the spruce on top, though. Never will.

Some problems with these things don't go away either. Look at their music, will you. Dots on lines printed on paper! Paper. You heard right the first time. They had to read this information before they got down to playing and then somehow get it into their heads and fingers. Damned indirect, I know. On top of all that they used to write little messages under and over their pitch code to tell you what to do. How could they ever have bothered?

Reminds me of a story about a crazy kid called Fidel who just had to have lessons with the local bigshot a few years back, a fellow called Moderno Simplicitas, who really did have all the answers. They just couldn't get along. They say it was over those little messages, but I can't believe anyone can get heated over that. Anyway, the story goes like this. Seems the kid got hold of an old acousticode which had imprinted a music trace inputted by this ancient player called Segovia. The kid was hooked. After a lot of looking, he came up with a guitar. What's more impressive is that he managed to get a facsimile of the original pitchcode. Simply amazing that any of that stuff lasted through the fire storms . . . you remember what those lunatics did to themselves. Anyway, Fidel has to hunt up a master of the lost art and, sure enough, old Moderno Simplicitas is at it—on the side, mind you. There's no full trade for a guitar teacher, is there? Moderno's fussy. He wants things his way and wants players who've already proven their merit, but he gives in. Fidel's persistence has to count for something.

Things went well at first. Fidel was missing strings, and the ones he had on were in the wrong places. Simplicitas set matters aright and taught Fidel about tuning. (Can you believe they had to *adjust* their pitch before they were ready to play!) This problem was solved back in the late twentieth, and Moderno had got hold of one of their machines—just to stay in the tradition, so to speak. "Tuners" they called them. Sensible name. Sensible device. Tells you exactly how many cycles per second you're generating and then you adjust to match the correct pitch. Fidel fell for these tuners. Built one himself.

The basics began and within a short time the kid was moving into regular pieces. Some of the facsimiles had opening messages, which looked a little like arithmetical equations; for instance, *M.M.* $\downarrow = 132$. "Ah," says Simplicitas, "Metronome indications." He explained that as far back as the nineteenth century, players and composers wanted to be *precise* (he used to say this with great drama, rising to the second syllable, which would come down sharply like the slice of a scimitar) about tempo. They invented their own astoundingly crude but (more astonishingly) effective machine—basically a gear-driven pendulum that sounded reasonably equal time intervals. They went through great technological development, increasing in accuracy and absorbing the twentieth-century fetishes about electrical circuitry. Simplicitas had one of these last models before they gave way to atomic clocks. Fidel matched enthusiasm for his master's knowledge, attacked the music with the Metronome, and learned within a short while to play different tempi very accurately. All the while, however, the memory of the former player Segovia remained with him. When would his efforts begin to seem like those of the ancients?

As the music became more advanced, the presence of messages accompanying the pitchcode became more pronounced—as did the urgency of Fidel's questions. He had decided by now that rigorous attention to the pitchcode and tempo markings alone did not (nor could they ever) make for the sounds of the long-dead Segovia. The secret, he concluded, must lie in the messages. This was the code he appealed to Simplicitas to break.

The master, truth to tell, found all of this a trifle histrionic. "What's the tragedy?" he used to say. "Haven't you been learning guitar? Why trouble yourself over the primitive acousticode?" To this Fidel could only reply: "Well, yes, I have been learning, but there is the music too." He wasn't sure about what he'd said then, but Simplicitas decided to humor his young pupil by responding to his every intemperate demand for detail. Delighted, Fidel lost little time. The messages would now be decoded.

He asked first about the long, narrow wedges that opened and closed under spans of pitchcode. Simplicitas was amused that this should be so intriguing. "They had to tell players then when to louden and when to soften the pitch. But they had no useful way of doing it. We took care of that a century ago with the Variable Decibel Monitor. You want to follow those wedges? Here. I will lend you my VDM." This brought forth further questions. "The instructions *rall. molto* or *molto rit. . . .* what is one to make of these?" Fighting the tedium, Moderno Simplicitas advances the obvious. Music can slow down and speed up. He condescends to reveal the vocabulary. He goes a step further. "If this troubles you, let me lend you my Accelerometer as well. It's a variable velocity device. Quite clever. A few weeks with this and you'll slow down and speed up with great accuracy. No need to leave matters to your most likely sloppy intuitions. Watch the meter. Remember the metronome. They just didn't get that far along. Probably their idiotic war." This slaked Fidel's thirst for a while and allowed him some entry into the intimate domain of a lost language. Segovia was still far away but, hopefully, closer. A matter of time and practice, perhaps.

The story should have had a happy continuation, but it doesn't. Somehow Fidel got hold of a copy of an old, old piece called "Sonatina Meridional," conceived by a man in a place they called Mexico in 1939.[22] It seems this writer, Ponce was his name, couldn't resist the messages. If Italian let him down, he threw in Spanish . . . anything. "What should I do with *sonoridad velada* and *sonoridad metallica?*" Simplicitas had a counter, as usual. "What they used to call 'tone color indications.' You strike the string one way and it sounds hard, another way and it sounds round—but these terms any fool can see carry no hard content, no precision. They knew but couldn't measure correctly the proportion of relevant upper partials to fundamental while a player played back then. So they relied on metaphors and connotations and other vague indicators; in a word, poetry." This last phrase was released with nothing short of contempt and the dawn of massive impatience. "Here, take my clamp-on Sound Spectrograph. It will keep you on track."

The next lot led to the break-up. Truth to tell, the last movement of the Sonatina was the culprit because Fidel couldn't stop. He thought he was near the end. Here's what he copied down from the movement called "Fiesta": *"violento, destacado con humor, robusto, con dulzura, ironica, con calor, lejano y humoristico, apasionado."*

I think Fidel expected more machines, more counters, more monitors. I think he reckoned on Simplicitas saying "Ah, yes, yes, yes. Those well-meaning backward writers. Here, boy, take this Affectometer. You'll find settings and instructions quite simple to follow." This isn't what happened. Simplicitas had quite had it. No machines, no counters, no monitors. "That, my boy," he said in a voice the patronizing quality of which far exceeded anything Fidel thought possible, "that is windy lyricism. The final vague stutters of a failed art. Do you wonder why a generation later they flocked to their computers, toylike though they were? I think we'd best move to proper music, precise music, don't you?"

Fidel never returned. Some say he devoted a great deal of time working on a counter to metricate things like violence and humor and irony and all the other features Ponce thought had to be incorporated into his piece. Others say he cast off Simplicitas's influence and spent all his time listening to the old Segovia acousticode, trying at the same time to imitate the sounds as he heard and felt them. Still others say he let his heart utterly dominate his mind. Whatever, we lost track. But you know, every year or so there are a few just like him trudging around with a wooden box with strings hunting down some master. Nobody sticks with it, though. Not for long. But they keep coming.

Teachers can teach technique. How can a teacher teach music? Or are they the same? Should we wait for an Affectometer? Will one ever turn up? Will it make any difference if it does? Is *music* a part of Simplicitas's culture?—s.G.

4-5. RECONSTRUCTION AND COMPOSITION

What have Alan Rawsthorne, Francis Cutting, and Richard Allison in common? They are all English composers, it is true, but they share a more peculiar distinction. Each has composed at least one work to which another hand has added something without the creator's explicit knowledge or consent.

Nothing is unusual about editorial amendments of other people's work. In music, as in literature, editors often make necessary grammatical alterations because they rightly assume, given the context and style of the piece, that certain aspects in the manuscript could not possibly have been meant. It is true that some editors have been downright abusive through ignorance of period style and manner—

such happened frequently in nineteenth-century editions of early music. But this type of butchery is now largely a memory, and the misguided corrections can be justified by appeal to the time and context in which they were made. In all cases of editorial revision at this level, no one would regard the editor as composing part of the piece. All he or she purports to do is correct rather than create.

This is not all that editors do, though, and it is interesting to consider at what point editorializing becomes composition in its own right. If and when this happens, the question of attribution becomes cloudy.

Alan Rawsthorne had been commissioned by Julian Bream to write a major solo work for guitar. Rawsthorne set to work and completed a fair portion of what was to have become a longer piece. Unfortunately, he died in 1975 before finishing it. Because what he had left was so magnificent, and because he had a series of sketches and ideas for the remainder, Bream himself completed the piece—at least that is how his contribution is described.[23] It is commonplace for composers to work with players in the course of creating the major works, simply because composers often do not know on their own enough about what can and cannot be done with an instrument. But these cases tend to be more consultative than creative, whereas Bream actually *wrote* a fair portion of Rawsthorne's piece. Let us call this a case of "creative completion."

Francis Cutting's story is a little more obscure. Cutting was a talented English lutenist of the late sixteenth century whose major works have come down to us in a series of manuscripts, not one of which is in his own hand. Many pieces are found in a splendid collection written down by Matthew Holmes, a house musician at one of the estates. The first of the Holmes manuscripts contains a piece of Cutting's called *Walsingham*, a series of variations on a well-known tune. Unfortunately, the top right-hand edge of the manuscript was extensively water-damaged—so much so that the first few measures of most of the variations are illegible. No efforts at removing the smudge have succeeded. Notwithstanding this, one modern editor has issued an edition of Cutting.[24] *Walsingham* is there, complete with a footnote stating that the first few measures have been "reconstructed." In this case, although there once was a Cutting original of the first few measures *of Walsingham* (via Holmes), it has been lost forever. A modern editor has filled in what he has taken to be a reasonable replacement for whatever Cutting might have put down himself. Let us call this, as is common, "reconstruction." It differs from creative completion in that it involves partial and often minor replacement of missing parts. It is as if the piece existed intact but is not musically functional because it lacks a portion that prevents it from being performed—rather like a road whose bridge has been washed out.

Creative completion, on the other hand, involves not only the replacement of parts but also the actual surveying, as it were, of the course of the piece.

In 1588, the Walsingham Consort Books were compiled. These were a series of part books for viols, lute, cittern, bandora, and flute and contained a number of extended chamber pieces for this combination (which has come to be known as broken consort music). Unfortunately, not all the part books have survived; for example, the lute part book is missing. This has not stopped the creation of a modern edition. Indeed, in 1977, Warwick Edwards issued full scores of these and other pieces in Volume 40 of the *Musica Britannica* series.[25] One composer often represented in this collection is Richard Allison, whose piece *The Lady Frances Sidney's Goodnight* contains a lute part that is described as a "reconstruction." Unlike the Cutting case, the lute part has been written *de novo* by Edwards. He has, of course, studied typical lute parts for typical consort settings extensively. He has also studied Allison's manner of writing for the lute. Even so, there is not one note of Allison's in the "reconstruction." The lute part is *by* Warwick Edwards. This is not a "reconstruction," as the term is applied to the Cutting case. A more appropriate expression is "proxy composition," which gives the flavor of a full-fledged composition that is not meant to be original. Here, though, we are far from Bream's task of reflecting Rawsthorne's ideas as best he could, because we do not know Allison's ideas concerning this piece. For all we know, the composition's lute part was rather experimental, indeed, Allison was known for his novelty. Edwards, of course, has played it safe and used as many stock-in-trade devices as he could to provide a "typical" or even "average" lute part. There is indeed a little joke that runs through early music circles about scholars who issue editions of lost works in full "reconstructed from the title."

All of these cases are to be distinguished from the more obvious of revisions. Consider, for example, Dionisio Aguado's version of Fernando Sors's Gran Solo, opus 14. As Aguado stated in the preface: "I have made certain additions without changing the essentials of the piece, additions which I judge will give it more brilliance."[26] Aguado sought to heighten "certain orchestral effects" present in the original. His additions largely consist of virtuosic expansions of existing passages, which add greater dazzle. This practice used to be very common among certain virtuosi and still persists. In such cases there is no intention to write or even to rewrite. These versions are, for want of a better term, "customizations" and represent certain technical preferences. Since improvisation has almost always been central to musical performance, it is no surprise that a great player may have wanted to use a given piece as a vehicle for technical display.

With these examples in mind we can ask a few questions. Are

creative completions, reconstructions, and proxy compositions all equally alterations of the original? Or, if we wish to reserve that phrase for customizations, are they not alterations at all? Would it be fair to call them aesthetic *intrusions*; that is, do they represent in some way unwarranted additions to the originals? Recall, when considering this question, the obvious analogy with the restoration of statues and paintings. A statue can, in some sense, do without a head or an arm; we still find room for aesthetic appreciation notwithstanding the mutilation of the piece. A musical work, alas, cannot be played if it lacks certain parts, and playability in this sense is essential to the very existence of the work. Suppose these editorial additions are not intrusions but *interventions* instead. On what basis could they be warranted? If they are warranted, do the completed works become the joint product of composer and editor? Suppose a half-dozen editors independently write six different lute parts, each of them compatible with the rest of the Allison piece. Does this work now have seven authors? In what way, if at all, is the editorial completion of a work unlike the editorial alteration of a work that is already complete? Suppose that creative completion, reconstruction, and proxy composition differ in degree only. By what scale could those differences be assessed? Would customization and complete composition lie on the same scale? Can there ever be so much of a piece missing that any "rebuilding" is simply composition? (Are there any links between this type of re-creation and the construction of facsimiles or models from scanty remains, for instance, the reconstruction of ancient cities on the basis of street plans or the fleshing out of dinosaurs from fragments of bone? Do problems about identity affect all these rebuildings equally?) Would any of the additions merit the term "re-composition," where what the editors do is likened to what a composer might do in his own work when he decides to reshape certain portions of it? If this is a fair likeness, what aesthetic barriers reasonably restrict the alterations and additions anyone might care to make of any work, whether complete or not? What value, in other words, ought we to place upon the *integrity* of a work, and why ought we to place any such value upon it at all?—S.G.

4-6. CUTTING *TINY ALICE*

When Edward Albee attended a San Francisco preview of the American Conservatory Theater's revival of his play *Tiny Alice*, he insisted that ACT read the following statement to the audience (ACT declined):

> William Ball, the director, has taken it upon himself to distort my play by cutting, juxtaposing and actually rewriting a good deal of the third act. . . . Of course this is inexcusable. And it is only out of concern for the

actors who have put so much dedication and talent into the production that I am permitting the play to be performed tonight. I'm sorry that you the audience aren't seeing the play as I wrote it.[27]

Who should have the final say about a performance of a play—the playwright or the director? Did the director's "distortions" mean that the audience was not really seeing Albee's play?—A.B.

4-7. EXACT REPLICATION

As a result of advanced experimentation in molecular physics, a small manufacturing company announces that it has perfected a process by which any work of visual art can be replicated on a molecule-for-molecule basis. In painting, this process makes possible replication of an entire work, including canvas, frame, and all lower as well as exposed layers of pigment. No human guesswork (or error) is involved, and the finished replica is indistinguishable from the original to the most sophisticated visual, physical, and chemical analyses.

1. The company applies for a permit to produce one replica each of the *Mona Lisa* and ten other very well known works at the Louvre as insurance, it says, against "natural disaster." The replicas are to be stored in a permanent underground vault and are not to be removed unless the originals are destroyed by calamities such as earthquake, vandalism, or nuclear war.
2. The company applies for a permit to produce 100 replicas of each of the above works to establish satellite museums in major cities and regional capitals throughout the world.
3. The company applies for a permit to produce unlimited replicas of the works, and announces that it plans to market the replicas in sundry and department store outlets for $14.95 each.

Would you grant any or all of the above permits? If you would grant one or two, why not all?—M.P.B.

4-8. NEW ORIGINAL ROTHKOS?

There are so few good examples of Mark Rothko's middle-period paintings that most people never get to see them, and even in large cities, you cannot count on finding one in a museum. The paintings might be exhibited in traveling shows, but moving them is difficult, expensive, and potentially damaging to the work. Besides, traveling exhibits take the paintings away from people who are fortunate enough to have access to them locally.

A brilliant computer scientist proposes to solve this problem by programming a machine to produce new Rothkos different from any of the paintings he did, but so similar in style to his best middle works that we can be sure Rothko himself would not have minded painting them. The machine's input consists of everything ever written by and about Rothko and his work, along with other relevant cultural and historical documents, together with features of Rothko's own paintings, which it scans and analyzes. The output is brand new "originals" that even the most competent critics and connoisseurs would judge to be no worse (or no better) than the best middle-period Rothkos. The computer program design requires no artistic aptitude or creativity; all it takes is a lot of technical computer ability, an educated layperson's understanding of the paintings, and the assistance of a good research librarian.

Should the new "originals" be produced? If so, what should be done with them, and how satisfactory a solution would they provide for the problem of the scarcity of Rothkos? How should their aesthetic value be judged? In particular, should the new "originals" be compared any differently to the first successful experiments through which Rothko devised his middle-period style than to later works, which were less innovative and tended pretty much to develop variations of the general format at which Rothko had already arrived?—J.B.

4-9. "HUB FANS BID KID ADIEU"

One of the most celebrated sports stories of all time is "Hub Fans Bid Kid Adieu," a minor masterpiece by the well-known novelist John Updike. This story is a loving and accurate account of the events in Boston's Fenway Park when Ted Williams took his last at-bats.

Suppose, however, that Updike were to reveal that "Hub Fans Bid Kid Adieu" was written in March 1960, six months before the historic game in which the Red Sox superstar took his last cuts at the plate. Suppose Updike had hoped to get the piece in print before the game, as an artistic account of how things should come out, but production delays prevented this. As it happened, the events of the game itself mirrored the picture presented in the prose with such accuracy that the story was subsequently published as nonfiction.[28]

Would the fact that the story eventually fit the actual events make a fiction piece nonfiction?—R.M.M.

4-10. POLISH MISTS

Suppose Frédéric Chopin, in his youth, composed a piano prelude, which he called "Polish Mists," performed it once, then put it in a drawer. He promptly forgot it, and so did all the listeners who heard it at its debut.

Now suppose that twenty years later, attempting to round out a set of twelve preludes, Chopin wrote a piece with exactly the same pattern of notes and rhythms as constituted "Polish Mists." He did not remember his earlier composition.

Is this untitled twelfth prelude the *same* piece as "Polish Mists" of twenty years earlier? What if Chopin were later to find the first manuscript at the back of his neglected drawer? Should that change anything?—J.L.

4-11. THE HORRIBLE JUNIOR HIGH CONCERT

Because you are anxious to make your two children aware of their cultural heritage, you have provided them with music lessons from an early age. Your thirteen-year-old plays the clarinet; your twelve-year-old plays the viola. Unfortunately, both children are still at the stage where the daily practice session is torture for student and family alike.

The music teacher at your children's school is extremely ambitious. He does not believe in compromising or introducing the children to second-rate works. Accordingly, he schools them in the classics of the Western symphonic tradition. This year, for their annual concert, the junior high orchestra has been working on Bach's first *Brandenburg* Concerto and Beethoven's Seventh Symphony. Despite the conductor's optimism, the music is much beyond the level of the students. You look forward to the year-end concert with trepidation. It is usually an agonizing occasion.

The concert is repeated three nights in succession. Out of a sense of loyalty, you have purchased a ticket for each performance. The *Brandenburg* opens the program, and on the first night it is played execrably. You know the piece well, and you realize to your horror that the orchestra has failed to play a single right note in the course of the piece. On the second night, the piece goes slightly better. You estimate that the group has managed to play about 40 percent of the notes as Bach wrote them. On the third and final night, the conductor has made a drastic decision: he has decided to alter the tempo and play the piece as slowly as is necessary to guarantee that the young musicians get every note right. He in fact succeeds in this goal, but at a rather high price: the performance of the Bach alone takes three hours! You exit from the concert exhausted, vowing to find another way to show your children the glories of classical music.

On any of the three school concert nights, did you hear a performance of Bach's first *Brandenburg* Concerto? If not, what did you hear? Are playings in practice, teaching, rehearsal, and similar situations performances of the work?—S.R.

4-12.   CORRECTING A CONCERTO

Suppose you are the mentor of one Paul-Jean-Henri Vitedigit, a celebrated concert pianist who is playing the Beethoven Piano Concerto no. 3. Vitedigit is technically very gifted, except that when he plays the Beethoven Piano Concerto no. 3 he inverts certain notes of the *fortissimo* arpeggio in the second movement. He has tried to relearn the piece and can play it correctly in practice, albeit at a slower tempo, but in performance he always plays it in inverted fashion. After considerable psychotherapy, Vitedigit has discovered the origin of the problem: as a boy, he played the concerto in his first public recital—and got the passage wrong. Despite his discovery of the truth, his playing remains faulty, at least during performance stress. Vitedigit is so ashamed of this flaw that he has considered dropping the concerto from his repertoire, but the remainder of his performance is so dazzling that critics and conductors alike encourage him to continue playing it.

Now, Vitedigit is recording the concerto. As is usual in recordings of orchestral music, artifactual noises, coughs, off-key notes, and other extraneous sounds are edited out by sophisticated electronic means. Furthermore, various features of the performance itself are customarily adjusted: pitches are made truer, scales are evened out, and so on. It would be possible—and not unusual within the recording industry—to substitute a correct arpeggio for the faulty one. This could be accomplished by recording Vitedigit at practice, speeding up the recording to reach the desired tempo, correcting for pitch, and splicing it into the performance recording. The conductor and the recording director approve. Vitedigit objects, saying he is sorry he ever agreed to record the concerto in the first place.

As his mentor, you believe you can persuade Vitedigit to do as you wish. You know that the recording of the concerto as a whole will be spectacular, and that the critics will hail it—with or without the dubbed passage—as the best made to date, indeed, the best likely to be made within the next several decades.

Suppose the problematic passage is not just a single arpeggio, but a figure that recurs repeatedly throughout the concerto. Would it be all right to "adjust" the figure in each of its many occurrences?

Suppose a whole movement of a symphony—say the *Andante*—is faulty? Could one electronically tamper with one's own performance, or let a stand-in do part of it, like a stunt man in the movies? How far should "adjustment" be permitted to go?

What should you tell Vitedigit to do?—M.P.B.

4-13. VARNISHING DAYS

Before the opening of an art exhibition at London's Royal Academy, artists were given a few days in which to put finishing touches on their canvases. The great landscape painter J. M. W. Turner relished this brief period, often completely transforming a work to the amusement of his artist colleagues. But he also often offered criticism and advice to other artists working on their canvases.

According to A. J. Finberg's *Life of Turner*, in 1847, Turner exhibited a painting that was hung next to a work by Daniel Maclise entitled *The Sacrifice of Noah after the Deluge*. Turner turned to Maclise and said,

"I wish Maclise that you would alter that lamb in the foreground, but you won't."

"Well, what shall I do?" asked Maclise.

"Make it darker behind to bring the lamb out, but you won't."

"Yes I will."

"No you won't."

"But I will," insisted Maclise.

"No you won't."

Maclise did as Turner proposed and then asked Turner if that would do.

Turner, stepping back to look at Maclise's alteration, said, "It is better, but not right," and then he went up to the picture, took Maclise's brush, and altered the lamb as he wished. He also introduced a portion of a reflected rainbow.

Maclise was very pleased and did not retouch Turner's work.[29]

To whom should we attribute the painting? To whom should we attribute the success of the painting? Is it possible to differentiate Turner's contribution in the completed work from that of Maclise? Is Turner's contribution confined to the darker background behind the lamb and the bit of reflected rainbow, or is it greater?—J.E.B.

4-14. "BODY AND SOUL"

The popular song "Body and Soul" was composed in 1930 by John Green, who wrote the music, and Edward Heyman, Robert Sour, and Frank Eyton, who wrote the melancholy lyrics about a lost love. The song has been played and recorded many times, but perhaps the most famous rendition is the instrumental version improvised and recorded by tenor saxophonist Coleman Hawkins in 1939. Hawkins's improvisation retained the original melody with only minor embellishments but included longer improvised passages containing many arpeggios and phrases not related to the original melody in any obvious way.

Nonetheless, the entire improvisation is clearly based on the harmonic structure of the original song.

In 1979 a vocal group, The Manhattan Transfer, recorded a version of "Body and Soul," which retained the basic harmonic structure of the original song, but substituted a completely new set of lyrics—an homage to saxophonist Hawkins and singer Eddie Jefferson (who himself introduced new words to recorded improvised solos). These words were sung, virtually note-for-note, to the melodic lines improvised by Hawkins in 1939. The Manhattan Transfer also added harmonic embellishments to Hawkins's improvised melodies.

Is the Manhattan Transfer performance a rendition of the original "Body and Soul?" Is it a performance of a new song? In either case, who is the composer of the song?—P.A.

4-15.   THE SEEDS OF FORGERY

Art forger David Stein's wife relates the beginning of her husband's notorious career:

> It was during his association with [Jean] Cocteau that the seeds of art forgery were planted in the back of David's mind. David would sit for hours and watch in admiration as Cocteau painted. But observing Cocteau did not turn David into a forger. What really served as his catalyst was a Picasso painting that David spotted in Cocteau's studio— or, at least, what David thought was one of Pablo's works.
>
> "What a marvelous Picasso," David remarked to Cocteau.
>
> "It is not a Picasso," Cocteau grunted. "I painted it myself. But when Pablo came here visiting one day and saw it, he was so taken aback at how much it looked like his own work that he insisted on signing it."[30]

What, exactly, is the seed of art forgery planted here, and ought any of the pejorative implications of forgery be applied to the "Picasso" too? What does a signature have to do with authenticity, anyway?—J.T.

4-16.   SEBASTIAN'S BAROQUE

Suppose that the Pulitzer Prize Committee finds among the nominees for its music composition prize one J. B. Sebastian, a talented young composer whose work has been strongly recommended for its technical merit and ingenious thematic development. Sebastian's music differs from that of the other nominees chiefly in its complete and stubborn fidelity to canons of composition that were abandoned three centuries ago. In fact, Sebastian is a modern-day baroque composer; his work is generally indistinguishable from that of Nardini, Tartini, and, at its best, Pachelbel. When interviewed, Sebastian said this of his music:

Long ago, I realized that the baroque fugue was not properly developed. It did not culminate in the *Kunst der Fuge*. Many more possibilities and tremendous potential for beauty lurked untapped in this form. In my admiration for the great baroque composers, I was determined to work with them in continuing their project, knowing that what they began was unfinished. I have therefore dedicated my energies to the further working out of this form, with its instruments, its musical architectonic, its limitations.

Should the Pulitzer Prize Committee hold it against Sebastian that his music is not "music of our time"? Should compositions more responsive to the most recent developments in musical tradition get the most credit in such competitions? Or should Sebastian's loyalty to the baroque composers, and his recognition that the project they had begun still remains unfinished, receive particular praise, involving as it does a sacrifice of currency with contemporary music? Does Sebastian's project differ in important ways from that of John Shmarb at the beginning of this chapter? How, in general, should "new-old" art in other media (e.g., contemporary Petrarchian poetry or Giotto-istic painting) be judged?—R.M.M.

4-17. REPHOTOGRAPHING NEIL

Contemporary artist Sherrie Levine is part of a group of artists known as "image appropriators," so called because members tend to lift parts or details from works of art by other artists. Levine is even bolder. Interested in Edward Weston's photographs of his son Neil, she simply photographed Weston's photographs and exhibited the virtually indistinguishable photos as her own works of art.[31]

Are these really original works of art by Levine, or are they simply copies of Weston originals?—H.R.

4-18. ART BY AARON

The "freehand" drawing (p. 137) was done by AARON, a computer program developed by artist Harold Cohen that is designed to model aspects of human art-making behavior. AARON uses a plotter to draw lines on a large sheet of paper; the computer is not programmed to produce a preformed design. Each drawing, which takes somewhere from 10 to 40 minutes to produce, depending on its complexity, is different, though the drawings do resemble each other in ways one might expect of drawings from the same artist. Cohen explains that AARON operates in accord with some twenty or thirty "things" it "knows"; it makes up the drawings as it goes along, without reference to input from the outside, relying solely on its internal rules instead.

Harold Cohen, *Black and White Drawing* (computer generated), 1986.
Photo: Becky Cohen.

Is your appreciation of this drawing affected by knowing that it was done by a computer? By knowing that the computer generates its own design?

Cohen has sold many of AARON's drawings, usually at a token cost of $10 or $20 (despite the much higher costs of the equipment), insisting that computer-generated art is a way for people of ordinary means to be able to have something that, although produced quickly and relatively cheaply by a machine, is nevertheless unique.[32] Does knowing the price further change what you think of the drawing? Does the fact that AARON's drawings are each unique give them greater value than ordinary prints of a drawing?

A majority of the viewers of AARON's work find recognizable shapes in it; the drawing above appears to contain human figures. But AARON here used only the twenty or thirty rules it usually uses, with no special reference to human beings. Does knowing this tell us something about the structure of representation?

Cohen has said, "At the risk of stating the obvious, it seems to me that one of the things human beings find interesting about drawings in general is that they are made by other human beings, and here you are watching the image develop *as if* it is being developed by another human being. . . . When the drawing is finished, it functions as a human drawing. . . . A large part of what we value in art is not the ability of the artist to communicate special meanings, but rather the ability of the artist to present the viewer with something that stimulates the viewer's own propensity to generate meaning."[33] Do AARON's drawings tell us something new about art?

One afternoon, the writer of an article on Cohen watched half a dozen people pay $10 and walk off with an original AARON. She reported: " 'It's a lot better than monkey art,' said one happy buyer to me. Harold Cohen's assistant happened to be standing nearby, and he responded: 'That's because AARON knows a lot more about art than monkeys do.' "[34] Is AARON's art really better than monkey art, and when AARON has been programmed to know four or five hundred things, as Cohen hopes, will it be better than human art too?—D.E.C.

4-19.   COPYRIGHT DISPUTE

In Washington, D. C., and in Indianapolis, Indiana, are two sculptures that look very much alike: both are human-size, dome-shaped structures made of iron bars. There are some differences in design and ornamental details, but, nonetheless, they are remarkably similar. One was made by the artist Nancy Holt in 1980; the other was made by a craftsman commissioned by Josie Orr, the wife of Indiana's governor, in 1981. Ms. Holt has charged violation of copyright laws; Ms. Orr claims that the work she commissioned is not a copy.[35]

How can such a dispute be settled? Is the second work a forgery? Are the aesthetic differences between the two relevant? To whom might our legal system turn for help in resolving this problem?—M.M.E.

4-20.   FAKES AND FORGERIES

On November 20, 1985, news services reported that a famous Rembrandt painting might not be his:

> A West Berlin art expert said Tuesday that *The Man in a Gold Helmet*, believed for centuries to be the work of Rembrandt, probably was painted by one of the Dutch master's students. Jan Kelch, an art historian and specialist in Dutch paintings, said *The Man in a Gold Helmet* probably was painted by one of Rembrandt's students about 1650. "The painting is not a fake," Kelch told the AP in a telephone interview. "It remains a great, masterful work." Kelch, head curator at the West Berlin Art Gallery, said important details in the painting do not match Rembrandt's style. He added there had been doubts about the painting for some time. The likeness it bears to his work testifies that the Dutch artist was "a great teacher", the curator said. "It looks like it really came from the hands of Rembrandt."

Is Kelch right that "the painting is not a fake?" What exactly is a fake? We can learn a lot about fakes and forgeries by considering imaginary cases and asking how we would be disposed to deal with them. Let us begin by reconstructing the story above.

Suppose Rembrandt instructed his most talented students to make exact copies of his best paintings because he wanted them for his own records, so to speak, and did not have the time or patience to copy the works himself. By some mix-up the student's copy of *The Man in a Gold Helmet* was given to the family that commissioned it. The painting remained hanging in the family seat until the present owner forsook tradition and handed it over to Sotheby's for auction. The painting was the object of international attention and, after fierce bidding, it finally fell into the hands of a major museum for a huge sum. Meanwhile, somewhere else in the Lowlands, an itinerant antique dealer was offered a remarkable painting of a man with a gold helmet by an old villager who also turned over a bundle of documents by the famous painter, including details of copies he had his students execute. Rembrandt explained in one letter to a friend that he had even taken measures to ensure that his students did not cheat him, by incorporating into the original paintings some seemingly minor detail. The matter reached public circles and, sure enough, the "original" turned out to be the very painting handed over by the villager. The one bought for millions was traced to a student.

Had Rembrandt commissioned fakes of his own works? Should we take into account the reason he asked students to execute copies when we pass judgment on the painting bought by the art museum? Suppose we change details. Suppose the so-called mixup was deliberate, that as Rembrandt was wrapping up his own painting for delivery, it was accidentally wrecked beyond repair and he could not repaint it if he was to retain the nobleman's commission. So, he grabbed the copy, changed the detail that was the secret key to its identification, wrapped it up, and sent it to his patron. How would this alter your judgment? Here there is no "original," but a copy which, from Rembrandt's perspective, is passable as the original; that is, Rembrandt had no qualms about letting his name stand as the creator of this piece even though he created the type and not this token. Is the painting a fake?

Change another detail: Rembrandt never sold his originals because he regarded his customers as charlatans, incapable of fully appreciating his art. The customers were quite happy with the copies, thinking them to be Rembrandt's own work. As to the originals, Rembrandt displayed them conspicuously in his studio, telling visitors they were copies done by his students for practice, and no one ever doubted him.

Or change yet another detail: Rembrandt teaches his students by requiring that they incorporate many of the telltale identifying features of his own work. He allows them to choose their own subjects but directs the composition in such a way as to yield the kind of painting *he* might have composed had he painted it himself.

These examples prompt us to consider when we would say of an artist that he fakes his own work. How far away from the original source, as it were, must we go before we begin to talk about the emergence of fakes? To what extent are we committed to restricting our talk about fakes to the context of some deliberate plan to deceive for personal profit?—s.g.

Performance and Reading

4-21. DISCUSSING THE TEMPO OF BEETHOVEN

A string quartet sits down to rehearse the first movement of Beethoven, op. 18/6. They read through the movement first, and then pause to discuss tempo:

Cello: How fast should this be?

Second Violin: I think it should be brisk but definitely unhurried (she sings the tune in a strongly rhythmical, vigorous way).

Viola: That sounds fine, and I could see playing it that way except that it's marked *Allegro con brio;* so I think it has to go faster to capture the "brio" feeling—more impulsive and propelled, more headlong, less deliberate. What you sang sounds like an *Allegro* to me, or even an *Allegro risoluto* or *Allegro moderato.*

Second Violin: I don't think we should worry about the words so much—just sing the melody and see how it wants to go, what feels best. Beethoven's words are obviously vague and allow us a great deal of latitude. We should get the tempo from the music itself.

Cello: But when I try to do that I'm never sure whether the tempo I come up with comes from the inner character of the music or from a recording that I heard so many times as I was growing up. What "feels natural" may just be what I'm used to hearing.

Viola: Exactly. And that's why we should stick to the score as much as possible. Even if it feels a bit unnatural to us at first, we'll probably get used to it. And we'll be trying our best to follow what Beethoven wanted.

Second Violin: I disagree completely. What is most important is that our playing is effective, convincing, and vital. So let's find the tempo and character that feels right to us, because that's obviously the way we'll give our best performance. Beethoven's markings are suggestions, and ultimately we're the ones who have to bring off the performance. I'm sure Beethoven wouldn't have wanted us to feel uncomfortable, and I'll feel very uncomfortable playing this movement any faster than I sang.

Viola: From all I've read about Beethoven, I don't think he'd care very much about whether you'd feel comfortable or not. He was a strong-willed person and he'd want the piece played the way he conceived it. I think he knew just what he wanted—he was a terrific performer, after all. Our job is to try to figure out what he had in mind and then to do it. After all, he's the composer! Are you going to suggest that we change dynamics and phrasings if they don't feel comfortable to *us?*

Second Violin: As a matter of fact, I could perfectly well imagine changing or ignoring some of the markings (and you know that most quartets do); we shouldn't be slaves to the score, after all. I don't think players in Beethoven's time felt that they had to follow every single marking in the score. Remember, this wasn't so long after the time when players were actually *expected* to ornament freely and do a passage differently each time it returned. We have to get at the essence of the music, which is very different from worrying about every detail of the score. We should go for the big picture and not get bogged down in details that don't work for us.

Cello: I'm not very happy about the idea of changing dynamics or articulations, but I've been thinking that tempo is different. Tempo seems more a performance matter. After all, a tempo that works well in a hall with very live acoustics may not work well in a hall with very dry acoustics. We've noticed that our faster tempi sound good in relatively dead-sounding halls, but they sound blurry and rushed in vibrant halls. So perhaps we should feel freer in connection with tempi than with other choices we have to make.

First Violin: You know, we have three other movements and two other quartets to rehearse. I suggest we take the slower tempo in tomorrow's concert, and then try it faster the next time.

How would the considerations expressed above be affected by the following facts (unrealistically assumed to be unknown to the players): Many years after the publication of this work Beethoven published metronome marks for this and all of his quartets through Op. 95. He indicated in letters that he was very excited about the possibility of indicating tempi through the newly invented metronome. The tempo indication for the first movement of 18/6 is: *whole note = 80,* which is extremely fast. The possibility that Beethoven's metronome was slow seems unlikely because some of his tempo indications are extremely slow—the second movement of this same work, for example—and are almost never played as slowly as indicated. The tempo indicated by the metronome mark is considerably faster than even that preferred by the violist. One other fact: the slow movement that follows has the metronome indication *sixteenth note = 80*. If the players want to preserve the relationship between the two movements that Beethoven seemed to have in mind, then, unless they play the first movement extremely quickly, the slow movement will be excruciatingly slow.—R.L.M.

4-22. BEETHOVEN'S FIRST SYMPHONY

After the introductory *Adagio molto* of twelve measures, which opens the first movement of Beethoven's First Symphony, the *Allegro con brio* constitutes the rest of the movement. The upbeat to the Allegro— a descending scale from G to D in the strings—resolves on C. As printed in the score, the upbeat appears in the Adagio, before the *Allegro* begins.

But this descending G-to-C figure (and others like it) is repeated many times within the *Allegro*. So, for the sake of aesthetic consistency, this figure as it appears in the *Adagio* preceding the *Allegro* (see circled passage) is almost always performed in the *Allegro* tempo, and it has become usual to regard the *Allegro* as actually beginning with

Allegro con brio.

the *Adagio*'s upbeat to the *Allegro*, not with what is actually marked as its beginning.

Is the usual performance wrong? Or is aesthetic consistency sometimes more important than fidelity to the printed score?—M.K.

4-23. ACTING GREEK TRAGEDY

You are to direct a performance of Aeschylus' *Agamemnon*. In the fifth century B.C., at the time Aeschylus was writing, the roles of the queen, Clytemnestra, and the captured Trojan princess, Cassandra, would have been played by male actors.

If the tragedy were performed with male actors today, would this increase our understanding of Aeschylus' play? Is it the same play, whether performed with male or female actors in the crucial female roles? Would it be the same play if performed by an all-female cast? Or is the original play simply unperformable in today's world?—M.P.B.

4-24. OBOE D'AMORE

You are the music director for a series of "musica antiqua" concerts, which will endeavor to reproduce early music in as authentic a way as possible. You are faced with the following problem: In Bach's Magnificat in D, the instrumental *obbligato* in the third number is scored for oboe d'amore. The oboe d'amore of Bach's day was a two- or three-keyed instrument, and although several of the original instruments are still extant and in playing condition, you are aware that to the modern listener this oboe has a somewhat archaic and peculiar tone. However, you are quite certain that it was not Bach's intention to produce a passage that might sound archaic or peculiar in any way, and you wonder whether Bach's intentions might not be better served by the modern French oboe d'amore instead of the instrument of Bach's day.

Keeping in mind that the purpose of the concert series is to reproduce early music authentically, which instrument would you use?—P.K.

4-25. HAYDN'S *FAREWELL*

In 1772, Franz Josef Haydn was given an excellent orchestra at the estate of Prince Esterhazy in Eisenstadt. He did much of his early composing there, including his memorable *Farewell* Symphony. In the dramatic finale of that work, Haydn had the instrumentalists, who all felt that they had been working far too long without a vacation at home, blow out their candles two by two and leave the stage. Two remaining violinists played the last notes, extinguished their candles, and exited from the stage, leaving the hall silent and dark. The message to the Prince was obvious, and it worked.

When the Symphony is played today, no one leaves the stage. However, after discovering that most listeners did not understand the dramatic *diminuendos* at the end, a certain conductor decided to perform the piece authentically by having the players tiptoe off stage two by two during the finale. Half the audience tiptoed out also, outraged that they had been cheated, or annoyed that a serious work had become a joke.

How should this symphony be performed? Suppose the auditorium has a complex series of elevators that allows each stand in the orchestra to descend slowly out of sight—would that add to or detract from the performance? Suppose the auditorium has a complex lighting system that allows each pair of musicians to remain on stage, while one by one the stands disappear into darkness? Or should *that* composition have been played only once, since there is no way to perform it a second time?—J.F.

4-26. EXPERIENCE AND ACTING

Heinrich Gottfried Koch refused to give the role of Phaedra to a certain actress because he felt that she had never experienced true love and thus would be incapable of rendering the part convincingly. W. H. Auden, on the other hand, argued that "if a man can be called to be an actor, then the only way he can be 'true' to himself is by his 'acting,' that is to say, pretending to be what he is not."

Which, if either, of these views of performance in theater is correct? Why?—J.F.

4-27. THE VIRTUES OF PORNOGRAPHY

Consider the argument that one of the most important (and indeed one of the distinguishing) features of fictional literature is its facility for engaging the reader actively in a way television and movies do not. Books, it may be said, make people fill in the details, exercise their imaginations, and work on and with the material that is presented, not merely take it in. But if this is so, shouldn't pornographic literature be especially welcomed? As Gore Vidal says:

> [B]y abstracting character and by keeping his creatures faceless and vague, the pornographer does force the reader to draw upon personal experience in order to fill in the details, thereby achieving one of the ends of all literary art, that of making the reader collaborator.[36]

Is this argument sound? Should pornography be welcomed on aesthetic grounds?—R.M.M.

4-28.   READING *RAMBO*

Three students have been discussing films and moral consciousness and come upon the following passage from a review in *Cahiers du Cinéma:*

> Morality is a matter of sentiment; it engages the spectator's subjectivity in an emotional way. It structures the spectator's pleasure. . . . Political discourse is different. It removes the innocence from the spectator's attitude, . . . it invests pleasure with worldly, material bases for violence. It deprives violence of its tragic, that is to say, metaphysical, halo.[37]

"The authors of this article ought to think well of *Rambo*," one student observes. "The film plainly treats Rambo's attacks on the Vietnamese as politically motivated acts."

"I agree," the second student chimes in. "*Rambo* is not sentimental. On the contrary, it encourages the spectator to be coldly realistic about the need to play hardball in international relations. According to the film's point of view, there are times when military privateering against a sovereign nation with whom you are not formally at war is justified."

"You're both wrong," the third student protests angrily. "*Rambo* is exactly the kind of film the writers of this article are criticizing." Which student (if any) has got it right?—F.L.

4-29.   ACTING *OTHELLO*

An actor is playing the title role in Shakespeare's tragedy *Othello*. He is, let us suppose, either (1) feeling nothing as he does so, or (2) thinking about his betrayal by his business partner, or (3) worrying over his suspicions of his wife's infidelity, or (4) imagining that the critic is about to pan him and thus becoming enraged.

Does the quality of the actor's performance, as judged by a spectator, depend on knowing anything about his inner state or real emotions, that is, whether (1), (2), (3), or (4) is the case? What does the actor's state of mind have to do with the effectiveness or worth of his performance, if anything?—J.L.

NOTES

1. Steven M. Cahn and L. Michael Griffel, "The Strange Case of John Shmarb: An Aesthetic Puzzle," *Journal of Aesthetics and Art Criticism*, 34, no. 1 (Fall 1975), 21–22. Reprinted by permission.

2. The quotation is from Percy Bysshe Shelley, Preface to *Prometheus Unbound*, in *Shelley's Poetry and Prose*, ed. Donald H. Reiman and Sharon B. Powers (New York: Norton, 1977), p. 133.

3. Plato, *Ion*, 534B.

4. Carl Gustav Jung, "Psychology and Literature," from *Modern Man in Search of a Soul*, trans. W. S. Dell and Cary F. Baynes (New York: Harcourt Brace Jovanovitch, 1955), reprinted in Stephen David Ross, *Art and Its Significance* (Albany: State University of New York Press, 1984), p. 514.

5. Vincent Tomas, "Creativity in Art," in *Problems in Aesthetics*, 2nd ed., ed. Morris Weitz (New York: Macmillan, 1970), p. 380.

6. Jack Glickman, "Creativity in the Arts," in *Philosophy Looks at the Arts*, ed. Joseph Margolis (Philadelphia: Temple University Press, 1978), pp. 145–146, quoting D. N. Morgan, "Creativity Today," *Journal of Aesthetics and Art Criticism*, 12 (1953), 14.

7. Monroe Beardsley, "On the Creation of Art," in *Art and Philosophy*, ed. W. E. Kennick (New York: St. Martin's Press, 1979), p. 157.

8. Glickman, "Creativity in the Arts," p. 146.

9. Glickman, "Creativity in the Arts," p. 154.

10. H. W. Janson, in *Perspectives in Education, Religion, and the Arts*, ed. Howard E. Kiefer and Milton K. Munitz (Albany: State University of New York Press, 1970), p. 302.

11. Beardsley, "On the Creation of Art," p. 159.

12. Beardsley, "On the Creation of Art," p. 159.

13. Beardsley, "On the Creation of Art," p. 159.

14. See, for example, Roland Barthes, *S/Z*, trans. Richard Howard (New York: Hill and Wang, 1974), passim.

15. Jean-Paul Sartre, *What Is Literature?* trans. Bernard Frechtman (New York: Harper & Row, 1965), p. 39.

16. Stanley Fish, *Is There a Text in This Class? The Authority of Interpretive Communities* (Cambridge, Mass.: Harvard University Press, 1980).

17. Nelson Goodman, *Languages of Art* (Indianapolis: Hackett, 1976), p. 186.

18. Andrew Porter, "Musical Events: Taking the Lead," *The New Yorker*, January 20, 1986, pp. 72–76; Wagner quotations are from p. 72.

19. "Bringing Paintings Back to Life," *The Economist*, December 25, 1982, pp. 95–100.

20. "Bringing Paintings Back to Life," p. 100.

21. Adapted from Norman Del Mar, *Orchestral Variations* (London: Eulenberg Books, 1981), pp. 203–208, 219–222.

22. Manuel M. Ponce, *Sonatina Meridional*, ed. A. Segovia (London: Schott: Guitar Archives, 1939).

23. Alan Rawsthorne, *Elegy*, completed and edited by Julian Bream (London: Oxford University Press, 1975).

24. Francis Cutting, *Selected Works for the Lute*, edited and reconstructed by Martin Long (London: Oxford University Press, 1968).

25. Warwick Edwards, ed., *Music for Mixed Consort*, vol. 40 of *Musica Britannica* (London: Stainer and Bell, 1977).

26. Dionisio Aguado, *Selected Works for Guitar*, ed. S. Wynberg (Monaco: Editions Chanterelle, 1983).

27. Dan Sullivan, writing in the *Los Angeles Times Calendar*, November 2, 1975.

28. John Updike, "Hub Fans Bid Kid Adieu," in *Assorted Prose* (New York: Knopf, 1965), pp. 127–147.

29. A. J. Finberg, *The Life of Turner* (New York: Oxford University Press, 1961), p. 416; and Diana Hirsch, *The World of Turner 1775–1851* (New York: Time-Life, 1969), p. 17.

30. Anne-Marie Stein and George Capozi, Jr., *Three Picassos Before Breakfast: Memoirs of an Art Forger's Wife* (New York: Hawthorne Books, 1973), p. 28.

31. See Douglas Crimp, "Appropriating Appropriation," catalogue essay for *Image Scavengers: Photography* (Philadelphia: Institute of Contemporary Art, University of Pennsylvania, 1983), reprinted in Richard Hertz, *Theories of Contemporary Art* (Englewood Cliffs, N.J.: Prentice-Hall, 1985), p. 159.

32. Pamela McCorduck, *The Universal Machine: Confessions of a Technological Optimist* (New York: McGraw-Hill, 1985), p. 124.

33. Moira Roth, "Harold Cohen on Art & the Machine," *Art in America*, September–October 1978, pp. 106–110.

34. McCorduck, *The Universal Machine*, p. 125.

35. See Douglas C. McGill, "Copyright Dispute Over 2 Artworks," *New York Times*, August 29, 1985, p. C20.

36. Gore Vidal, *Reflections on a Sinking Ship*, quoted in Irving Buchen, ed., *The Perverse Imagination: Sexuality and Literary Culture* (New York: New York University Press, 1970), p. 131.

37. Pascal Bonitzer and Serge Toubiana, "État du siege," *Cahiers du Cinéma*, no. 245–6 (April–June 1973), 50.

CHAPTER 5

ART
and
OTHER
VALUES

THE DESTRUCTION OF MONTE CASSINO

In February 1944, in one of the most controversial actions of World War II, two hundred fifty Flying Fortresses leveled the Benedictine monastery at Monte Cassino with the highest concentration of explosive power used up to that time. In a single day, at the orders of a single person, General Bernard Freyberg, an artistic and historical monument that had been begun in the sixth century was completely destroyed.

Allied leaders who had obeyed General Freyberg's orders immediately protested their innocence and their powerlessness to prevent the bombing. Although precautions were to have been taken in the campaign to avoid any damage to the abbey, General Freyberg insisted that the abbey was occupied by German soldiers who threatened the lives of his advancing men. For this reason, he maintained, it had to be destroyed.

Assuming that General Freyberg was correct in his assessment, was it acceptable to destroy an artistic treasure such as Monte Cassino? One might say that it was a military necessity. (Actually, there was apparently no evidence of a military presence within the monastery, and there had been widespread skepticism about its being the keystone of the German defenses of the Liri valley.) But surely, one could have replied, millions of people died in World War II, so what are a few thousand more casualties relative to the worth of such a monument? Indeed, an incalculable number of people had lived and died in the fourteen centuries Monte Cassino survived. But, on the other hand, is any monument, any artwork, worth saving if it results in even one death? Does art have any real importance or value compared with the value of human life?

If war inescapably distorts our way of looking at values, let us imagine a fictional peacetime dilemma:

THE FIRE IN THE LOUVRE

The Louvre is on fire. You can save either the *Mona Lisa* or the injured guard who had been standing next to it—but not both.

What should you do?

Is a human life more valuable than an artwork, even an extraordinary artwork, or less so? Would it make any difference if the person about to die in the fire were not a guard, but a thief who had come to steal the painting, or a convicted terrorist who had murdered other people? Or suppose the guard had already fallen to the floor unconscious and would not have suffered in the fire—how would that affect your decision? What if he were very old and ill and not likely to live much longer anyway—would this provide a reason for saving the painting rather than the man? Or ought one save the painting under any circumstance, even if this requires the sacrifice of human life?

ROTHKO'S BEST WORK?

Suppose that before he died, Mark Rothko told you in a sworn, notarized statement that one of the paintings attributed to him was executed by the incorrigible nephew of a visitor to his studio who got hold of a brush and paint and vandalized an empty canvas. By mistake the canvas was consigned to a gallery and later sold to a museum at a very high price, where it now occupies a prominent place. It clearly contributes to the reputation of both the museum and Rothko, and the critics consider it among Rothko's best works.

As an admirer of Rothko and a friend of the museum, should you keep this secret of twenty years, or tell the truth?

How would you justify telling all when you are very fond of the canvas and consider it better than most real Rothkos?

Consider the consequences of your revealing what you know: not only will there be endless lawsuits and deep embarrassment on all sides, but people will view the canvas differently and perhaps even remove it from the museum in which it hangs. Yet people may get more delight from a canvas about which they are misinformed than from one about which they have learned the truth; why should anyone want to change things? After all, the authenticity of a work may properly affect its economic value, but what has it to do with aesthetic value? On the other hand, is it not important to tell the *truth?*

THE PRICE OF A RAPHAEL

Suppose that Raphael had faked a painting of his studio assistant Giulio Romano and signed it with Romano's name. Discovered undamaged, it was sold for $12,000. When it was later demonstrated that the painting was not a real Romano, its market value dropped to the price of the frame. When it was still later proved that it was Raphael's work instead, a museum offered $1,200,000 for it. Curators and museum directors claimed that the price was right because they could see things in it when it became known as a Raphael that they could not see when it was known as a Romano.

We obviously can be mistaken about the immediate cash value of a painting, and that value is, like most things, variable over time. Can we be mistaken about the aesthetic value of a work of art? Can it change over time? In what way, if any, is the aesthetic value of a work related to its market value?

ROCK LYRICS

Many persons, especially teachers and parents, have expressed concern over rock lyrics that are sexually explicit or vulgar and that express approval of violence, incest, murder, torture, and mutilation.

One rock musician recently defended his work by replying, "When I say 'Sleep with your sister, it'll blow your mind,' I am saying that if the United States would start being friendly with the Soviet Union, who knows how much good would be accomplished?"

An organizer of rock concerts responded to the charges of being a corrupting influence by saying, "It is not my job to police the morality of society. The performers are all artists, and no one has the right to tell an artist what to do."

Do overtly obscene lyrics undermine conventional morality, and if so, should they be suppressed? Or are artists beyond usual moral constraints, even the dominant moral rules in a culture? Does a society have the right or the responsibility to make sure that its arts do not subvert its accepted moral principles? *Can* the arts alter a society's fundamental moral stance?

"HAIL, MARY"

From time to time, commercial motion pictures have outraged various religious groups. In Jean-Luc Godard's film *Hail, Mary,* Mary, who is nude in several scenes, is portrayed as an avid basketball player who works at a gas station. Joseph is a cabdriver; Gabriel is an unsavory bum. All of them discuss divine insemination casually, and often in obscene language.

The film was widely picketed by Catholic groups, which claimed it blasphemed their most sacred religious beliefs. Their chief complaint was not so much that the morals of a society were directly threatened by the film, or even that Catholic youths who saw it would fall into sin, but that a desecration of religion itself had taken place.

Does an artist have the right to offend the moral or religious sensitivities of a community? Should whatever aesthetic values we find in film, painting, literature, or any of the other arts yield to other societal values? If so, under what conditions? Is it always wrong to offend anyone with your art? If not, when does it become wrong? How severe an offense to the majority would make it wrong? How severe an offense to a specific minority? Can there be redeeming aesthetic values in a work in the face of which religious, moral, or other societal values become unimportant or less important?

These cases point to just a few of the kinds of conflict one can discover whenever art is, as inevitably it must be, part of the life of a people. Art is valued for a host of reasons. You might, for example, value an engraving you own because its lines are subtle and delicate, because it calls to mind a devotional theme, because it covers a crack in the wall, or because an art dealer is willing to pay you a thousand dollars for it. If another object would cover the crack more efficiently, or if you would prefer to have a thousand-dollar coat rather than the engraving, one of your reasons for valuing the artwork may compete directly with others and lose out to them. In instances like these, determining the outcome of a conflict of values may be an easy matter. Difficulties arise, however, as soon as we try to assess the competition between aesthetic and other values. What is the importance of the engraving's cash value as compared to the subtlety and delicacy of its lines? This difficult question points to two more basic difficulties, which must be faced at the start of any discussion of the relation between aesthetic and other kinds of value.

The first difficulty has to do with ambiguities in the concept of *value* itself. Sometimes we speak of value as one big class or kind of thing, so that moral values, economic values, religious values, political values, historical values, aesthetic values, and so on are subclasses of human value, and one general theory of value provides the criteria for judging each. At other times, we are concerned more with the distinctive characters of different sorts of value than with similarities between them. We speak of each field of value as having its own individual nature, so that comparisons among different kinds of value are difficult to make. If the differences between the kinds of value are substantial—if, for example, ethical values are held to be universally binding, whereas aesthetic values are not—quite separate theories may be required to account for them.

The second basic difficulty, already raised in earlier chapters, involves a lack of conceptual clarity about the nature of aesthetic value. Is aesthetic value something that an artifact possesses—a quality we can find among the other objective properties of the work— or is it something that happens to an artifact when we esteem it in a certain way? When we say that an object is "aesthetically valuable" or that it has "aesthetic value," do we mean that the object *has* value, independently of being perceived and appreciated, or do we mean that it has been *judged* valuable? Does a piece of classical sculpture buried forever under volcanic ash have aesthetic value even though it will never be seen again?

The history of aesthetics, as we have seen, has had defenders of each view. With respect to the conflict of values, however, the theoretical problem of where aesthetic value lies is less consequential than that of the nature of the enterprise of valuing. Whether or not the value is in the artifact or in the eye of the beholder, it is the value that produces the tensions. The buried sculpture, valuable though it may be, is unlikely to be involved in any quarrel. Only when we have a publicly perceivable artwork does aesthetic value—however that may be judged—conflict with other, different values in our society.

ETHICAL VALUES

Every social group has its standards for acceptable behavior. But some moral principles, it is widely believed, transcend local cultures. For instance, a great many people believe that respectful treatment of other persons is a moral imperative, and that causing unnecessary pain in others is an action universally to be deplored. Consequently, if aesthetic values were to come into conflict with these ethical values, they might be expected to do so in all societies. Nevertheless, the nature of the resulting conflicts, their characteristic terms and results, will continue to vary from culture to culture, as the qualities of the values involved are assessed differently by different people. Something that is universally to be deplored may be more deplorable in some societies than in others. It may also have differing relationships to aesthetic values (which may themselves be weighed differently). One can speak of value conflicts in the abstract, but the tensions between aesthetic values and moral values always occur in particular societal settings.

The recognition that ethical and aesthetic values may conflict with or reinforce each other is hardly new. In Book 3 of the *Republic*, Plato argued that it is necessary to restrict the artist in his ideal state on the grounds that art affects human behavior. Art that produces undesirable behavioral consequences must be excluded, and art that yields good behavioral consequences should be produced for the benefit of the populace. Thus, poetry that sets bad models, such as Homer's description of Achilles weeping over the death of Patroclus or of Zeus' impatience to sleep with Hera, must be expunged from the literature of the state, and poets should write only of brave, pious, upright actions. Such views of art, not simply as an autonomous activity but as deeply affecting the whole of our lives, were not restricted to the Greeks. In the nineteenth century, Tolstoy saw art as a force that could elicit the loftiest ethical behavior—if the artist sincerely experienced the highest of human feelings and possessed the ability to communicate them to others through his works. In both Plato's and Tolstoy's eyes, ethical (and religious) goals were the determinants of aesthetic value.

Sexual Ethics

Artworks, or artifacts offered as artworks, often seem in our culture to create friction with ethical values in the area of sexual mores. At a time when sexually explicit films can be seen in any city, in theaters and on videotapes, it is hard to imagine that before the release of *The Moon is Blue* in 1953, the words "pregnant," "seduce," and "virgin" were never spoken in Hollywood films. In retrospect the lawsuits over this film, its being banned in Boston, and the moral outrage of the Roman Catholic Legion of Decency over what today is thought to be a harmless comedy seem quaint and unreal. But the issue was real enough at the time: a motion picture offended the moral sensibilities of a large segment of the population; and this fact was accepted by many people as a basis for suppressing it.

Furthermore, the issue did not disappear when the Production Code was eventually replaced by the audience-rating system in use today. Nor has the fundamental conflict between pornography and traditional morality been resolved by distinguishing between "hardcore" and "softcore" pornography. This is not simply because it is difficult to find a clear definition of pornography, but because pornography is often *intended* to be a challenge to conventional morality. If the very point of a pornographic work is to violate moral norms, the question becomes: Does this specific work nevertheless possess socially redeeming features to merit its acceptance? Those who answer yes often construe these features in aesthetic terms and argue that positive aesthetic values may override ethically negative ones. Indeed, some argue that aesthetic values always override ethical ones. Those who answer no may hold either that aesthetic values never override ethical ones, or that they do not do so in the present case. How such disputes are to be adjudicated must depend, of course, on a more general account of the relative weights of aesthetic and ethical values, an account by no means subject to easy agreement.

The "Work Ethic"

Because American society has traditionally valued hard work, Americans tend to admire those who are industrious and diligent and tend to abuse those they perceive as lazy or facile. This value in large part motivates the cliché expressed by detractors of the more abstract arts, "anyone could have done it." But even if an artist demonstrated little effort or skill in creating a work, would this warrant critical judgment against it? Clement Greenberg, proponent of the avant-garde, once said of the painter Piet Mondrian that his pictures with their white grounds, straight black lines and opposed rectangles of pure color radiate clarity, harmony, and grandeur. "Mondrian" he insisted "was one of the greatest painters of our time."[1] Frederic Taubes responded that Greenberg was under the influence of some rhapsodic afflatus and did not realize that "even without the use of masking tape any semiskilled practitioner could easily achieve similar grandeur without unduly straining his creative faculties."[2]

Assuming that you are at least semiskilled, could you achieve what Mondrian achieved, armed only with three cans of spray paint and a roll of masking tape? How does, or should, the presumption that any semiskilled person could have executed a work affect its value? Is it a moral or an aesthetic demand that a great work take great effort?

RELIGIOUS VALUES

Religion is an area of human enterprise that uniquely blends conflict and cooperation, the competition of values and their accommodation. Religious devotion has inspired—and been fostered by—much of the greatest music, architecture, poetry, and visual art of all cultures. Cathedrals, which are among the grandest architectural accomplishments in history, can be understood only in terms of religious belief. The same is true of oratorios, requiems, and many great literary works. Yet some religious artifacts (plastic dashboard Madonnas, household icons, cinder-block churches, mass-produced menorahs, flea-market Buddhas, sentimental devotional verse) have negligble aesthetic value. And, conversely, some works apparently devoid of both religious intent and content have such evident and overpowering aesthetic value that many people are inclined to insist that they are religious. For example, Paul Tillich called Picasso's *Guernica* an altarpiece and considered it a masterpiece of modern religious painting, even though he would not be tempted to regard Picasso as a religious person.[3]

Obviously, the reasons why something is prized aesthetically and the reasons why it is prized religiously can interact in complex ways. The aesthetic greatness of Verdi's *Requiem* fuels its religious power. And, in spite of Clive Bell's remark that it does not matter a straw whether a crucifixion painting is of Jesus Christ or John Smith,[4] the religious content of Grunewald's *Crucifixion* seems to contribute to its aesthetic power.

Fra Filippo Lippi is reported to have been a blasphemer and a nun-seducer. He never renounced his orders, but painted many moving paintings and fathered another famous painter, Filippino Lippi. Fra Angelico, also a painter, was revered as a pious and faithful friar all of his life. Both Fra Filippo Lippi and Fra Angelico painted a number of paintings of religious subjects. It seems doubtful that anyone not aware of the biographical accounts could look at their paintings and tell which of the painters was the more genuinely religious. Yet a great many of the devout consider Fra Angelico's work not only more deeply religious, but aesthetically superior as a result. (Indeed, perhaps the fact that a large number of Fra Angelico's paintings are still in unusually good condition today reflects the religious community's esteem for him; such a concern for artworks because of the artist is commonplace.) Nevertheless, there is an important distinction between valuing artists, or the character of artists, and valuing their works. While this distinction may seem to be a clear one, it may also be asked whether aspects of the character of the artist insinuate themselves into the work in such a way that they affect its aesthetic value, so that judgments of the artist and the artwork are never wholly independent.

J. S. Bach wrote a celebrated mass, as did Leonard Bernstein. Bach made a point of identifying his work with deeply held and specific theological beliefs; Bernstein did not. Are the aesthetic qualities of these works affected by these attitudes? Is one mass more "religious" than the other? Indeed, what makes a piece of music religious?

Of course, some paintings *are* more religious than others. Surely representational content plays a role: a painting of the Crucifixion, no matter how good or how bad, is usually thought to be more religious than a painting of a bowl of fruit, simply because it portrays a religious event. Of course, the matter is not always so simple. A painting of the Crucifixion might be intended to show the cruelty of religion, and hence be antireligious, whereas a bowl of fruit might be intended to convey thanks for God's bounty. But it is also maintained that certain stylistic qualities make some works, even abstract works, more religious than others: profundity versus triviality, for example, or reverence versus superciliousness. While reducing these qualities to simple descriptive characteristics may be an impossible task, it would also be absurd to deny that there is something that could be called religious style—even in works that have no overt connection with religious subjects or even religious artists. Similarly, certain pure musical compositions strike us as appropriately called "hymns" or "requiems" or "prayers," even though they lack words that might indicate religious content. Does this mean that some blurring of the categories of religious value and aesthetic value is inevitable?

HISTORICAL VALUES

People enjoy artworks for various reasons. Much of the so-called art of antiquity draws attention primarily because the works are old. Even the *Venus de Milo*, exquisite as it may be, is often viewed as one would view the Acropolis at Athens or Fountains Abbey—as a ruin, more important historically than aesthetically. When an alleged antique krater from ancient Greece, loudly praised for its beauty, is discovered to be a bowl made in the nineteenth century, it is scorned and its presumed aesthetic qualities seemingly disappear. Is an object more beautiful if it is authentic than if it is a fake? This is to extend a question introduced in our discussion of creativity in Chapter 4; we may now ask whether aesthetic value depends upon historical factors and, if so, to what degree.

In the previous chapter, we considered whether Jan van Meegeren's Vermeer forgery *Christ and the Disciples at Emmaeus* could be considered creative. When Van Meegeren confessed in 1945 that he sold six of his own paintings as Vermeers—including *Christ and the Disciples at Emmaeus*—they were regarded as among the finest of all of Vermeer's works and had hung in major galleries for years. Van Meegeren's very effective forgery brought the matter of historical authenticity and aesthetic value to an obvious head: of course it is *morally* wrong to fake a painting, but did the revelation in 1945 that the paintings were not by Vermeer point out any *aesthetic* difference? Not surprisingly, some critics immediately changed their minds about the value of the paintings. Authenticity became the criterion of aesthetic value, but had the paintings changed? Where had their beauty gone?

Some works that are genuine, and done by artists of certifiable talent, are nevertheless criticized as being unoriginal. In Chapter 4 we considered originality as a variety of creativity; here the question is whether originality is a historical or an aesthetic property. When Handel or Mozart built complex works out of simple, familiar melodies, were they unoriginal? Surely originality in music does not mean using only unfamiliar tunes any more than originality in literature means using only sentences that have never been written before. Originality seems to involve what the artist does with the material in relation to the history of the medium more than what he or she does with the material itself. But, like authenticity, originality is clearly an aesthetic as well as a historical property.

POLITICAL VALUES, MARXISM, AND THE ISSUE OF AESTHETICISM

In the previous discussion of conflicts between aesthetic and other values, we asked whether aesthetic values should yield to ethical, religious, or historical values, or the other way around. We have assumed that the values were more or less distinct and have dealt largely with questions of priorities among them.

The conflict between aesthetic and political values also seems at first to involve a question about priorities. Frequently, however, theorists understand this conflict in such a way as to deny, or undercut, any need to establish priorities among values. Some argue, for instance, that the *only* value of artworks is aesthetic. This is the radical aestheticist position. More moderate aestheticists hold that whereas art has other values, aesthetic values always have priority, and hence there is no real conflict. Others maintain that art naturally excludes itself from contact (and hence, conflict) with other values. Marxists, among others, differ from aestheticists in that they do not deny conflict between aesthetic and other values, but insist that aesthetic value is merely a function of other values, and therefore not in conflict with them.

Aestheticists defend their views by pointing out that we would not call an artifact *art* except for its aesthetic qualities, no matter what other qualities it possessed. Since they understand aesthetic value to be autonomous, they tend to locate it in formal features of the work, not in its utility or moral significance. This is the background from which "art for art's sake" theories are derived, theories that insist that art has nothing to do with morality, religions, politics, or any other area of human activity. Taken to its logical conclusion, however, this idea suggests that art is in total conflict with all other human concerns (because it is at odds with all other values) yet that it cannot conflict at all (because it is disconnected from these values). In this view, the realms of art and social concerns are by their natures distinct, and the artist is completely alienated or separated from society.

Marxists make much of this alienation, insisting that the "art for art's sake" view of the aestheticists defends a social order marked by class exploitation. This exploitation will end, they say, when aesthetic value is recognized to have its roots in economic relationships and to have importance only because art is important to the life of man in his society. An artwork's real value, they insist, depends on its function in its social setting.

Lenin was in many respects the clearest, as well as the most radical, of the early theorists. Literature, he insisted, "cannot be a means of enriching individuals or groups: it cannot, in fact, be an individual undertaking, independent of the common cause of the proletariat. . . . Literature must become *part* of the common cause of the proletariat."[5] In other words, any literary activity that does not serve the common cause, as found in the efforts of the party, is to be condemned. Literature, as all art, is a tool, a shaper of political attitudes. Its function is social. It arouses and enhances the awareness of social realities. Thus, in every setting Marxists have considered the function of art as ideological; indeed, if an artist were to fail to serve an ideology, any value accorded his or her work would be based on a false idea. Furthermore, art based on a false idea produces a contradiction that leads inevitably to the deterioration of aesthetic value itself. Properly understood, Marxists maintain, the work of art is both an expression of and a reaction against social conditions. Appropriately designed, it becomes a weapon in the class struggle.

ECONOMIC VALUES

That the price tag on an artwork does not coincide with its aesthetic value, however the latter is measured, is obvious. We know many other factors that affect economic value: among them, supply and demand, inflation, and fads. Is an Impressionist painting that was bought for a few hundred dollars in the nineteenth century ten thousand times better today? Not long ago Sotheby's sold two Degas paintings for slightly over seven million dollars and a Tissot of the same period for about two hundred thousand dollars. Is one Degas worth almost twenty Tissots, not just in the marketplace, but aesthetically? Is the Van Gogh *Irises,* sold for almost 50 million dollars in 1987, twenty-five times better than his *Bouquet de Fleurs des Champs,* sold by Sotheby's in 1981? These questions may not seem to make much sense, because aesthetic values do not readily lend themselves to quantitative measure. Art thieves do not steal the most beautiful objects; they steal the ones with the highest price tags. A person who prefers to contemplate a Mary Cassatt or an Adolphe Bouguereau canvas rather than a Renoir may be exercising good sense or good taste, but whoever gets a chance to buy a Renoir at a Cassatt price and chooses the Cassatt as an economic investment may be doing a very unwise thing. Of course, it may be that Renoirs are currently overpriced and Cassatts are not yet at the top of their market; perhaps the buyer was right. How to outguess the financial market in art is one problem; the important question is what difference, if any, *aesthetic* values should play here.

Works of art can do many things, and these may cut across the traditional boundaries of values. Art is not unique in being subject to different kinds of evaluation, nor are aesthetic values the only values that conflict with others. The contest between the religious and the ethical, for instance, is among civilization's oldest, and the struggle between the political and the ethical among its most controversial. Here we have been specifically concerned with problems raised by the aesthetic, a value realm that seems to have more than its fair share of competitors. Can any characteristic patterns be seen in these oppositions? Is any generalization possible?

Because art objects can be used in so many ways, the corresponding evaluations are hardly a surprise. Paintings can be a good investment, as they may appreciate faster than stocks or bonds do. Music can soothe or excite us, cover the sounds of traffic or of the quarreling couple upstairs, induce us to buy more in the supermarket or play a better game of backgammon, or even reduce pain during childbirth. Literature can inspire self-improvement or make us frustrated with life. Some sculpture can even keep us warm if we run out of firewood.

Aristotle's observations about the functions of objects are applicable here. An object can have all sorts of uses, he pointed out, and can function effectively in a number of ways. An acorn can serve as food for a squirrel or a missile for a child to throw at a squirrel. It can be varnished and mounted on a stand. It can signal that autumn has come. It can also develop into an oak tree. But of all these functions, the last is the *distinctive* one, since, while other things can serve as food, weapons, decorative objects, or natural symbols, nothing but an acorn can grow into an oak tree. Similarly, art can have many values attached to it, but only one value is distinctive. This is what we have called "aesthetic value." Just what aesthetic value consists in has puzzled philosophers since they began thinking about it, but two things seem clear: aesthetic value has to do with appreciating something for its own sake, rather than for other considerations, and it has to do fundamentally with the act of perceiving. Aestheticians sometimes combine these ideas in the claim that aesthetic value arises when something is recognized as "worth contemplating for its own sake."

But what *is* worth contemplating for its own sake? Can aesthetic theory provide useful guidance here? The task is difficult because strongly held values are as complex as they are diverse. Each of us has a loose catalogue of things, attitudes, and actions we prize. Judgments about them are not always compatible in concrete situations. They may even show a mutual hostility within one realm of value. In the realm of ethics, for instance, one may be obliged both to tell the truth *and* to preserve human life, yet find oneself in situations where one obligation can be satisfied only if the other is violated. Moreover, contests of values may cut across entire value systems. I may admire a work aesthetically that offends me religiously. I may buy a painting that is a poor investment, or profit from a painting that I loathe. I may appreciate the art of Bruckner's music, yet prefer to listen to music whose aesthetic value I acknowledge to be inferior (it may be hard work to listen to Bruckner, and I may be tired; indeed, some serious musicians cannot stand chamber music at breakfast).

If, despite all this, aesthetic theory is to guide us in determining what is worth contemplating for its own sake, it will begin either by underscoring or denying the autonomy of our aesthetic judgments. In declaring a painting aesthetically valuable one may have to ignore how well it covers the cracked plaster, how much of a bargain it was, how strongly it inspires one to charity or nobility, whether it offends or reinforces one's faith or morality, and so on. According to the opposite point of view, however, the claim that a painting is aesthetically valuable may imply that its beauty is *enhanced* by its utility or by how it functions morally, religiously, economically, historically, and so on. There is no consensus as to which is the right alternative or even whether other alternatives may exist. As in so many aesthetic matters, this fundamental question has so much compelling evidence on either side that it does not permit easy resolution. Furthermore, it is not a question to be resolved lightly, for the answer determines whether General Freyberg was right in bombing Monte Cassino, whether the *Mona Lisa* or the guard should be rescued from the fire in the Louvre, whether the secret of the "Rothko" canvas should be told, whether the Romano is undervalued, whether certain rock lyrics should be suppressed, and other practical dilemmas, which are presented in the cases that follow.

CASES

Art and Ethics

5-1. BLOOM COUNTY

Bloom County by Berke Breathed. © 1983 Washington Post Writers Group, Reprinted with permission.

Is it *wrong* to enjoy something aesthetically if it is unethical? Can one enjoy aesthetically a fictional portrayal of horrible events without enjoying aesthetically the horrible events themselves?—M.M.E.

5-2. DANGEROUS BODY ART

During the late 1960s there was a great deal of interest in "Body Art" in both Europe and the United States. In such art, the physical body of the artist was a central element in the work and was used in extremely dangerous ways. American artist Chris Burden, for example, had himself shot in the arm with a .22 caliber bullet in *Shoot* (1971), crawled (almost naked) through broken glass in *Through the Night Softly* (1973), and had himself "crucified" with nails in his hands onto the back roof of a Volkswagen in *Transfixed* (1974).[6] Members of the *Wiener Aktionismus* group—Otto Mükl, Günter Brus, and Rudolf Schwarzkogler—were even more extreme.[7] Schwarzkogler created what he called "artistic nudes—similar to a wreckage," in which he mutilated himself, cutting his penis.[8] In 1969, he died from these self-mutilations.

As a gallery director, not only must you decide whether or not this is art, but what your responsibilities are to human life and its preservation. Considering the circumstances and your knowledge of his previous "works," what should you do if an artist like Schwarzkogler wanted to perform in your gallery?—H.R.

5-3.   STOLEN MAYAN ART

As the director of a large museum, you are offered the opportunity to purchase an important Mayan sculpture for your museum's Pre-Columbian collection. However, you realize that the sculpture has been stolen and smuggled into this country. If you and other museum directors do not purchase such pieces and preserve them in your museums, this sculpture and others like it will be destroyed. What should you do, break the law and thereby encourage pillaging of artworks, or let the work be forever lost to the world? (Note: this practice goes on all the time; does that make a difference?)—H.R.

5-4.   EARTHWORKS AND ENVIRONMENTAL DEVASTATION

In the 1960s and 1970s, works of art known as earthworks became popular. Although it was not much noticed at the time, these artworks are in many ways similar to various kinds of environmental devastation. For example, Walter De Maria's *Las Vegas Piece* (1969) consists of four "earthmarks" in the desert 95 miles northeast of Las Vegas: each earthmark is 8 feet wide and ½ to 1 mile long. The work resembles a bulldozer scar on a virgin desert landscape; in fact, it was constructed with a bulldozer. Similarly, Michael Heizer's *Double Negative* (1969–1970) is a 50- by 30- by 1,500-foot double cut in Virgin River Mesa, Nevada, which displaces 240,000 tons of rhyolite and sandstone. It is reminiscent of the results of mining operations, in particular the highwall cuts and skyline notches produced by Appalachian coal mining. Another striking example is Robert Smithson's *Asphalt Rundown* (1969), constructed by dumping a truckload of asphalt down the side of a quarry. It resembles the consequences of certain kinds of industrial pollution.

   The similarity in appearance of such works to the environmental devastation caused by industry, mining, and construction is not accidental. Smithson once remarked that the "processes of heavy construction have a devastating kind of primordial grandeur" and that the "actual *disruption* of the earth's crust is at times very compelling."[9] In fact, he once contacted industry in an attempt to actualize a proposal for a set of works called *Projects for Tailings*. His vision was to construct earthworks of the millions of tons of waste "tailings" and spoil produced by modern mining operations. Michael Heizer even characterizes himself by saying, "you might say I'm in the construction business."[10]

Robert Smithson, *Asphalt Rundown, Rome, Italy, 1969.*
Courtesy of John Weber Gallery, N.Y.

By the 1970s and 1980s, public response to the environmental devastation produced by technology had become extremely negative. In many states, legislation was passed both restricting the extent of allowable industrial pollution and requiring the reclamation of devastated environments. Indeed, one can imagine an industry leader responding to an earthwork such as Smithson's *Asphalt Rundown* with the comment: "If my company had dumped that eyesore out there, the government would make me clean it up!"

Why should artists such as De Maria, Heizer, and Smithson not be treated in the same manner as the industry leaders? Is there any good reason why public response to earthworks should be different from what it is to the environmental devastation caused by industry, mining, and heavy construction? Should De Maria, Heizer, and Smithson be required to clean up their earthworks?—A.C.

5-5.   JACKSON POLLOCK'S THERAPY

In 1939 to 1940, Jackson Pollock gave his analyst a series of forty-three drawings as a means of expressing himself. The analyst, Dr. J. Henderson, sold the drawings in 1959 to a San Francisco art gallery, but Pollock's widow, Lee Krasner, objected to having them publicly exhibited. She said, "anything that goes on between analyst and patient is private—about as private as a confessional."[11]

Pollock's widow died in 1985. Should her wishes concerning her husband's drawings be respected? Or is it appropriate to exhibit them now? Should her wishes have been respected prior to her death, or would it have been all right to exhibit the drawings despite her objections, since she did not own them? Was the analyst justified in selling the drawings in the first place, or should he have kept them and had them destroyed at his own death? Does the fact that these drawings were part of Pollock's therapy have any bearing on their status as art?—M.P.B.

5-6. DYING WISHES

Virgil, fatally ill aboard the ship that was carrying him back to Italy, is said to have made a deathbed wish that the unfinished manuscript of the *Aeneid* be destroyed. Felix Mendelssohn made a similar wish concerning the manuscript of his Italian Symphony. And Aubrey Beardsley, also on his deathbed, ordered his illustrations for *Lysistrata* to be destroyed because he considered them obscene.

None of these wishes was carried out. Should any or all of them have been honored? Do we need additional information to answer this question?—B.H.

5-7. *ROCKY ISLAND WITH SIRENS*

The year is 1912. A patron who has commissioned a mural entitled *Rocky Island with Sirens* is distressed to discover that the artist has painted the sirens naked. The patron has a second artist touch up the mural so that the sirens appear dressed. The original artist, who had accepted the commission fee, nevertheless holds that he has a right to present his work in its original form.[12]

Who should have prevailed in this case, the patron or the artist? Is this merely a legal issue, to be settled by determining whether the case took place in the United States, which does not recognize an artist's "moral rights" of integrity in the artwork, or, say, Germany, which does? (Because *Rocky Island with Sirens* was a German case, the court held that the artist had the right to present his work in its original form; it probably would have been decided against the artist in the United States.) Or are there aesthetic principles that dictate what the law should be? —M.P.B.

5-8. THE COLOR OF *PITTSBURGH*

In 1958, Alexander Calder's mobile *Pittsburgh* was donated by a private collector to Allegheny County, Pennsylvania, for installation in the Greater Pittsburgh International Airport. The mobile was originally black and white, but when it was installed, it was painted green and gold, the official colors of Allegheny County. Calder protested, but the work was not restored to black and white during his lifetime.[13]

Having already relinquished ownership of the work when it was sold to the collector, did Calder, as the creator of the work, still have a right to insist that it not be altered? Even if he did not, was it wrong for Allegheny County to alter the artwork against his wishes? Could we say that the artwork itself had a right not to be altered, regardless of whatever rights Calder or Allegheny County might have had?—R.M.M.

5-9. MAHLER'S SUPERSTITIONS

Mahler's Symphony no. 6 is allegorical and highly personal. In the last movement, Mahler traces the adventures of a fighting hero who falls and rises twice in battle. These events are marked by two hammer strokes, and in the first version of the score, they are followed again by a third hammer stroke. This last hammer stroke marks the hero's being fatally struck down, "like a tree."

Mahler so strongly identified with the hero of the first version that he feared that the third hammer stroke would foretell and precipitate his own death. So, in the official second version he suppressed the third hammer stroke entirely.[14]

Are only artistic considerations pertinent in giving credence to the intentions of a composer? Are we under a moral obligation not to perform the first version? Should we disregard Mahler's personal feelings of identification? Which of the competing intentions of the composer is decisive, if any? Is the fact that Mahler is already dead relevant?—M.K.

5-10. TAKIS AND "THE MACHINE"

On January 3, 1969, the Greek-born sculptor Takis (Panayotis Vassilakis) went to the Museum of Modern Art in New York City and attempted to remove one of his sculptures from the museum's exhibition "The Machine." As critic Lucy Lippard reported in *Studio International* magazine, Takis contended that "an artist had the right to control the exhibition and treatment of his work whether or not he had sold it." Lippard went on to say that this was "not a revolutionary proposition, except in the art world."[15]

Art law has become a more complicated field in recent years.[16] It is widely claimed that works of art are part of a separate category of objects, distinct from all other classes of objects and, therefore, not subject to the laws and restrictions placed upon other material goods.

Is this claim philosophically defensible? Or was Takis simply stealing?—H.R.

5-11. CLOTHING NUDES

Joe Brown, a noted sculptor of athletes who lived in Princeton, New Jersey, did a larger-than-life bronze of two gymnasts for the campus of Temple University, in Philadelphia. The male figure, dressed in shorts, both feet on the pedestal, holds the unclothed female high over his head in a dramatic handstand. Mr. Brown, in response to feminist complaints that the sexes are not treated equally in his work, replied that he had at first intended both figures to be unclothed, but a nude male at street level in a city would invite vandals to spray paint or decorate it in various ways, so he added the shorts.

Should such issues affect the aesthetic qualities of artworks? Should the sculptor have left both figures unclothed? Both clothed? Clothed the female and left the male unclothed? Or do what he did? Are the shorts an artistic mistake?—J.F.

5-12. REVISING *KING LEAR*

During the eighteenth century, Shakespeare's *King Lear* was regarded as a great but flawed play. Critics complained that the play concluded with the undeserved death of Cordelia, the "virtuous" daughter. As the great eighteenth-century critic Samuel Johnson complained: "His [Shakespeare's] first defect is that to which may be imputed most of the evil in books or in men. He sacrifices virtue to convenience . . . he makes no just distribution of good and evil."

Eighteenth-century producers were quick to solve this problem. In the so-called Tait ending of *King Lear* Cordelia not only survives but is rewarded for her virtue. Is Johnson's complaint about Shakespeare a just one? Do considerations of morality justify changing Shakespeare's original in the Tait ending?—A.S.

Art and Religion

5-13. THE TRIAL OF VERONESE

In Venice in 1573, Paolo Veronese was tried before the Tribunal of the Inquisition on charges of having introduced unacceptable figures into a religious painting called *Feast in the House of Simon*, executed for the Refectory of S. S. Giovanni e Paolo. The following is an excerpt from the minutes of the trial:

Q. What picture is this? . . .

A. This is a picture of the Last Supper that Jesus Christ took with His Apostles in the house of Simon.

. . . . .

Q. At this Supper of Our Lord have you painted other figures?

A. Yes, milords. . . . There is the owner of the inn, Simon; besides this figure I have made a steward, who, I imagined, had come there for his own pleasure to see how the things were going at the table. . . .

Q. . . . What is the significance of the man whose nose is bleeding?

A. I intended to represent a servant whose nose was bleeding because of some accident.

Q. What is the significance of those armed men dressed as Germans, each with a halberd in his hand?

A. This requires that I say twenty words!

Q. Say them.

A. We painters take the same license the poets and the jesters take and I have represented these two halberdiers, one drinking and the other eating nearby on the stairs. They are placed there so that they might be of service because it seemed to me fitting, according to what I have been told, that the master of the house, who was great and rich, should have such servants.

Q. And that man dressed as a buffoon with a parrot on his wrist, for what purpose did you paint him on that canvas?

A. For ornament, as is customary.

Q. Who are at the table of Our Lord?

A. The Twelve Apostles.

Q. What is St. Peter, the first one, doing?

A. Carving the lamb in order to pass it to the other end of the table.

Q. What is the Apostle next to him doing?

A. He is holding a dish in order to receive what St. Peter will give him.

Q. Tell us what the one next to this one is doing.

A. He has a toothpick and cleans his teeth.

Q. Who do you really believe was present at that Supper?

A. I believe one would find Christ with His Apostles. But if in a picture there is some space to spare I enrich it with figures according to the stories.

Q. Did any one commission you to paint Germans, buffoons, and similar things in that picture?

A. No, milords, but I received the commission to decorate the picture as I saw fit. It is large and, it seemed to me, it could hold many figures.

Q. Are not the decorations which you painters are accustomed to add to paintings or pictures supposed to be suitable and proper to the subject and the principal figures or are they for pleasure—simply what comes to your imagination without any discretion or judiciousness?

Paolo Veronese, *The Feast in the House of Levi.*
Art Resource, N.Y.

A.   I paint pictures as I see fit and as well as my talent permits.

Q.   Does it seem fitting at the Last Supper of the Lord to paint buffoons, drunkards, Germans, dwarfs and similar vulgarities?

A.   No, milords.

Q.   Do you not know that in Germany and in other places infected with heresy it is customary with various pictures full of scurrilousness and similar inventions to mock, vituperate, and scorn the things of the Holy Catholic Church in order to teach bad doctrines to foolish and ignorant people?

A.   Yes that is wrong; but I return to what I have said, that I am obliged to follow what my superiors have done.

Q.   What have your superiors done? Have they perhaps done similar things?

A.   Michelangelo in Rome in the Pontifical Chapel painted Our Lord, Jesus Christ, His Mother, St. John, St. Peter, and the Heavenly Host. These are all represented in the nude—even the Virgin Mary—and in different poses with little reverence.

Q.   Do you not know that in painting the Last Judgment in which no garments or similar things are presumed, it was not necessary to paint garments, and that in those figures there is nothing that is not spiritual? There are neither buffoons, dogs, weapons, or similar buffoonery. And does it seem because of this or some other example that you did right to have painted this picture in the way you did and do you want to maintain that it is good and decent?

A.   Illustrious Lords, I do not want to defend it, but I thought I was doing right. . . .

The judges required Veronese "to improve and change his painting" within three months of the trial and decreed that if he did not "correct the picture" he would be liable to penalties imposed by the Holy Tribunal. However, Veronese did not change the picture; instead, he changed its title to *The Feast in the House of Levi,* thereby satisfying the Inquisition.[17]

Is Veronese's painting still a painting of the Last Supper, or is it now a painting of a feast at Levi's house? Did Veronese change anything in the picture in changing the title? Was the Inquisition too easily satisfied?—A.T.

5-14.   TREASURES OF ISLAM

During the summer of 1985, the Musée Rath in Geneva held a major exhibition of Islamic art, emphasizing miniatures and Arabic calligraphy. Organizers and donors were criticized by Islamic fundamentalist groups, who claimed that many of the works were blasphemous or too sensual to be displayed.

Claude Lapaire, director of the Geneva Museum of Art and History, which organized the show, said he had been under pressure to remove a fifteenth-century Persian miniature depicting Prince Ardashir in bed with the slave girl Gulnar, a seventeenth-century Indian picture of a Qadi, or judge, "caught by surprise with a young man," and an eighteenth-century Persian picture showing Susannah naked before the Elders. Lapaire also said that the fundamentalists considered the display of Arabic calligraphy blasphemous because the texts were all taken from the Koran: "They felt that the exhibition extols the beauty of the *script* when for them the real beauty lies in what the writing *says*, which is the Word of God."[18]

What weight should be given to the fundamentalists' objections, either in continuing the Musée Rath exhibition or in planning a future one? How similar are the fundamentalists' objections to the display of the miniatures and to the display of the calligraphy? Should these objections change the ways in which other persons view the exhibition?—M.P.B.

5-15.   MIXED VOICES IN THE CHURCH

In a letter to Franz Liszt, dated June 23, 1865, Giocchino Rossini wrote:

> If it were given me to live in the Vatican as you do, I would throw myself at the feet of my adored Pius IX to plead for the grace of a *new* Bull permitting women to sing in church together with men. Such a step would give new life to sacred music, which is now in total decay. It is my feeling that His Holiness who, I know, loves music and is not ignorant of my name, would acquire new glory in Paradise by issuing such a Bull, and Catholics of every land would bless him for this act of justice (since both sexes mingle in church attendance) and true harmonic sensibility. Our holy religion, though some wretches would like to trample it

underfoot, will always remain at its most sublime and music will ever be a great aid to the devout.[19]

Is Rossini right that allowing men and women to sing together in the church would achieve "true harmonic sensibility" for sacred music? Does the fact that most, if not all, of the sacred music of the time was written for men's and boys' choirs make a difference in whether "true harmonic sensibility" could be achieved? Do Rossini's reasons for recommending this change to the Pope appear to be primarily aesthetic, social, or religious?—J.F.

5-16. SAWING APART THE GHENT ALTARPIECE

In the late nineteenth century, the Berlin Museum, which then owned part of the paintings belonging to the Ghent Altarpiece, separated the painted fronts of these panels from their backs, which were also painted, by sawing them apart. This harsh measure was intended to facilitate the exhibition of the panels and their inspection by an art-loving public. But it also served to obscure the fact that the panels were created as ecclesiastical objects for display in a church, and to stress their character simply as art.[20]

Is there something wrong with the display of religious objects as *art*? Did the Berlin Museum mistreat the Ghent Altarpiece by facilitating its public display, or should religious art be displayed like other works of art?—M.P.B.

Historical and Political Values and the Problem of Aestheticism

5-17. PHOTOGRAPHING THE CIVIL WAR

Civil War photographer Matthew Brady frequently repositioned and rearranged bodies of dead soldiers and other objects in composing war scenes to be photographed. Is there anything about Brady's practice that should disturb us?—M.P.B.

5-18. DRAMATIC CONFRONTATIONS

Maximilian, sent by Napoleon III to be emperor of Mexico, never met Benito Juarez, the revolutionary leader whose forces finally captured and executed him. The makers of the film *Juarez* followed history, documenting the events of the Mexican revolution, and did not invent a confrontation scene between the two leaders—even though this could have dramatized powerfully their opposing political philosophies.

In *Maria Stuart*, the German poet Friedrich von Schiller invented a meeting between Queen Elizabeth and Mary Queen of Scots in which an attempt by Lord Shrewsbury to reconcile the two queens is marred by insults from Elizabeth and a vehement denunciation of Elizabeth by Mary. This confrontation confirms Elizabeth's resolve to have Mary executed and leads directly to Mary's death. It is one of the most powerful scenes in dramatic literature, though it departs widely from the historical facts.[21]

Did the makers of *Juarez* miss an aesthetically important opportunity which Schiller did not, thus consigning their work to lesser significance? Or did Schiller take unwarranted liberties with his subject, given that his materials were historical ones? Can the merits of *Juarez* and *Maria Stuart* be evaluated on the same basis, and if not, what differences should there be in the bases on which they are judged?—J.H.

5-19. DAMAGING STEREOTYPES

Oliver Twist's Fagin, the Merchant of Venice, the Pisan *Cantos*, clowning blacks in old movies, W. S. Gilbert's use of "nigger" time and again in his lyrics—are these not arguably pernicious, sustaining the most damaging stereotypes? Even if they contribute to artistic merit, should works that may do social harm continue to be preserved and enjoyed?—J.E.B.

5-20. RIEFENSTAHL'S *TRIUMPH OF THE WILL*

In 1933 the well-known German filmmaker, Leni Riefenstahl, was commissioned by Adolf Hitler to make a documentary of the Nazi Party rallies that were to take place in Nuremberg that year. Riefenstahl was known in Germany both as an actress and as a creative and innovative director, but she was not an expert in the documentary film style nor was she a member of the Nazi Party. In fact, she was preoccupied with film as an art form and had little interest in German politics. Under this commission Riefenstahl made three films of Nazi Party rallies. The most famous, *Triumph of the Will*, portrayed the rally of 1934. This film won a number of awards, including the grand prize at the 1935 Venice Film Festival and the International Grand Prix at the 1937 Paris World Exhibition.

As an artistically and technically superb documentation of the rise of Hitler and the Nazi Party, the glorification of German nationalism and the innate superiority of the Aryan race, *Triumph of the Will* has raised a number of criticisms and questions:

1. Is the film a documentary or a piece of propaganda? In general, can one distinguish between documentary and propaganda?
2. Can a film disinterestedly record an event? What is the role of the editor or director?
3. (a) Are documentaries works of art, or can they be?
    (b) Are pieces of propaganda works of art, or can they be?
    (c) Can one distinguish between art and documentary/fact, or art and propaganda?
4. Can a great work of art represent or express evil, or can the subject matter and content of a work, especially when it is radically sexist, racist, or violent, irremediably damage the work? Should works that present inherently evil notions through aesthetically dramatic means be censored on that account?
5. Can artists aesthetically distance themselves from an evil they portray in a positive or sympathetic way in an artwork, or are they somehow morally responsible for the way that evil is depicted, even in a work of art?—P.W.

5-21.   CONDUCTING WAGNER

After World War II, the Jewish conductor L. K. emigrated from Europe to the United States and settled in Ohio, where he was appointed music director of a symphony orchestra. It was suggested that he include works of Wagner in his programming. L. K., who had lost his parents in the Nazi concentration camp at Auschwitz, refused on the grounds that Wagner was an anti-Semite and that his views had been appropriated into Nazi ideology.

Israel also forbids the playing of Wagner's music. Should its reasons for doing so be understood in the same way as L.K.'s, or is there some difference in how individuals and countries should act in such a situation?—M.K.

5-22.   THE GREAT PYRAMID

In *Civilization on Trial*, the English historian Arnold Toynbee said:

> When we admire aesthetically the marvellous masonry and architecture of the Great Pyramid or the exquisite furniture and jewellery of Tut-ankh-Amen's tomb, there is a conflict in our hearts between our pride and pleasure in such triumphs of human art and our moral condemnation of the human price at which these triumphs have been bought: the hard labour unjustly imposed on the many to produce the

fine flowers of civilization for the exclusive enjoyment of a few who reap where they have not sown. During these last five or six thousand years, the masters of the civilizations have robbed their slaves of their share in the fruits of society's corporate labours as cold-bloodedly as we rob our bees of their honey. The moral ugliness of the unjust act mars the aesthetic beauty of the artistic results.[22]

Can/should the ugliness of the unjust act of creation mar the beauty of the Great Pyramid? Are persons who respond in this way being softhearted, or are they right? Despite the harm it might do to the Egyptian national identity, the tourist industry, and local pride, would it be a significant achievement to have the Great Pyramid razed to remind us that aesthetic values ought never be given priority over ethical ones? Or should we treasure the Great Pyramid no matter what it cost in unjust human suffering?—R.M.M.

5-23. MURDER AS A FINE ART

One of the assigned texts in a course on nineteenth-century English literature is Thomas De Quincey's satirical essay, "On Murder Considered as One of the Fine Arts." A student in the course finds the essay lackluster and tedious until she comes upon the following passage:

> [S]omething more goes to the composition of a fine murder than two blockheads to kill and be killed—a knife—a purse—and a dark lane. Design, gentlemen, grouping, light and shade, poetry, sentiment, are now deemed indispensable to attempts of this nature.[23]

She is instantly inspired and determines to become the leading artist of this exciting genre. She sets about at once to design and execute murders of the highest artistic quality. Judges of the law will presumably find her work culpable, but should judges of artworks—art critics and aestheticians—evaluate it in the terms, and according to the standard techniques, of aesthetic assessment usually applied to more conventional art genres? Is the immorality of murder a bar to one's aesthetic appreciation of it? Isn't immorality sometimes a source of aesthetic appreciation (as it appears to be in the works of Edgar Allan Poe, Charles Baudelaire, and others)?—R.M.M.

5-24. *ASIAN FLOODWORK*

Aestheticism, the view that works of art are not, or should not be, subject to moral judgment, is often associated with the nineteenth-century writers Theophile Gautier, Walter Pater, and Oscar Wilde. As

Wilde once put it: "I must admit that, either from temperament or from taste, or from both, I am quite incapable of understanding how any work of art can be criticised from a moral standpoint. The sphere of art and the sphere of ethics are absolutely distinct and separate."[24]

Recently one author has asked us to consider a hypothetical work he calls *Asian Floodwork*:

> Imagine that Christo [famous for pieces such as *Running Fence* and *Valley Curtain*] announces at a press conference that he's going to dam the entire river system of an Asian alluvial valley. The object of the art project is to show Third-World agriculture under water. Jacques Cousteau will make photographs which will be shown in the Tate Gallery. At the end of the press conference Christo points out, "I know some of you object to this because of the billion people living there who are dependent on that agriculture. Such concerns, I must remind you, are irrelevant. This is a work of art."[25]

Does *Asian Floodwork* constitute a *reductio* of aestheticism?—A.C.

Economic and Social Values

5-25.   THE PRICE IS RIGHT

In Milan in 1957, Yves Klein exhibited ten blue monochrome paintings. The paintings appeared to be exactly the same in every respect. However, the prices were all different. According to one account, this provoked the viewers "to examine them minutely so as to discover the unique essence of each."[26]

Were the viewers looking for something that could not have been there—differences in the paintings that were a function of price alone? Or could differences in the prices *create* differences in the paintings, or in the way the viewers saw the paintings? How does or should the price of a work enter into aesthetic appreciation of it?—M.P.B.

5-26.   BUDGET CUTS IN THE SCHOOLS

Because of your legislature's ever-zealous enthusiasm for budget cutting, the funds for art instruction at the elementary school of which you are principal have been reduced to five thousand dollars for the entire school year. The school has two kindergartens and six grade levels with about one hundred twenty students each, for a total of nearly one thousand students. Of these students, about 3 percent have been identified as gifted and 1.5 percent as learning disabled. Twenty percent come from economically deprived backgrounds, 65 percent are middle class, and another 15 percent come from quite well-to-do circumstances. The art teacher reports that there are three children, one a first grader and two in the fifth grade, who appear to have uncommon artistic ability.

As principal, you must decide how to spend the funds your legislature has appropriated. You can purchase only two of the following:

1. A series of weekly art-appreciation films.
2. The services of a half-time art teacher who meets the usual certification tests.
3. The services, on a tutorial basis, of a prominent and gifted artist living in the area, for a quite limited number of hours of individual instruction per week.
4. Remedial art supplies designed for students working below grade levels.
5. Materials to equip one art room for crayon and pencil drawing and water painting; this would accommodate five groups of forty children per day, throughout the year.
6. Elaborate materials and supplies, including kiln, oils, sculpture equipment, and so on, to service a very small number of students on a reasonably intensive basis.

Which two will you choose? As principal, you can also consider siphoning off funds from other programs, such as mathematics or athletics, for use in the art program; or you can consider distributing all of the art funds to programs elsewhere in the school. All other programs, in your opinion, are also underfunded.—M.P.B.

5-27. THE NEW-MUSIC DILEMMA

In 1983, the New York Philharmonic instituted a series of new-music concerts designed to introduce contemporary music to symphony audiences. During the first year, the concerts drew an average of 2,000 customers a night; they were discontinued only several years later, after the average attendance had dropped to 1,212. "A hundred years ago," remarked music critic Donal Henahan in commenting on this situation, most music was new music, and "people went to concerts eager to test new pieces, to thump and squeeze them like produce customers in search of a tasty melon. But now," he continued, "we find on one side a small but influential group vociferously pressing for recognition of new works and on the other a resistant majority made up of those who know what they do not like and refuse to buy the rationale that they have a duty to be bored on behalf of art. . . ."[27]

Because Philharmonic patrons voted with their feet by staying away from concerts devoted to contemporary music, should this music be inserted into the regular subscription program, so they must hear it if they want to hear any music at all? Or should the Philharmonic simply discontinue its efforts to introduce symphony audiences to contemporary music?—A.S.

5-28. OROZCO

One of José Orozco's greatest murals, *Prometheus*, depicts an enormous human figure surrounded by flames and strange animals. The face is anguished, the lines and shapes are contorted and tense, and the colors are strident and unsettling.

Prometheus is painted on the wall of the Frary Dining Hall at Pomona College, Claremont, California. The location of the mural gives it a captive audience: it is hard to eat in Frary without looking at it. Thus, the vast majority of people who see the mural are the diners. And almost all of them—even those who greatly admire the mural— find it an unwelcome dining companion, particularly at breakfast, when it bothers almost everyone.

From time to time, people have argued that no matter how good the mural is, unwilling viewers should not have to be subjected to it and so it should be painted over. In deciding to paint a *mural* rather

José Orozco, *Prometheus*, 1930.
Pomona College, Claremont, California.

than a movable canvas, they claim, Orozco accepted such an eventuality. In any case a mural should not control the use of the building that supports or houses it, but the other way around.

In view of the genuine, repeated, and well-documented discomfort it causes, as well as its acknowledged greatness, should the mural be preserved?—J.B.

5-29. THE CASE OF THE RECLUSIVE ART-OWNER

Imagine that from a recently discovered document of the early sixteenth century, a certain Baron, descendant of an ancient family, turns out to be the rightful owner of the *Mona Lisa*. A series of courts examines evidence concerning the original document and its successors, and ownership is definitely attributed to the Baron.

The Baron is a recluse who lives in a wood-frame cottage on the northern coast of Finland. He admits no visitors. He travels nowhere. He will permit no reporters, photographers, art historians, or copyists to enter his cottage. He hangs the *Mona Lisa* on the back wall of his pantry and looks at it only rarely. His eyesight is not very good. He writes a will ordering that the *Mona Lisa* be destroyed at his death.

The Baron also owns a Picasso canvas, given to him personally by the artist in 1938 and signed on the back in Picasso's own handwriting, "I give this to my friend for his own." The Baron hangs this painting on another wall of his pantry and also orders in his will that it be destroyed upon his death.

On the third wall of the Baron's pantry hangs a third canvas. This is a quite mediocre still life by a second-year art student at a provincial art school in the south, who has since abandoned art to go to dental school. This canvas is also to be destroyed at the Baron's death.

Is the Baron doing something wrong, either in his treatment of these paintings or in the provisions of his will, in any, some, or all of these cases?—M.P.B.

5-30. ACCESS AND THE PRIVATE COLLECTOR

Suppose a well-established senior painter is to be the subject of a one-woman show at a major New York museum. The show is to be a retrospective of her work during her long, fruitful, and very influential career. The museum has been assembling works from various collectors; it pays transportation costs, insurance, and an honorarium or rental fee for the borrowing of the work. Among the works the painter considers most important in her development is a canvas done almost twenty years ago, *Whenever I Look at Her*. This canvas was sold shortly after its completion to a collector who now refuses to permit the work to be exhibited. The collector acknowledges that no work borrowed by this museum has ever been damaged, and that, indeed, security is not his principal motive for refusal; nor would he mind being without the work for the six-month duration of the show. The honorarium is not too small. He simply does not want *Whenever I Look at Her* in the show. The museum argues in behalf of the artist that the canvas is a major milestone in her career and crucial to an understanding of her development.

Does the collector have any obligation to make *Whenever I Look at Her* available to the show, and if so, what sort of obligation would it be?—M.P.B.

NOTES

1. Clement Greenberg, *Clement Greenberg, the Collected Essays and Criticism*, vol. 2, ed. John O'Brien (Chicago: University of Chicago Press, 1986), p. 15.
2. Frederic Taubes, *A Judgment of Art* (Westport, Conn.: Northern Lights Publishers, 1981), p. 129.
3. Paul Tillich, *Christianity and the Existentialists*, ed. C. Michalson (New York: Scribner's, 1956), p. 138.
4. Clive Bell, *Since Cézanne* (New York: Harcourt Brace, 1922), p. 94.
5. From V. I. Lenin, *Collected Works*, reprinted in *Marxism and Art*, ed. Maynard Solomon (New York: Knopf, 1973), p. 180.
6. See "Chris Burden," in *Contemporary Artists*, 2nd ed. (London: Macmillan, 1983), p. 145.
7. Thomas McEvilley, "Art in the Dark," *Artforum*, Summer 1983, reprinted in *Theories of Contemporary Art*, ed. Richard Hertz (Englewood Cliffs, N.J.: Prentice-Hall, 1985), pp. 294–295.
8. Rosalee Goldberg, *Performance: Live Art 1909 to the Present* (New York: Abrams, 1979), p. 106.
9. Robert Smithson, "A Sedimentation of the Mind: Earth Projects," *Artforum*, 7 (1968), 83.
10. John Gruen, "Michael Heizer: 'You might say I'm in the construction business,' " *ARTnews*, 76 (1977), 98.
11. "The Therapist's Duty—To Patients, Art, or History?" *The Hastings Center Report*, 17, no. 2 (February 1986), 2.
12. *Rutgers Law Review* 30 (1977), 456, n. 28, citing 79 RGZ 397, June 8, 1912.
13. See Stephen Weil, "The 'Moral Right' Comes to California," *ARTnews*, 78, no. 10 (December 1979).
14. Norman Del Mar, *Mahler's Sixth Symphony—A Study* (London: Eulenberg, 1980); and Frederik Prausnitz, *Score and Podium* (New York: Norton, 1983).
15. Lucy R. Lippard, *Get the Message: A Decade of Art for Social Change* (New York: Dutton, 1984), p. 11.
16. Leonard D. Duboff, *Art Law: In a Nutshell* (St. Paul: West Publishing, 1984).
17. From Paolo Veronese, "Trial before the Holy Tribunal," pp. 246–248 in Elizabeth Gilmore Holt, ed., *Literary Sources of Art History: An Anthology of Texts from Theophilus to Goethe*, Copyright 1947, © 1975 renewed by Princeton University Press. Reprinted with permission.
18. Paul Lewis, "Exhibition of Islamic Art Provokes Controversy," *New York Times*, August 26, 1985, p. Y16.

19. Giocchino Rossini, Letter to Franz Liszt, June 23, 1865.
20. Lotte Brand Philip, *The Ghent Altarpiece and the Art of Jan Van Eyck* (Princeton, N.J.: Princeton University Press, 1971), p. vii.
21. Based on a case in John Hospers, *Understanding the Arts* (Englewood Cliffs, N.J.: Prentice-Hall, 1982), p. 271.
22. Arnold Toynbee, *Civilization on Trial* (New York: Oxford University Press, 1949), p. 26.
23. Thomas De Quincy, "Romances and Extravagances," in *On Murder Considered as One of the Fine Arts* (Boston: Houghton Mifflin, 1877), p. 532.
24. Oscar Wilde, "Letter to the Editor," *St. James Gazette*, June 25, 1890, reprinted in *The Artist as Critic: Critical Writings of Oscar Wilde*, ed. Richard Ellmann (New York: Vintage, 1969), p. 236.
25. Peter Humphrey, "The Ethics of Earthworks," *Environmental Ethics*, 7 (1985), pp. 7–8.
26. "Yves Klein," *Flash Art*, January–February 1981, p. 52
27. *New York Times*, October 7, 1983, sec. 3, p. 28.

CHAPTER 6

CRITICAL
JUDGMENT

Is aesthetic appreciation a private affair, to be savored in silence rather than openly discussed? Some people equate appreciating art with enjoying ice cream or perfume; they insist that aesthetic judgment should not be debated, because valuing art is as much a matter of personal preference as the taste of chocolate or the scent of sandalwood.

Although experiencing art probably bears some resemblance to experiencing tastes and smells, we should not hastily conclude that public assessment of the merits and defects of art is as peripheral to appreciating art as it is to tasting and smelling. One prominent difference is that ice cream and perfume are much more ephemeral than most artworks. Indeed, during the greatest part of our cultural history, art objects have been fashioned to serve as enduring objects of public appreciation and have been situated for the greatest public exposure. Whether published or performed, whether presented for worship or propaganda or pure decoration, art is experienced in public contexts that encourage critical discussion. Such discussion often occurs when people need to reach an agreement about the value of an aesthetic object.

In the following testimony, excerpted from the transcript of a public hearing, critical judgments are used in the attempt to resolve a practical question: should a very large, obtrusive sculpture be moved, or remain at the site for which it was originally commissioned? As this testimony reveals, differences in critical judgment often arise from disagreements about the issues explored earlier in this book. Differences about how to judge a particular work of art are typically occasioned by disagreements about the definition of art, whether aesthetic value is objective or subjective, what we can learn from art, the nature of creativity, and the relative importance of aesthetic values versus other values. Most of the questions raised in philosophical aesthetics relate, in one way or another, to the considerations brought to bear in judging works of art. But another question must be addressed if we are to understand how verdicts about art should be formulated: Are critical judgments susceptible to rational support, and, if so, what sort of reasoning process concludes in critical judgment? Answering this question requires developing a philosophical theory of the foundations of critical judgment.

THE DISPUTE OVER *TILTED ARC*

(From a transcript of a hearing in New York City in March 1985 on the issue of whether to relocate Richard Serra's *Tilted Arc*, a sculpture commissioned by the federal government for the plaza of the Jacob Javits Federal Building in lower Manhattan.)

Representative Ted Weiss: Imagine, if you will, this curved slab of welded steel twelve feet high, 120 feet long, and weighing over seventy-three tons bisecting the street in front of your house, and you can imagine the reaction to *Tilted Arc* of those who live and work in the area.

Adding to the shock effect is the sculpture's natural oxide coating, which gives it the appearance of a rusted metal wall. Many who first viewed *Tilted Arc* regarded it as an abandoned piece of construction material, a relic perhaps too large and cumbersome to move.

The artist is said to have intended with this piece to "alter and dislocate the decorative function of the plaza." If that was the intent, one may conclude from the sculpture's harsh, disorienting effect that the artist has eloquently succeeded.

But what of those who live and work nearby? The sculpture cuts a huge swath across the center of the plaza, dividing it in two and acting as a barrier to the building's main doorways. Access to the building is awkward and confusing, and the normal walking patterns of those who enter and exit the building are disrupted.

The time has come to find a new location for *Tilted Arc*.

Mr. Serra argues that because his work is site specific, moving it to another location would destroy it. It has, he maintains, a proprietary claim upon the plaza just as real as that of a painting to its canvas. I suggest that there are other valid claims upon the plaza that conflict with Mr. Serra's, and that the scales tip in their favor. The community—those thousands of people who live and work in the area—has the right to reclaim this small oasis for the respite and relaxation for which it was intended.

Mr. Serra, I do not wish to see your work destroyed. I simply would like to see it in a more felicitous location.

Richard Serra: My name is Richard Serra and I am an American sculptor.

I don't make portable objects. I don't make works that can be relocated or site adjusted. I make works that deal with the environmental components of given places. The scale, size, and location of my site-specific works are determined by the topography of the site, whether it be urban, landscape, or an architectural enclosure. My works become part of and are built into the structure of the site, and they often restructure, both conceptually and perceptually, the organization of the site.

My sculptures are not objects for the viewer to stop and stare at. The historical purpose of placing sculpture on a pedestal was to establish a separation between the sculpture and the viewer. I am interested in creating a behavioral space in which the viewer interacts with the sculpture in its context.

One's identity as a person is closely connected with one's experience of space and place. When a known space is changed through the inclusion of a site-specific sculpture, one is called upon to relate to the space differently. This is a condition that can be engendered only by sculpture. This experience of space may startle some people.

When the government invited me to propose a sculpture for the plaza it asked for a permanent, site-specific sculpture. As the phrase implies, a site-specific sculpture is one that is conceived and created in relation to the particular conditions of a specific site, and only to those conditions.

To remove *Tilted Arc*, therefore, would be to destroy it . . .

It has been suggested that the public did not choose to install the work in the first place. In fact, the choice of the artist and the decision to install the sculpture permanently in the plaza were made by a public entity: the GSA. Its determination was made on the basis of national standards and carefully formulated procedures, and a jury system ensured impartiality and the selection of art of lasting value.

The selection of this sculpture was, therefore, made by, and on behalf of, the public.

The agency made its commitments and signed a contract. If its decision is reversed in response to pressure from outside sources, the integrity of governmental programs related to the arts will be compromised, and artists of integrity will not participate. If the government can destroy works of art when confronted with such pressure, its capacity to foster artistic diversity and its power to safeguard freedom of creative expression will be in jeopardy.

Judge Dominick DiCarlo: I had my first encounter with *Tilted Arc* after learning that I was being considered for appointment to the United States Court of International Trade. I was driving on Centre Street when I saw it. What is it? It's a 120-foot-by-twelve-foot rusted piece of iron. Having just returned from visiting our embassies in Rome, Islamabad, Rangoon, and Bangkok, I concluded that this rusted iron object was an anti-terrorist barricade, part of a crash program to protect United States government buildings against terrorist activities. But why such a huge barricade? Was this an overreaction? Why in cities where terrorist activity is much greater are comparatively attractive highway dividers and concrete pillars sufficient to do the job?

After my appointment to the court, I was told that this was art. Was it a thing of beauty? Could be, since beauty is in the eyes of the beholder. Could its maker be making a political statement? Perhaps it was a discarded and rusted piece of the iron curtain. Or perhaps its author was expressing his views on trade policy. This is the Court of International Trade. Was his iron barrier symbolic of a protectionist viewpoint?

We don't have to guess why the iron wall was placed in the plaza. Those responsible have told us. It was to alter and dislocate the decorative function of the plaza, to redefine the space, to change the viewers' experience of that plaza. Simply put, their intention was to destroy the plaza's original artistic concept, the concept of its architects.

To object to the removal of the iron wall on the basis of an honest, moral right to preserve the integrity of the work is astounding, since the sculptor's intent was to destroy another artistic creation . . .

Peter Hirsch: I am the research director and legal counsel for the Association of Immigration Attorneys. We are constantly at 26 Federal Plaza, since that is where the Immigration Service is located.

My membership has authorized me to say that we are entirely opposed to *Tilted Arc*. My own personal view is that a good place to put *Tilted Arc* would be in the Hudson River.... I am told that they are going to have to put artificial things in the river to provide shelter for the striped bass. I think *Tilted Arc* would make a very fine shelter.

Fred Hoffman: I am an art historian and curator of contemporary art associated with many of the leading cultural organizations in Los Angeles.

We can learn more about ourselves, about the nature of our social relations, and about the nature of the spaces we inhabit and depend upon by keeping *Tilted Arc* than we ever could by languishing in the alleged pleasures of a Serra-less plaza.

One of the fundamental realities about an important work of art such as *Tilted Arc* is that it does not simply sit down, roll over, and play dead. This work does not have as its intention pleasing, entertaining, or pacifying. By structuring an experience that is continually active, dynamic, and expansive, *Tilted Arc* makes sure that we do not fall asleep, mindless and indifferent to our destiny and to the increasing scarcity of freedom in an increasingly banal, undifferentiated, and style-oriented world....

William Rubin: I am director of the Department of Painting and Sculpture at the Museum of Modern Art.

Like many creations of modern art, *Tilted Arc* is a challenging work that obliges us to question received values in general and the nature of art and of art's relation to the public in particular.

About one hundred years ago the Impressionists and post-Impressionists (Monet, Gauguin, Cézanne, for example), artists whose works are today prized universally, were being reviled as ridiculous by the public and the established press. At about the same time, the Eiffel Tower was constructed, only to be greeted by much the same ridicule. Leading architects of the day as well as writers and philosophers, to say nothing of the man on the street, condemned the tower as a visual obscenity.

As these examples suggest, truly challenging works of art require a period of time before their artistic language can be understood by the broader public.

I must say that I have never heard of a decision to remove a public monument being settled by popular vote. If that is what is being contemplated here, it seems to me a most dangerous precedent. Moreover, the decision should, it seems to me, involve the sentiments of a much wider circle than simply those who work in the immediate neighborhood. For society as a whole has a stake in such works of art.

Certainly the consideration of any such move should not be a response to pressure tactics and, above all, should not take place before the sculpture's artistic language can become familiar.

I therefore propose that a consideration of this issue be deferred for at least ten years.

Joel Kovel: I am a writer and a professor at the New School for Social Research.

This very hearing proves the subversiveness, and hence the value, of *Tilted Arc.* Its very tilt and rust remind us that the gleaming and heartless steel and glass structures of the state apparatus can one day pass away. It therefore creates an unconscious sense of opposition and hope.

This opposition is itself a creative act, as, indeed, this hearing is a creative act. I would submit that the true measure of a free and democratic society is that it permits opposition of this sort. Therefore, it is essential that this hearing result in the preservation of Serra's work as a measure of the opposition this society can tolerate.

Joseph Liebman: I am the attorney in charge of the International Trade Field Office, Civil Division, U.S. Department of Justice, with offices located at 26 Federal Plaza.

I have worked at 26 Federal Plaza since 1969. While the plaza never fulfilled all my expectations, until 1980 I regarded it as a relaxing space where I could walk, sit, and contemplate in an unhurried manner. Every now and then rays of sunshine bathed the plaza, creating new vistas and moods for its vibrant, unchallenged space.

I remember those moments. I remember the cool spray of the fountain misting the hot air. I remember the band concerts. I remember the musical sounds of neighborhood children playing on the plaza while their mothers rocked baby carriages. I remember walking freely in the plaza, contemplating the examination of a witness, undisturbed by the presence of other people engaged in conversation or young lovers holding hands. I also remember my dreams of additional seating areas, more cultural events, temporary outdoor exhibits of painting and sculpture, and ethnic dance festivals.

All of those things are just memories now.

Regardless of the thoughtfulness and artistic accomplishment of its creator, *Tilted Arc* fails to add significant value to the plaza. The arc has condemned us to lead emptier lives. The children, the bands, and I no longer visit the plaza. Instead, the arc divides space against itself. Whatever artistic value the arc may have does not justify the disruption of the plaza and our lives.

The arc, a creation of mortal hand, should yield. Relocate it in another land. Reprieve us from our desolate condemnation . . .

Donald Judd [sculptor]: We need to revive a secular version of sacrilege to categorize the attempt to destroy Richard Serra's work in Federal Plaza in Manhattan.

Art is not to be destroyed, either old or new. It is visible civilization. Those who want to ruin Serra's work are barbarians . . .

Holly Solomon: I have a gallery in SoHo and now I've moved to Fifty-seventh Street. I don't feel qualified to discuss the law part of this and I don't feel I have time to discuss the taste or the art historical importance of this piece. I can only tell you, gentlemen, that this is business, and to take down the piece is bad business. Mr. Serra is one of the leading sculptors of our time. I sell many paintings. I try very hard to teach people about contemporary art, but the bottom line is that this has financial value, and you really have to understand that you have a responsibility to the financial community. You cannot destroy property.

Phil La Basi: I have been a federal employee for twenty-two years, about eleven years in this building.

First of all, I would like to say that I really resent the implication that those of us who oppose this structure are cretins or some sort of reactionaries.

It seems to be very typical of self-serving artists and so-called pseudointellectuals that when they disagree with something someone else has to say, they attack the person. So I am not going to attack the artist.

What I see there is something that looks like a tank trap

to prevent an armed attack from Chinatown in case of a Soviet invasion. In my mind it probably wouldn't even do that well, because one good Russian tank could probably take it out.

To be very serious, I wouldn't call it *Tilted Arc*. To me it looks like crooked metal or bent metal. I think we can call anything art if we call that art. I think any one of these people here could come along with an old broken bicycle that perhaps got run over by a car, or some other piece of material, and pull it up and call it art and name it something. I think that was what was done here . . .

Frank Stella [painter]: In the matter under discussion here the government and the artist, Richard Serra, have acted in good faith and have executed their responsibilities in exemplary fashion.

The objections to their efforts are without compelling merit. The objections are singular, peculiar, and idiosyncratic. The government and the artist have acted as the body of society attempting to meet civilized, one might almost say civilizing, goals—in this case, the extension of visual culture into public spaces.

The attempt to reverse their efforts serves no broad social purpose and is contrary to the honest, searching efforts that represent the larger and truer goals of society.

Satisfaction for the dissenters is not a necessity. The continued cultural aspirations of the society are a necessity, as is the protection of these aspirations.

The dissenters have accomplished enough by having their objections heard, discussed, and publicized. Whatever merit their case may have, it is not part of the public record and will have its proper influence in future decisions involving matters of this kind.

To destroy the work of art and simultaneously incur greater public expense in that effort would disturb the status quo for no gain. Furthermore, the precedent set can only have wasteful and unnecessary consequences.

There is no reason to encourage harassment of the government and the artist working toward a public good. There are no circumstances here to warrant further administrative or judicial action. If the matter stands as it is, no one will experience any serious harm or duress and one more work of art will be preserved.

This dispute should not be allowed to disrupt a successful working relationship between government agencies and citizen artists.

Finally, no public dispute should force the gratuitous destruction of any benign, civilizing effort.

Danny Katz: My name is Danny Katz and I work in this building as a clerk. My friend Vito told me this morning that I am a philistine. Despite that, I am getting up to speak. Listen fast, because I hear seconds being counted and tempers are high.

The blame falls on everyone involved in this project from the beginning for forgetting the human element. I don't think this issue should be elevated into a dispute between the forces of ignorance and art, or art versus government. I really blame government less because it has long ago outgrown its human dimension. But from the artists I expected a lot more.

I didn't expect to hear them rely on the tired and dangerous reasoning that the government has made a deal, so let the rabble live with the steel because it's a deal. That kind of mentality leads to wars. We had a deal with Vietnam.

I didn't expect to hear the arrogant position that art justifies interference with the simple joys of human activity in a plaza. It's not a great plaza by international standards, but it is a small refuge and place of revival for people who ride to work in steel containers, work in sealed rooms, and breathe recirculated air all day. Is the purpose of art in public places to seal off a route of escape, to stress the absence of joy and hope? I can't believe that this was the artistic intention, yet to my sadness this for me has been the dominant effect of the work, and it's all the fault of its position and location.

I can accept anything in art, but I can't accept physical assault and complete destruction of pathetic human activity.

No work of art created with a contempt for ordinary humanity and without respect for the common element of human experience can be great. It will always lack a dimension.

I don't believe the contempt is in the work. The work is strong enough to stand alone in a better place. I would suggest to Mr. Serra that he take advantage of this opportunity to walk away from this fiasco and demand that the work be moved to a place where it will better reveal its beauty.[1]

The witnesses whose testimony is transcribed in this case all expressed critical judgments. DiCarlo, Hirsch, Weiss, Liebman, La Basi, and Katz agreed that the Serra sculpture should be removed from the plaza. Some of them reached this conclusion by denying that *Tilted Arc* is art or has aesthetic value. Others did so by denying that whatever aesthetic value *Tilted Arc* brings to the plaza fails to compensate for the loss of other values. Serra, Hoffman, Rubin, Kovel, Judd, Solomon and Stella all supported the continued presence of *Tilted Arc* at its present site, but they did not all appeal to the same criteria to justify their views.

Do you think that those who testified at this hearing understood each other when they talked about art or aesthetic value? Is there a rational procedure for resolving this disagreement? If you were the national director of the General Services Administration, how would you decide this case?

Not all our encounters with art issue in critical judgments. Often, we appreciate (or detest) art objects without formulating or communicating anything about whether the work is good or bad, worthy of display in a public setting or best discarded, to be recommended to others for appreciation or to be avoided. However, more often than we may recognize explicitly, we find ourselves making assertions about the value of art objects. We do so when we say such things as: "The work is beautiful," "This painting will continue to command admiration throughout the ages," "The King made a contribution to civilization when he commissioned the Eleventh Symphony," "People who paid good money for those terrible pictures of the children with the black-hole eyes have no taste at all," "Don't bother to stand in line for that movie; it's a grade-B potboiler."

Sometimes we use purely evaluative expressions such as "beautiful" or "good" or "terrible" to convey our critical judgments. But very often our evaluations are not overtly expressed. Instead, our approbation or disapprobation is indicated by how we choose to describe or interpret art.

Not all cases of critical judgment involve communicating with other people. Sometimes we come to comprehend through direct experience and without guidance from other people why a particular artwork—perhaps a work that originally left us unmoved—is considered great. Such cases can be explained by supposing that some factor in our assessment of the work has changed: we have come to perceive aesthetically relevant properties that we had previously failed to notice, or we have revised our views about whether some or all of the work's properties are aesthetically meritorious.

We may think of cases like these as occasions when one communicates critically with oneself, perhaps questioning one's aesthetic principles, perhaps asking oneself why one's present response diverges from those reported by others or even from one's own earlier experience. The public contentiousness surrounding *Tilted Arc* is not unique; art has been subject to public controversy in practically every culture and age. But it is important to realize that, although critical debate may be stimulated by cases calling for public adjudication, the appeals to critical judgment so emphatically present in the *Tilted Arc* case are equally applicable when you consider whether you personally should value any work of art.

Some philosophers believe that only evaluations that derive from general theories of aesthetic value qualify as critical judgments. In this view, no judgment can be involved in recommending works of art unless the recommendations can be the conclusions of reasoned argument. If this is the case, then we need to ask how expressions like "This is a good painting" and "I recommend that you buy tickets to the drama department's production of *Hamlet* before it is sold out" function. Do they function as conclusions supported by reasoning? In cases like the controversy about removing *Tilted Arc*, as well as in instances in which someone wishes only to form a private opinion of an art object, is the evaluative process subject to rational guidelines or constraints? Or is it impossible to distinguish between good critical reasons and considerations that are bad or inappropriate or not reasons at all?

The different approaches to the question of beauty introduced in Chapter 2 can be generalized to distinguish different views about the proper basis of critical reasoning. "Is beautiful," "is good," and "has aesthetic value," expressions considered in Chapter 2, are among the common predicates we use to express our critical judgments about artworks. There are many others as well. Some of the judgments that appeared in the discussion of *Tilted Arc* include: "*Tilted Arc* is a challenging work," "*Tilted Arc* fails to add significant value to the plaza," "Those who want to ruin Serra's work are barbarians," and "The work is strong enough to stand alone."

In the testimony about *Tilted Arc*, each of these expressions is offered as a critical judgment that is supposed to justify either preserving *Tilted Arc* at its current site or relocating the sculpture. Of course, there are only two possible ways to resolve this case: either move *Tilted Arc* or let it remain in the plaza. But often even the witnesses who testified in favor of the same resolution of the case were not in agreement as to the particular considerations they cited. For instance, some of *Tilted Arc*'s supporters appeared to rely on objectivist accounts of aesthetic value, while other supporters, who agreed that *Tilted Arc* should remain in place, gave reasons that appealed to subjectivist analyses of aesthetic value. (See Chapter 2 for a review of the difference between objectivist and subjectivist analyses.) The question raised here concerns how divergences in the conception of aesthetic value affect the prospects of resolving disputes about art.

In understanding the different approaches that different people take in making and defending their critical judgments, we can see why some of the *Tilted Arc* testimony may convince us, while some strikes us as irrelevant and unpersuasive. Furthermore, we can comprehend how disagreements about the value of art result in controversies like the one created by *Tilted Arc*. And perhaps we can also determine whether there are methods appropriate for resolving such controversies.

Although in their testimony Richard Serra (the sculptor of *Tilted Arc*), Joel Kovel (who claimed that its value is the subversiveness), and Fred Hoffman (who said it keeps us awake) all urged that *Tilted Arc* remain at its present site, how far and deep does their agreement reach? For instance, if some people reported that *Tilted Arc* depressed them, would Kovel and Hoffman have agreed about the appropriateness of this response? In view of the reasons they gave for their judgments, would Serra, Kovel and Hoffman have continued to agree that *Tilted Arc* should remain if the buildings surrounding it were torn down and the site turned into a park? If Serra, Kovel and Hoffman appealed to incompatible principles of aesthetic judgment, but arrived at the same recommendation regarding *Tilted Arc*, is it appropriate to consider that recommendation a rational conclusion supported by good critical reasons?

Judge DiCarlo objected to *Tilted Arc* but admitted that it might be beautiful. His reason, he said, was that beauty lies in the eye of the beholder. Is Judge DiCarlo's theory about the nature of beauty helpful in determining whether *Tilted Arc* should remain in the plaza? Phil La Basi also objected to *Tilted Arc*, saying, "we can call anything art if we call that art." Are the premises of La Basi's argument consistent or inconsistent with the premises of DiCarlo's argument? Which argument is more effective or appropriate?

Holly Solomon testified that taking down *Tilted Arc* would be bad for business and would destroy property. Is this a relevant objective consideration that overrides subjective considerations? Joseph Liebman testified against *Tilted Arc* because he could no longer sit in the plaza and enjoy the sunshine, the cool spray of the fountain on hot days, and the sounds of children playing. Is this argument more or less relevant, more or less convincing than Solomon's? Is there a place in critical debate for appeals to values that are not strictly aesthetic values?

Consider another issue raised by the discussion of *Tilted Arc*: How great a voice should the public itself have in choosing public art? Most members of the general public are not artists, nor are they familiar with the traditions of art or of public art. In its hearing on *Tilted Arc*, the General Services Administration invited comment from members of the general public—including office workers and the custodian—but it did not decide the disposition of *Tilted Arc* on this basis. Rather, it charged the National Endowment for the Arts with evaluating possible alternative sites for the work. This was to be done by a panel of experts who would formulate criteria for judging how various alternative sites would enhance or detract from the sculpture's aesthetic value.[2] The members of the panel included an artist, two architects, a deputy museum director, an art historian, a city council member, and a labor negotiator,[3] but not office workers, private citizens, or custodians. It may be asked, then, whether members of the general public should be among those whose reasons are considered in judging the presence or absence of aesthetic value, especially when it is public art that is at issue, and how much weight, if any, their reasons should be given compared with those of experts.

The hearing and expert-panel procedure used by the General Services Administration presumes that judgments about aesthetic value can be reached through reasoned argument, that reasoned argument is sufficient to generate criteria for such matters as the aesthetic impact of relocating the sculpture to an alternative site, even though no one can test how the sculpture would look at any of the alternative sites without its actually being moved (after all, *Tilted Arc* is so big that it fills an entire plaza; it cannot be moved about in the way that a big picture can be hung on different walls to see how different sites affect it). But should criteria for judging how different sites affect a work be decisive in judging its aesthetic value; could any such criteria be justified; or is there no rational basis for predicting which sites would be appropriate for *Tilted Arc* and which would not? Must we wait until the *Tilted Arc* is installed at a new site to see whether its aesthetic value is damaged, unchanged, or perhaps enhanced, and should these observations decide what is to be done with the work?

Some philosophers believe that critical judgments are not the conclusions of reasoning that attributes properties either to art objects themselves or to subjects who are responding to the objects. They believe that critical judgments are not *reasoned* at all. Among contemporary philosophers, for instance, Arnold Isenberg insists that even if a critic's reasons were correct in the properties he or she attributes to the work, such reasons do not add the slightest weight to any evaluative

Richard Serra, *Tilted Arc.*
Photo: Dith Pran, New York Times
Pictures.

verdict about the work. He says, "There is not in all the world's criticism a single purely descriptive statement concerning which one is prepared to say beforehand, 'If it is true, I shall like that work so much the better.' "[4]

However, Isenberg admits that critics do tell us something about the works they criticize, and that what they tell us helps to convince us whether or not to accept their verdicts. Isenberg cites the following description by the critic Ludwig Goldscheider, which supports a favorable judgment of El Greco's painting *The Burial of Count Orgaz:*

> Like the contour of a violently rising and falling wave is the outline of the four illuminated figures in the foreground: steeply upwards and then downwards about the grey monk on the left, in mutually inclined curves about the yellow of the two saints, and again steeply upwards and downwards about . . . the priest on the right.[5]

The purported reason for the favorable verdict lies in the value attributed to the steeply rising and falling curve, Isenberg comments, but the same quality—indeed, the same curve—could be found in hundreds of other contexts without being a reason for attributing aesthetic value. Isenberg concludes that Goldscheider's reason does not prove his verdict but supports it by drawing our attention to another property of the work. This other property is so subtle or complex or unique it cannot be described in words. But we—or at least those of us who are sensitive—can perceive it directly if we attend to the part of the painting with the steeply rising and falling line.

Thus, for Isenberg, critical judgments do not derive from general aesthetic principles or theories, nor do critical reasons support critical judgments the way reasons support conclusions in logical arguments. In other words, critical reasons cannot demonstrate or prove that critical judgments are either false or true. Nevertheless, Isenberg proposes, critical reasons can cause people to accept a critic's verdict by helping them to perceive in the work the indescribable properties that the person who rendered the verdict perceived.

Two centuries ago David Hume had also denied that saying an artwork is good involved attributing a special aesthetic property to it or to subjects who were affected by it. Nevertheless, Hume did believe that some artworks were more worthy than others. In remarks echoed in William Rubin's testimony on *Tilted Arc*, Hume observed that art was subjected to the test of time and that some works satisfied this test by continuing to be acclaimed despite the passage of time and despite changes in cultural interests and expectations. He noted: "The same Homer, who pleased at Athens and Rome two thousand years ago, is still admired at Paris and at London. All the changes of climate, government, religion, and language, have not been able to obscure his glory."[6] The test of time does provide reasonable support for some judgments about aesthetic worth. For instance, it is reasonable to support the judgment that Shakespeare's plays are great art by pointing out how many centuries they have been acclaimed. But, of course, this could not have been the reason why Shakespeare's contemporaries acclaimed his work.

Can we reasonably judge which contemporary works will withstand this test and continue to be appreciated as great art by generation after generation? Such assessments are not reasoned conclusions, Hume thought; they are mere expressions of taste. However, he also thought that some people's tastes were better than others': "Though men of delicate taste be rare, they are easily to be distinguished in society, by the soundness of their understanding and the superiority of their faculties."[7] Because the superior critic can perceive subtle aesthetic properties, draw comparisons among many artworks, and not be prejudiced by irrelevant personal or cultural considerations, there is a high probability that future generations will agree with this critic's assessment of praise or blame. Indeed, this facility to respond as others will in the future is central to making some critics superior to others, according to Hume. Consequently, the rare but good critic's tastes are indicative of how art objects will stand the test of time.

Hume may have anticipated Isenberg's view that, while critics cannot offer reasons that prove their conclusions, some critics can direct other people's attention to the valuable (or defective) aspects of any work. In doing so, they elicit agreement with their own response to the work, even though this agreement is, in general, caused not by reasoned argument but by the critic's skill in showing others how to see or hear the work the way the critic sees or hears it:

> Many men, when left to themselves, have but a faint and dubious perception of beauty, who yet are capable of relishing any fine stroke, which is pointed out to them. Every convert to the admiration of the real poet or orator is the cause of some new conversion.[8]

Although no critic can demonstrate the truth of a conclusion, Hume suggested, we can test purported critics to distinguish better from worse ones. The crucial considerations include whether such persons have the delicacy of perception needed to apprehend subtle differences in the aesthetic surface of a medium, practice in perceiving art so that they can look or listen or read without confusion, experience with many artworks so that they can compare the degree to which the object is meritorious or defective against the merits and defects of other works, freedom from prejudice so they can remain unaffected by the idiosyncrasies of their own society and biography, and good sense and sound understanding. Approval or blame expressed by a critic who satisfies these criteria is more likely to elicit agreement. On this account, the average person who wishes to express verdicts that others accept should strive to satisfy these criteria as well. If Hume's view is correct, public confidence in the verdict rendered by the National Endowment's panel ought to be determined by how well the panelists meet these standards of good taste.

As noted, some philosophers even deny that critical judgments are any kind of judgment at all. Some do so because they think that such expressions as *"Hamlet* is a great artwork" are simply the sounds that go with our having a feeling of approval, much as a cat will purr when it feels pleased or young children will say "yucky" when faced with anything they dislike. If the director of the Visual Arts Program at the National Endowment upheld this belief, he could not expect anyone to formulate acceptable criteria for evaluating the relative aesthetic merits of alternative sites for public works of art. Indeed, this would be true if he agreed with any of the positions that deny that critical judgments are subject to reasoned argument. However, if he agreed with Hume and Isenberg that persons who are effective in showing others how to appreciate particular works are thereby able to produce agreement about the works' value, it would be plausible for him to establish a panel of excellent critics who could cause the public to share their approbation or disapprobation for each alternative site. The question of who should decide about the acquisition and preservation of public artworks thus depends greatly on whether aesthetic assessment is a reasoned procedure that results in judgments that are subject to rational defense.

Further discussion of the *Tilted Arc* case continued in an opinion piece written by lawyer Alvin Lane for the *New York Times:*

> The General Services Administration has modified its guidelines for the Art-in-Architecture program by providing for consultations with local groups and leaders before a work of art is commissioned. This plan will mitigate dissension, but it may have the distasteful side-effect of corrupting the selection panel's freedom.
>
> If we leave the selection of public art to the residents of a community—or even permit their strong influence on the process—we will end up with an esthetic common denominator of sterile, benign and conventional art that will neither offend nor stimulate anyone.
>
> The purpose of Government-sponsored art is to elevate the public's appreciation of all art. . . . Selection, therefore, cannot be left to a popular vote. Only a panel of recognised art experts . . . can properly choose the high caliber of public art that justifies the expenditure of public funds. This is an elitist approach, but it is necessary to preserve the objectivity of a panel's choice and the integrity of the artist and his work.
>
> Chaotic hearings held by the General Services Administration on the "Tilted Arc" highlight the need for rules to guide reviews of public art. Re-evaluation might be done by a panel consisting mainly of art experts. . . . A panel's findings should not be based solely on the artist's esthetic achievement but also should take account of the needs and desires of the community.[9]

Who should select art purchased by public funds? Should selection be left to a popular vote? Should selection be left to the experts? Are there justifiable theories, rules, or guidelines that should be applied in reviewing art?

If we compare activities that clearly are regulated by principles, rules, or laws (such activities as conducting a trial in a court of law, playing a game of baseball, or doing scientific research) with aesthetic evaluation, we may suspect that these activities differ fundamentally from the activity of rendering judgment about the value of artworks. Rule-governed activities seem to be characterized by decision procedures that are conclusive. We do not usually end ball games and trials undecided about who won; nor are we typically accepting of research that has no detectable result. So, when we engage in rule-governed interactions with other people, we typically and reasonably expect that disputes will be resolved and agreement reached.

In contrast, we are not ordinarily disturbed when debates about art end inconclusively. This difference inclines some people to believe that there is no disputing tastes. They contend either that there are no rules, principles, or laws that legitimately direct reasoning about whether art is good or bad, or else that the aesthetic rules we formulate are so weak and loose as to have little effect in bringing about agreement in critical judgment. If we do not have aesthetic rules, or do not have effective ones, we lack a decision procedure for resolving disputes. Thus, some people hold, there is no point arguing about aesthetic evaluations; the outcome of such disputes will always be inconclusive.

Nevertheless, many cases resemble that of *Tilted Arc* both because they concern art that is meant for public appreciation and they evoke critical judgment that affects more than a few people. Hence, we insist that critical judgments not be merely idiosyncratic. Moreover, there do seem to be regularities that characterize good works of art. It seems at least initially plausible to suppose that these regularities can be summarized or generalized to provide guidelines for judging aesthetic value. Consequently, throughout the history of the arts, artists, critics, and philosophers alike have attempted to formulate rules, principles, or law-like theories to guide the creation and criticism of art.

Ancient Greece was both the inspiration and the source of much great work in Western art. Art was public for the Greeks, whether it was sculpture commissioned for religious or civic sites, dramatic works submitted for judgment in open competition (for the Greeks, performances of tragedy commanded even greater public attendance than football games do for us), or poetry, which was read aloud and served instead of textbooks to transmit various kinds of information and attitudes to the young. Like the ancient Greeks, we are inclined to discuss in public the merits of particular art objects and to desire rational means for adjudicating disputes.

Observing how the form of tragic drama had evolved in his own culture, and noticing which dramas elicited the most public approval, Aristotle sought in the *Poetics* to explore the nature of tragic art and identify the bases for artistic excellence. From this analysis, he derived a set of subsidiary rules to which, he claimed, good tragedies conform. For instance, beginning with a distinction between tragedy, defined as the imitation of the actions of superior men, and comedy, defined as the imitation of men who are inferior but not altogether vicious, he recognized that the downfall of a virtuous man is not tragic but, rather, offensive. Consequently, he formulated the rule that, in tragic drama, "a man who is not outstanding in righteousness, or in wickedness and vice ... should fall into misfortune through some flaw of moral character or mental judgment."[10]

The *Poetics* contains many principles of this sort, ranging from guidelines for constructing the most effective tragic plots to rules for selecting the poetic devices that will embellish the language of the play most appropriately. Aristotle's principles were designed to make a play coherent, so that all its parts contributed effectively to ensuring that a single, albeit complex, action was depicted and to make the play at the same time produce the proper tragic response in audiences. Scholars disagree about the precise meaning of the Greek term *catharsis*, which Aristotle used to characterize this tragic response, but Aristotle clearly believed that a successful tragedy elicited pity and fear, either as expressive properties of the play or as emotions felt directly by the audience:

> Tragedy ... is an imitation not only of a complete action, but also of incidents arousing pity and fear. Such incidents have the very greatest effect on the mind when they occur unexpectedly and at the same time in consequence of one another; there is more of the marvelous in them then than if they happened of themselves or by mere chance. Even matters of chance seem most marvelous if there is an appearance of design as it were in them; as for instance the statue of Mitys at Argos killed the author of Mitys' death by falling down on him; ... for incidents like that we think to be not without a meaning. A Plot therefore, of this sort is necessarily finer than others.[11]

Aristotle's principles continue to this day to influence critics in judging drama. However, as with other attempts to formulate the rules of aesthetic excellence, Aristotle's permit exceptions. For instance, many critics contend that Arthur Miller's modern tragedy *Death of a Salesman* achieves the effects Aristotle acknowledged as characteristically tragic, despite the central character's being a salesman who is neither famous nor prosperous, as Aristotle seemed to require. Similarly, the events depicted in Shakespeare's *King Lear* take longer than a single revolution of the sun. Such tragedies violate Aristotle's rules but are as effective in eliciting aesthetic responses—and hence as deserving of aesthetic approval—as, say, Sophocles' *Oedipus*, which does comply with the rules given in the *Poetics*.

Some philosophers and critics propose canons of aesthetic value. These function somewhat more loosely than rules and simply indicate what properties make art objects likely to deserve praise or blame. Monroe Beardsley, in a theory that has been extensively discussed by recent aestheticians, holds that there are three general canons—unity, complexity, and intensity—all of which are involved in the evaluation of any work of art in any medium.[12] The critic's job is to show the degree to which the work possesses each kind of property. Thus, to applaud a work's strong composition is to praise it for being unified; to say it is good because of its juxtaposition of contrasting effects is to praise it for being complex; and to mention its pervasive spirituality is to praise it for being intense. Of course, a work that possesses less of one property may be better than a work possessing more of that property if the former exceeds the latter with respect to the remaining two properties. For instance, a complex work that expresses profound spirituality may be better than a well-organized but banal work.

Other theorists believe that critical judgments can lay claim to universal agreement even though there are no rules to determine the value of individual art objects. Immanuel Kant, for example, argued in the eighteenth century that our aesthetic experience differs from scientific and practical experience because we cannot assess objects aesthetically by subsuming them under concepts, applying definitions, or evaluating them according to rules. Rather, Kant said, when we experience a very special kind of pleasure—namely, aesthetic pleasure—it is legitimate to issue a positive critical judgment about that pleasure's object.[13]

As we observed in Chapter 2, Kant said that aesthetic pleasure is occasioned by our experiencing the "free play" of our imagination with our understanding. Such free play occurs when we experience images that do not elicit systematically reasoned or practical responses from us. Nevertheless, Kant said, when we are truly experiencing aesthetically, the nature of this experience compels us to suppose that the object would be experienced by others in a similar way. Thus, even though there are no justifiable *rules* for determining the value of particular works of art, the nature of aesthetic experience promotes our forming presumptions about whether other people should experience objects aesthetically.

Kant's view that the recognition of aesthetic value cannot be the result of applying rules, principles, or generalizations was adopted by nineteenth-century Romantic poets. These poets, especially Coleridge, insisted that critical judgment was the product of the imagination.[14] As such, both the process of creating art (as we have seen in Chapter 4) and the process of evaluating it must differ greatly from the unimaginative procedures stressing repetition and reason that characterize everyday, practical thinking. In Kant's view, trustworthy critics were those who accurately and reliably recognized whether their experiences of objects were aesthetic ones. Such a critic, serving on a panel to recommend whether *Tilted Arc* should be moved or whether *Death of a Salesman* should win the Pulitzer Prize, presumably would function differently from a critic who sought unity, complexity, and intensity in aesthetic objects, or from a critic who applied the Aristotelian rules to establish what value the judged works possessed.

In weighing the advantages of having a panel of experts judge art against those of appealing to a public vote (or equivalent evidence of public approval, such as the sale of tickets), we must consider that there is no generally accepted methodology for arriving at critical judgments. This seems to be the case even though the history of aesthetics is richly endowed with different rules, principles, and canons that have dominated aesthetic evaluation at different times in the past and that still may be applicable to judging some art. Therefore, to resolve disputed cases like the one involving *Tilted Arc*, two stages of justification may be required: justifying the method of arriving at critical judgments may have to precede justifying the critical judgments themselves.

Does the *Tilted Arc* case represent a typical context in which critical judgments are made, or is it atypically contentious? Public hearings in which testimony is taken about an object's aesthetic value are not uncommon. Other famous cases include the U.S. Customs Service's hearing to decide whether Constantin Brancusi's abstract sculpture *Bird in Space* was an artwork that could be imported free of tax or a piece of metal on which duty had to be paid. A trial determined that James Joyce's novel *Ulysses* possessed sufficient aesthetic merit to outweigh its offensive sexual explicitness. Likewise, the art dealer Sir Joseph Duveen was tried on the charge of manipulating the market value of certain Renaissance paintings by permitting his expert authenticator, art historian Bernard Berenson, to change his mind about who painted the works.[15] More typically, however, critical judgment occurs in contexts like the review excerpted below. In this discussion of a retrospective exhibition of Serra's works at the Museum of Modern Art in New York City, the critic's judgment functions as a recommendation about how to appreciate aesthetic objects rather than as a way of adjudicating disagreements about the value of the works.

> With all that has been said and written recently about Serra, the retrospective is still likely to change the way we see him.... It is important to recognize that the work of the contemporary artist who has been supported and attacked as few others, can be understood as an ongoing Passion play in which signs of provocation and suffering are equally present.
>
> Another of the paradoxes of Serra's work is that while its meaning is always dependent on context, each sculpture seems absolutely distinct and finished. From the moment we enter the show, we have a clear sense of the human and sculptural drama that awaits us. The first work, the 1969 "Cutting Device: Base Plate Measure," looks like a campsite that has just been made or broken. Steel poles, blocks of stone and wood, and strips and rolls of lead seem scattered about the floor in a roughly circular pattern. What makes the work so impressive is Serra's mastery of the entire gamut of formal relationships—including circle and square, open and closed, light and dark, hard and soft ...
>
> In the work Serra made for the museum's sculpture garden ... [there are] religious associations.... From the 53rd Street side, the almost square slab suggests late medieval and Renaissance images.... Only there is no image ...
>
> Serra's sculpture does indeed have a political dimension. But it is also steeped in tradition. For a work that continues to retain so much of its radical force, it could not be otherwise. If only a reaction against

tradition can establish a work's radical potential, only the weight of tradition can sustain it. In this exhibition we encounter some of the most convincing ways of thinking about art that have been developed during the past 20 years. But they are so convincing because in almost every gallery we feel part of basic psychological and religious ritual.[16]

The critical judgments contained in this review are meant to enhance appreciation of Serra's work for at least three types of readers: those who had seen the 1986 Museum of Modern Art retrospective, those who were planning to see it, and those who, like most of us, would never see it. In cases like this, where the function of critical judgment is primarily to enhance appreciation rather than to resolve a dispute, critical conclusions about aesthetic worth are closely entwined with descriptive and interpretive claims about the work. For instance, in the review just quoted, Serra's sculpture *Cutting Device* is described as emphasizing formal contrasts, "circle and square, open and closed, light and dark." But the same sentence also evaluates the sculpture as exhibiting "mastery" of the gamut of such relationships. Some philosophers hold that the most important elements of critical judgment are attributions which, like this one, function both by describing art objects in ways that constitute reasons for attributing worth to the objects and also function as conclusions by directly attributing aesthetic value to the objects. In other words, it may not be possible to decide whether many of the expressions typical of criticism are descriptive or evaluative.

The contemporary philosopher Frank Sibley believes that many of the expressions used in criticism are aesthetic terms. Applying aesthetic terms requires aesthetic discrimination or perceptiveness, which Sibley equates with appreciation or taste. Aesthetic terms refer to aesthetic properties, but there are many more such properties than there are terms used to name them. Critics must employ complex mixtures of aesthetic and nonaesthetic terms to cite such unnamed aesthetic properties as reasons for their judgments: "By merely drawing attention to those easily discernible features which make the painting luminous or warm or dynamic, we [bring] someone to see these aesthetic qualities."[17]

While Sibley believes we are brought to accept critical judgments by having our attention directed to aesthetic properties that are perceivable although not necessarily nameable, Arthur Danto proposes that "something the eye can't descry" is crucial to art. Danto supplies another dimension to the process of critical judgment by contending that appreciation and assessment of art is conditioned by references to the history of art:

There was a certain sense of unfairness felt at the time when [Andy] Warhol piled the Stable Gallery full of his Brillo boxes; for the common-

place Brillo container was actually *designed* by an artist, an Abstract
Expressionist driven by need into commercial art; and the question was
why Warhol's boxes should have been worth $200 when that man's
products were not worth a dime. . . . In part, the answer to the question
has to be historical. Not everything is possible at every time, as Heinrich
Wölflin has written, meaning that certain artworks simply could not be
inserted as artworks into certain periods of art history, though it is
possible that objects identical to artworks could have been made at that
period.[18]

Further discussion about the *Tilted Arc* case, again from the *New
York Times*, exemplified both Sibley's contention that critical reasons
direct perception and Danto's point that some reasons relate the work
to the history of art instead of to what can be directly perceived in the
work.

> The largest sculpture in the show . . . enables the public to consider some
> of the ideas behind "Tilted Arc." The curve, which is 10 feet tall and 60
> feet long, seals off the space between a column in the middle of the room
> and a corner. From the convex side that greets us, the sculpture pushes
> toward us assaulting us like a crowd in a city street at rush hour. From
> the concave side, however, the work offers a refuge so absolute that it
> seems like an abandoned amphitheater or monastery. It is as if Serra had
> in some way combined the active movement of Francesco Borromini's
> Baroque facades with the heavy passivity and latent energy of Michel-
> angelo's "Slaves."[19]

Another complexity in evaluating art is the variety of reasons
that are typically, and often convincingly, offered to support critical
judgment. Sibley's account construes critical reasons as referring to
properties whose presence is established only by being directly perceived. Danto's account directs attention to critical reasons of a very
different sort, reasons referring to properties that cannot be perceived
at all. Are these accounts inconsistent? If very different kinds of
reasons are conjoined in evaluating a work, does doing so enrich
appreciative experience, or does it detract from a coherent approach to
appreciating the work?

Each of the previous chapters of this book addresses one or more
of the kinds of reasons that have been thought to be relevant for critical
judgment. But how do these reasons relate to each other when one is in
the actual process of assessing aesthetic objects? If you are moved by
certain reasons in appreciating one work, does consistency require you
to give those reasons weight in considering the value of similar or
dissimilar works? Or is each instance of critical judgment unique, so
that no guides, canons, principles, or rules usefully apply in subsequent
cases? Does the procedure used to evaluate a single case sometimes

have the power to affect the shape of subsequent critical judgments by changing the kinds of reasons we find relevant or by changing taste itself?

The *New York Times* review of the Serra retrospective show and the testimony for and against *Tilted Arc* resemble each other because both contain critical judgments. Yet the contexts in which they were made differ: In the context of the review judgments provided guidance in appreciating art, whereas in the context of the public hearing, they were aimed to resolve a dispute. By comparing these cases, both in their similarities and in their differences, we can learn more about how critical judgment should be made and how we can generalize from the case of *Tilted Art* to judgments about other works. Even though the operation and objectives of criticism are extraordinarily complicated, puzzling cases which illustrate the different applications of critical judgment both challenge and illuminate how we understand aesthetic appreciation and aesthetic valuation.

CASES

Critical Judgment

6-1. LEAVING THE THEATER

"I never said it wasn't good. I merely said I hated it."

Drawing by Modell; © 1985 The New Yorker Magazine, Inc.

Is this excuse defensible on philosophical grounds?—R.M.M.

6-2. CAN THIS MARRIAGE BE SAVED? (A HYPOTHETICAL LETTER TO DEAR ABBY)

Dear Abby:

I own three paintings, which I'll call A, B, and C. I like them all, but I like A the best. David and I will be married in June, and we will move to an apartment where there is room for only one of my paintings.

I asked David to choose the one he liked best. First he carefully compared A and B and said he preferred B. Then he compared B and C and said he preferred C. Then he spent a lot of time comparing C and A and said he preferred A. "I suppose," he said, "that I cannot have a favorite among the three."

I told David he was irrational and that his decisions were self-contradictory and impossible. I told him that if he preferred B to A and C to B, he'd have to prefer C to A.

David told me that the problem was not his. He blamed the nonobjectivity of aesthetic values. He said that objective properties like age and weight have transitive relationships and that if B is older or heavier than A and C is older or heavier than B, then C has to be older or heavier than A. But if aesthetic value is not a property like weight or age, then the transitivity of relationships will not be relevant to choosing one of my paintings. He said that his preferences exhibit the nonobjectivity of aesthetic value rather than his own irrationality.

Abby, I'm afraid that David is so irrational and indecisive he'll change his mind about marrying me. Do you think the flaw lies in David, or is it in the nature of aesthetic value?

Nervous in New Haven

What advice should Dear Abby give Nervous?—E.M.Z.

6-3. LEO STEIN AND THE MATISSE

Art collector Leo Stein relates the story of his having purchased a Matisse that he came to dislike because he felt the treatment of the arm was wrong. He put the painting in the attic. One day his dealer made an offer for it, and Stein, in need of money, felt very tempted. He went to the attic to get the painting, and lo! the arm had come right!

José Ortega y Gasset has said that the way an apple *really* looks is the way it looks when we are about to bite into it. Would it follow that the way a painting really looks is the way it looks when we are confronted with a choice between keeping it and selling it? Does this story suggest that in moments of crisis, conventional constraints fall away and we see things as they really are, or do crises merely cause us to see things differently, but not necessarily better? Should the psychological circumstances of the viewer be considered relevant to the critical judgment of the work perceived?

C. I. Lewis has suggested that whatever the viewer *must* bring to the presentation of a work of art, in order to understand it correctly, belongs to the work of art.[20] Does it follow from this that Stein ultimately saw the work of art objectively because he brought something to its perception that he had previously failed to provide?—M.L.

6-4.   THE ART-LOVING ANTHROPOLOGIST

Suppose that an anthropologist who loves art visits a remote island, where the natives show him their carvings, dances, and songs. He discovers that this culture does not distinguish between high art, intended for the elite, and low art, made for the masses. When he tries to explain this distinction, the natives laugh at him, saying they do not understand what he means. Any carving, song, or dance that is not liked by most people, they insist, simply is not *art*, and they do not see why it should be praised so highly.

Without a distinction between high and low art, could the people of this culture judge art as we do? And would their aesthetic judgments be better or worse?—J.M.

6-5.   MADE IN ROME

From the fourteenth through the eighteenth century, European collectors held the Greco-Roman marbles in high regard. These sculptures of gods and goddesses, which had been excavated in Italy, were Roman copies of Greek originals believed lost. Then, in the nineteenth century, a number of true Greek sculptures were brought to Europe by Lord Elgin and others, and art-lovers had their first experience of the originals of which they had previously known only copies. The Greco-Roman sculptures fell out of favor, even though they too had originated in antiquity.

Many people regard this change in taste as a correction of a mistake in critical judgment. Was it?—A.S.

6-6.   CRITICIZING BEETHOVEN

In 1881, John Ruskin said, "Beethoven always sounds to me like the upsetting of bags of nails, with here and there also a dropped hammer."[21] In 1837, William Gardiner, observing that Beethoven had been deaf for nearly a decade, wrote, "His compositions have partaken of the most incomprehensible wildness. His imagination seems to have fed upon the ruins of his sensitive organs."[22] And in 1857, A. Oulibicheff stated that because Beethoven's hearing was faulty, "accumulations of notes of the most monstrous kind sounded in his head as acceptable and well-balanced combinations."[23]

Does the later critical appreciation of Beethoven show that these early critics were wrong? Or were they perceptive in a way that these later critics are no longer able to understand? How should we interpret these assessments?—M.P.B.

6-7. POEMS AND *TREES*

Joyce Kilmer's famous poem begins, "I think that I shall never see a poem as lovely as a tree."[24] Suppose he originally wrote this poem for a creative writing class and received the following comments from his instructor:

> Although it is sometimes a good idea to begin a poem with a paradoxical thought, this simply will not do. Your first sentence assumes that a meaningful comparison can be made between the beauty of trees and the beauty of poems. But this idea is completely crazy. Lovely poems and lovely trees have absolutely nothing in common. A beautiful tree is one thing, and a good poem is something quite different. There is no way to compare them. So the thought with which your poem begins is totally confused. Perhaps you should try to get into the School of Business.

Can you help Joyce Kilmer make a good rebuttal to these charges? Or do you agree that he should, at the very least, have revised the first line of the poem?—D.W.C.

6-8. COMPARING WORKS OF ART

Is Beethoven's Fourth Symphony aesthetically as good as or better or worse than his Fifth Symphony? Is it as good as Haydn's First Symphony? As Mozart's G major String Quartet? As Raphael's *Sistine Madonna*? As the cathedral at Chartres? As any painting of Robert Motherwell's? Are the overall aesthetic values of two different works of art comparable when the works are by different composers or artists, in different styles (e.g., Fauvist or Cubist) or media (e.g., paint and sound), or from different periods? Is there any basis on which comparative judgments of works of art can be made?—B.V.

6-9. A CRITICAL JUDGMENT OF HER OWN

Virginia Woolf wrote in her diary: "I finished *Ulysses* and think it is a misfire. . . . The book is diffuse. It is brackish. It is pretentious. It is underbred, not only in the obvious but in the literary sense. A first rate writer, I mean, respects writing too much to be tricky."[25]

Given Woolf's own diffuse style, on what basis can she object to Joyce's diffuseness? If she thinks Joyce's work is a "misfire" because it is diffuse, must she think her own work misfires too?—A.S.

6-10.   OH NO, NOT THAT SAME STORY AGAIN!

Lord Byron criticized Shakespeare as follows: "Shakespeare's name, you may depend on it, stands absurdly too high and will go down. . . . He took all his plots from old novels, and threw their stories into dramatic shape, at as little expense of thought, as you or I could turn his plays back again into prose tales."[26]

Is Shakespeare's use of familiar stories an aesthetic defect? Is Byron an undependable critic because his own poetic style and aesthetic values appear to be so different from Shakespeare's?—A.S.

6-11.   SHOOTING CLAY PIGEONS

Paul Ziff says that the sport of clay pigeon shooting is of "no aesthetic interest." The same is true, he says, of tiddlywinks, shuffleboard, archery, baseball, basketball, bicycling, bowling, canoeing, curling, golf, and fishing. But some sports do have distinct aesthetic aspects: gymnastics, ski-jumping, figure skating, high-diving, and bullfighting. He explains:

> The relevant difference between the first and second group is this: form is a grading factor only for the second. How one does it counts in the second group of sports but not in the first. Sink the ball hit the target: that's what counts in the first group. Form doesn't. Hold the club any way one likes look like a duffer: if one manages somehow to sink the ball expeditiously enough one may end up a champion.[27]

Is Ziff right in dividing sports up in this way? Should the judging of all sports be revised to take aesthetic aspects into account? Does a sport remain a sport when it is judged on aesthetic grounds?—M.P.B.

6-12.   THE CASE OF THE PERISHABLE PLAYING

In a *New York Times* article of October 24, 1985, music critic Bernard Holland wrote:

> Listening to Vladimir Horowitz record Schubert [made me] regret that these moments survive on tape. It was music for the moment. Encased . . . in permanence, it will never be the same again. . . . Its principal

fascination was its unpredictability, the anticipation it inspired, the excitement of discovery growing within the listener. What would this man do next?

But Mr. Holland went on to say that he was not sure he would like the record made on that occasion:

> The second thoughts will start. My brain will ask, "Is this classical grammar . . . that line was not meant to be shaped as Mr. Horowitz has done. Those exaggerated evocations of inner voices . . . what in the world do they have to do with Schubert?"[28]

Which would be the preferable critical judgment of Horowitz's performance, the one made without reflection when the performance was first heard, or the one made at a second hearing, when there is time to reflect on one's knowledge of the history of music?—A.S.

6-13. COLD AND HUNGRY

Reviewing Robert Altman's film *Quintet*, a critic wrote:

> The film proceeds with a deliberate, infuriating slowness. Its rhythm is the rhythm of its people, half-frozen and at the same time half-crazed. *Altman doesn't let us perceive anything faster than we would if we were always cold, always hungry.* He keeps what we perceive at a bare, glazed minimum. We see the city as though we're walking with our heads down, depressed, only occasionally looking about us.

Do you think the critic's remarks support a favorable or unfavorable judgment of the film? Is there anything in the remarks themselves that should determine what sort of critical judgment they can support? In fact, this critic used these remarks as the basis for an unfavorable verdict, but almost identical remarks were made by other critics as the basis for a favorable verdict on the same film. Are some of the critics right in basing their judgments on remarks such as these, while others are wrong? Or could these remarks be appropriate in both favorable and unfavorable judgments? What is the function of remarks such as these in criticism generally?[29]—J.H.

6-14. JIM MANGRUM'S VOICE AND A. R. AMMONS'S WORDS

Some people think scientists may disagree about what conclusions should be drawn from the available evidence, but not about the evidence itself. Similarly, you might think that although competent and careful critics may disagree about the aesthetic merit of a work, they should not disagree about factual descriptions of features of the work on which they base their evaluations. With this in mind, consider the following examples:

1. In 1971 *Rolling Stone* praised a record called "Black Oak Arkansas" for the singing of Jim Mangrum. The reviewer said it was "incredibly sinister," that it had "a randy malevolence," and described Mangrum as "growling ferociously."[30] In 1979, another *Rolling Stone* reviewer (who listened to a physically similar copy of the same record on equipment not very different from what was used in 1971) complained that Mangrum's singing was "mealy mouthed."[31] How could Mangrum's singing on the same record have been ferocious in 1971, and mealy mouthed in 1979? And how could a competent critic mistake mealy mouthed singing for ferocious, malevolent, incredibly sinister growling?

2. A passage from A. R. Ammons's *Sphere: The Form of a Motion* was praised by one critic as "extravagantly pell mell" and condemned by another for being "wordy."[32] How is this sort of disagreement possible?—J.B.

6-15.   PINK AND BLUE

A professor of psychology was a practical joker. He had never done a painting before in his life, but when an art museum announced a competition for painters, he painted the left half of a rectangular piece of plywood pink and the right half blue, framed it, and gave it the title *Composition for Two Violins*. His piece won an honorable mention in the show, while some works by professional artists received no recognition.

Did the judges make a mistake? Do you think they would have judged as they did if they had known of the hoax? Suppose the piece had no title? What if it had been titled *Plywood in Pink and Blue*?—V.A.

6-16.   THE STUDENT SHOW

The late Alan Jarvis, director of the National Gallery of Canada, was asked to judge a show of paintings by art students. It turned out that the painting to which he awarded the prize had been produced the night before the exhibition by a disgruntled art student who sprayed paint at random onto a prepared canvas. There was a lot of bad publicity to the effect that even an expert could not tell good from bad in contemporary art, but Jarvis stood by his decision, insisting that the painting had a freshness and vitality that the other contenders lacked. The rest, he claimed, were laborious and contrived.

Must Jarvis have been wrong, since the paintings he rejected represented serious efforts by young artists whereas the winner was not serious? For Jarvis's judgment to be justified, do we have to suppose that the winner unconsciously imparted to the spraying the acquired skill of a trained hand, or unconsciously expressed the authentic rage and despair that prompted the gesture? Or do we have to say that the art school must be destroying creativity in its serious students?

We have only the winner's word that his work was intended to be a hoax. Do we commit a fallacy when we equate the artist's word about what he intended to do with what actually was achieved? How can we really know an artist's intention? How should we judge the merits or demerits of the disgruntled student's "work"?—F.S.

6-17. RAUSCHENBERG'S *BED*

Robert Rauschenberg's 1955 work *Bed* consists of his own quilt, sheets, and pillow attached to a stretcher. In the upper half, the linen is lavishly painted with clots, runnels, and swipes of various colors; in the lower half, the quilt, itself brightly colored, shows only a splash or two of paint.

When in 1958 Rauschenberg was invited to participate in the Festival of Two Worlds in Spoleto, Italy, he submitted *Bed*. The officials were shocked and refused to show it in the main gallery. *Bed* was placed, instead, in the storage room of the exhibition building.[33]

What could have been the cause of the officials' shock, and what sort of artwork would be required to produce a similar response today? Or is "shock" of this sort no longer possible in the art world?—M.P.B.

6-18. ADDITIVE AESTHETIC VALUE

Consider two paintings. The first painting is admired and considered good because it is a faithful and revealing representation of something interesting, for instance, a group of peasants peeling potatoes. The second painting also is admired and considered good for these reasons, but in addition it makes an interesting allusion to a great work of the past: Its subjects are posed in the same way, the composition is similar, and so on. It is considered good not only for all the same reasons as the first painting but also for an additional reason.

As described, there are more things that are good about the second painting than the first. Does that make the second painting a better work of art than the first painting? Or is there something wrong with the above line of reasoning?—D.W.C.

6-19.   THE CASE OF THE SHRINKING FRAMES

Suppose that one night, all the frames on all the paintings in the Metropolitan Museum of Art in New York, and in the Museum of Modern Art in the same city, shrink by one half, and the parts of the paintings left exposed outside the frames by the shrinkage disintegrate. The next night, all the reduced-size paintings expand to their original sizes, so the frames are the same size as they were before, but the pictures they frame look strikingly different, since part of the surface of each original painting no longer exists.

You are commissioned to assess the damage to the paintings, and you are asked to pay particular attention to any loss of aesthetic value. What is the extent of damage? Are the paintings in some styles—for instance, Renaissance paintings—more damaged than paintings in other styles—for instance, cubist or abstract expressionist works? —R.M.M.

6-20   WHILE ROME BURNS

The Roman emperor Nero considered himself to be an artist. He is also said to have intentionally put Rome to the torch. Suppose he made the following claim for himself: "In the *Poetics*, Aristotle claimed that a good tragedy purifies the soul by arousing pity and fear. You can hardly deny that watching your neighbors burn to death fills you with pity and fear, more pity and fear than you are likely to experience in watching any staged drama. Therefore, whatever you may think of my moral character, my great tragedy, *Rome in Flames*, is a very successful drama, and I am a greater artist than Sophocles, having inspired more pity and fear than he did."

Do you agree with Nero? If not, is the Nero argument a refutation of Aristotle's theory?—E.M.Z.

6-21.   THE PEALE BROTHERS AND THE GERANIUM

Suppose the National Gallery of Art recently paid four million dollars for a portrait by the early American painter Rembrandt Peale. The portrait shows the artist's brother, Rubens Peale, examining a geranium. The portrait is praised not only for its realistic technique and sensitive portrayal of an individual but also because its rendering of the geranium is so accurate and detailed that botanists use it to identify an early American variety of the plant and to help date the introduction of scented geraniums into America.

Does the accuracy of the rendering of the geranium make Rembrandt Peale's portrait of his brother a better painting? A better portrait? Or does the botanical value of the painting of the geranium have nothing to do with the aesthetic value of the portrait as a work of art?—A.S.

6-22.   THE GREAT SAN JOSE ART MYSTERY

While walking to lunch one day in April 1986, David Allen, San Jose's newly appointed art-in-public-places coordinator, noticed that something was missing from a little urban-renewal park across from a construction project. That something was a twenty-foot-high, seven-thousand-pound constructivist steel sculpture entitled *Great Planes Study #7*, by David Bottini. Installed in 1976, it had been the first work of art the city of San Jose had purchased with public money.

As Allen's persistent inquiry later revealed, *Great Planes Study #7* had been removed eight months before to protect it from damage during the construction project, but since it had been "severely bent and scarred" in the process, a city official had ordered it destroyed. Yet no one had noticed that the sculpture was missing, until its absence struck Allen eight months later, and it was only with some difficulty that he determined what had happened to the piece.[34]

Does the fact that no one noticed that *Great Planes Study #7* had disappeared have any bearing on its value as art? As public art? As art that was purchased with public funds and on permanent public display? If no one missed it, does this mean that it was all right to destroy it? Does it mean that the sculpture was not successful as art, or perhaps was not really art at all?—G.I.

6-23.   COLLECTOR'S CHOICE

Eskimo carving is extremely varied, though most of it is immediately recognizable as Eskimo. Many of the Inuit Eskimos produce carvings, occasionally or regularly. For some it is just a chore, others like to do it for a change, a few are dedicated artists. The iconography is sometimes personal; often it is based on the vanished way of life; sometimes it is related to beliefs common to the culture. Several villages have distinctive styles, often incorporating themes and mannerisms inaugurated by powerful artistic personalities; many individuals develop their own styles and *oeuvres*.

Assume that a collector of Inuit carving is considering purchasing one of several desirable pieces. One is a modest carving by a famous Inuit artist whose work the collector has long wanted to own. Another is by a good artist whose work the collector already owns but that, when displayed with these other pieces, will help viewers see and appreciate the artist's style and development. A third choice is a stunning work by an artist no one has ever heard of, and the collector does not know whether this artist has made or will make other equally stunning pieces. Yet another piece is appealing because it has characteristics of which the collector is particularly fond; for instance, it has animal as well as human figures, or is small enough to fit into a person's hand. Still another piece is interesting because it is unusual for Inuit carving; the collector has never seen another piece like it. Another strikes the collector as a lot of fun, a piece that would be a source of continuing pleasure and amusement. Finally, there is the piece whose execution is exceptionally skillful and whose artistic quality is usually beyond the collector's price range; it seems to be a bargain.

The collector can afford only one piece. If, on first sight, all of these pieces attract her about equally, is there any general principle that can guide her choice?

If you yourself sometimes buy art, what is the significance to you of what you buy? The artistic significance? How did your relationship to art change, if at all, when you began collecting art? Whether or not you have bought art, how do you think you should be guided in making the sorts of decisions that would turn you into a collector, that is, the maker of a collection that would have a character you might never have foreseen, but for which you would be responsible?—F.S.

6-24.   IS THIS VAN GOGH STILL LOST—OR FOUND?

One of Van Gogh's paintings of sunflowers was destroyed in a bombing raid on Yokohama in 1945. Until recently, the only reproduction of it known to art historians was a black-and-white photograph taken in 1941. In 1986, however, an edition of a book on Van Gogh's sunflowers was published in Japan, and a guest at a dinner party celebrating the publication asked the author why he had chosen a black-and-white photograph to illustrate the lost painting. She then showed him a limited-edition art book made in Japan in 1941 that contained a detailed, colored woodblock of the Van Gogh.

On the basis of this reproduction, an expert determined that the lost painting was the only major sunflower picture in which Van Gogh had placed the flowers against a dark blue background. The critic also claimed that the lost painting was clearly the most dramatic of the sunflower paintings by Van Gogh.

Can supportable critical judgments of a work of art be made if the work has been destroyed but descriptions or reproductions of it are available? How can we determine how reliable such judgments are?
—A.S.

6-25.   THE REAL MICHELANGELO'S FORGED *CUPID*

In an essay in the *New York Review of Books*, Joseph Alsop called Michelangelo "the first clearly identifiable faker in the history of Western art." The reason: in 1495, Michelangelo sculpted his *Sleeping Cupid* in a conspicuously classical style. He was then advised by Lorenzo de Pierfrancesco de' Medici to treat the statue "so that it seemed to have been buried in the earth." "I would send it to Rome," Lorenzo suggested, "and pass it for an antique, and you would sell it for a far better price." Michelangelo followed this advice, and the purportedly ancient *Cupid* was sold for two hundred ducats, a very large sum for an art object in those days. However, a row ensued when the purchaser discovered he had acquired a fake.[35]

Did Michelangelo commit fraud by treating the *Sleeping Cupid* so that it could be (and was) mistaken for a Greek or Roman antique? Since Michelangelo's own work possesses exceptional aesthetic value, would you be disappointed to find that your purported Roman sculpture was really made by Michelangelo? Would learning this change your appreciation or critical judgment of the sculpture?—A.S.

6-26.   SCHUMANN AND THE ANGEL

Schumann claimed that the main theme of his violin concerto, written in 1853, had been dictated to him by an angel during a dream or vision. The violin concerto is one of Schumann's least known, least performed, and least regarded larger works. During the period of its composition, Schumann was suffering from some sort of mental illness, probably manic-depression; on two occasions, he threw himself into the Rhine. Not long afterward he entered a sanitarium, where he died.

Can a piece of music written by a mentally disturbed, delusionary individual be any good? Are critics justified in taking into account these facts about Schumann's life in judging the worth of his last compositions to the extent that they do so?—J.L.

6-27.   THE CASE OF THE DISAPPEARING SYMPHONY

A composition identified as Beethoven's *Jena* Symphony used to be performed occasionally at concert, and at least half a dozen recordings of it were made. Then scholars persuaded themselves it was not by Beethoven, and it disappeared from concert programs and record catalogues. Yet the *Jena* is the same work now as it was before being pronounced spurious Beethoven. A similar fate overtook Haydn's *Toy*

Symphony after it was discovered that it was by somebody else, probably Leopold Mozart.

Could changing the attribution of a composition cause us to appreciate it differently? Is a change in attribution a good reason to revise critical judgment of a work?[36]—A.S.

6-28. *SWAN LAKE*

The ballet *Swan Lake* has undergone continual revision since the first production of its canonical version in St. Petersburg in 1895. Anyone mounting the ballet now has to decide how it should be performed in the light of the many variations in past performances, together with those that may seem called for by the talent and resources available. If *Swan Lake* exists, it exists as this history of changing practice within the constants of Tchaikovsky's music and the choreography of Petipa and Ivanov.

In 1895, the leading role of the Prince had to be given to the senior dancer Paul Gerdt, who was too old to partner the ballerina properly. Ivanov accordingly added an extra male character—Benno, the Prince's friend—to help out. Should Benno be included in productions now? Here are some of the pros and cons:

Con: "Benno was never more than a concession to necessity, so there is no reason to keep him."

Pro: "Yes, but Ivanov did choreograph the part, and, if Benno had been absent, the Prince's part would be different."

Con: "But the Russians themselves often left him out later."

Pro: "All sorts of changes are made, but, if we abandon the original production, we have no benchmark to go by."

Con: "But it is ludicrous to have a third person in a *pas de deux*."

Pro: "On the contrary, it is important to the ballet that the Prince is a prince, burdened by protocol, and princes have equerries who follow them around just as presidents have bodyguards."

Con: "If there were no Benno in the original production, no one would have suggested he be there."

Pro: "But he is there."

Consider as well this feature of the canonical *Swan Lake*. In 1895, Pierina Legnani was the only ballerina in the world able to do thirty-two *fouettes,* and her audience expected to see them in her performance as the Black Swan. But thirty-two fouettes are well within the competence of today's superbly athletic dancers. Should today's productions of *Swan Lake* continue to include them? Again, here are some pros and cons:

Con: "Any good dancer nowadays can do thirty-two fouettes, so they miss their original point."

Pro: "But they are what was originally devised for that moment in the ballet."

Con: "But only because they were a brilliant feat then; a modern revival should substitute something that is a comparably brilliant feat now."

Pro: "But the fouettes are motivated. They represent the malicious, inhuman triumph that distinguishes the Black Swan from the White Swan."

Con: "Any other brilliance would serve the same purpose."

Pro: "Not so. Anything else would look gratuitous. Just try to imagine something else; you can't."

Con: "But the fouettes don't have that effect. They are too famous. When she starts spinning, we stop watching and start counting. It stops the show in the worst possible way."

Pro: "But if that is true, any substitution would be even worse. Instead of watching what was being danced; we would be seeing what she did *as a substitute.*"

Con: "If we are too frivolous to look at a dance properly, that's our fault."

Nowadays, the Benno is usually discarded, although the thirty-two fouettes are usually retained. The cases seem similar, but are the same factors relevant in deciding them? Is one way of deciding better than another? Or does the decision depend on circumstances?— F.S.

6-29.   THE BLACK SWANS

The New York City Ballet's "Swan Lake" [is a] problematic production. . . . Although Odette, the Swan Queen, is still in white, all the swan-maidens now wear black. . . . The black costumes often cause the swan-maidens to fade from sight in the shadows at the sides of the stage. . . . Perhaps one trouble with the black swans is that they no longer seem brilliant enough . . .

Black is associated with evil. Who, then, are these black swans? Could they even be accomplices of Rothbart, the sorcerer, sent to guard Odette so she does not escape? . . . I hasten to assure the flabbergasted balletomanes that I do not advance this suggestion with total seriousness. But neither is it completely frivolous in its intent, for in the production Rothbart is encased in an enormous black costume that makes him resemble a monster from a science fiction movie. . . . However, the real trouble with Mr. Vaes's costumes is not that they are odd, but that their oddity does not possess much significance. The black swans do not seem to be evil spirits, innocent maidens or anything else; they are merely dancers in black costumes.[37]

The black swans *are* dancers in black costumes. Why should their seeming to be what they are detract from the value of the production? Traditionally, the swans' costumes are white. Is the reviewer inconsistent if he fails to criticize productions in which the swans are costumed in the traditional white but also do not have costumes possessing much significance?—A.S.

6-30.   ARNHEIM ON TALK ABOUT ART

According to Rudolf Arnheim:

> Art may seem to be in danger of being drowned by talk. Rarely are we presented with a new specimen of what we are willing to accept as genuine art, yet we are overwhelmed by a flood of books, articles, dissertations, speeches, lectures, guides—all ready to tell us what is art and what is not, what was done by whom and why and because of whom and what. We are haunted by the vision of a small, delicate body dissected by crowds of eager lay surgeons and lay analysts. And we feel tempted to assume that art is unsure in our time because we think and talk too much about it.[38]

Is art enhanced by talk and, in particular, by critical discourse? Or is art stifled by art criticism and other talk about art? Is there something ironic about Arnheim's adding his own voice to other critical voices? Isn't he just generating more talk and, worse than that, talk about talk about art? Or is he illuminating the "art of criticism" as critics can illuminate art?—R.M.M.

NOTES

1. Edited transcript copyright 1985 by Harper's Magazine. All rights reserved. Reprinted from the July 1985 issue by special permission.
2. On December 15, 1987, the advisory committee to the General Services Administration (a committee consisting of an artist, two architects, a deputy museum director, an art historian, a city councilman, and a labor negotiator) agreed with Serra's claim that *Tilted Arc* is "site-specific" and decided, by unanimous vote, that the work could not be removed or relocated without destroying its artistic value. See Douglas C. McGill, "Advisory Panel Backs 'Tilted Arc,' " *New York Times*, December 16, 1987, p. Y25; and Douglas C. McGill, "Art People" *New York Times*, December 18, 1987, p. Y24.)
3. See Douglas C. McGill, "Advisory Panel Backs 'Tilted Arc,' " *New York Times*, December 16, 1987, p. Y25.
4. Arnold Isenberg, "Critical Communication," in *Philosophy Looks at the Arts*, ed. Joseph Margolis (Philadelphia: Temple University Press, 1978), p. 408.
5. Ludwig Goldscheider, cited in Isenberg, "Critical Communication," p. 406.
6. David Hume, "Of the Standard of Taste," in *Aesthetics: A Critical Anthology*, ed.

George Dickie, R. J. Sclafani, and Ronald Roblin (New York: St. Martin's Press, 1989), p. 245.

7. Hume, "Of the Standard of Taste," p. 602.
8. Hume, "Of the Standard of Taste," p. 609.
9. Alvin Lane, *New York Times*, July 13, 1985, p. 21.
10. Aristotle, *Poetics*, 13.
11. Aristotle, *Poetics*, 9.
12. Monroe Beardsley, *Aesthetics: Problems in the Philosophy of Criticism* (Harcourt, Brace & World, 1958), passim.
13. Immanuel Kant, *Critique of Judgment*, passim.
14. Samuel Taylor Coleridge, *Biographia Literaria* (1817), ed. J. Shawcross (London: Oxford University Press, 1958).
15. Several of these cases are presented in Laurie Adams, *Art on Trial* (New York: Walker, 1976).
16. From an unsigned review, *New York Times*, March 16, 1986.
17. Frank Sibley, "Aesthetic Concepts," in *Philosophy Looks at the Arts*, ed. Joseph Margolis (Philadelphia: Temple University Press, 1978), pp. 81–82.
18. Arthur Danto, *The Transfiguration of the Commonplace* (Cambridge, Mass.: Harvard University Press, 1981), p. 44.
19. *New York Times*, March 1986.
20. C. I. Lewis, *An Analysis of Knowledge and Valuation* (La Salle, Ill.: Open Court, 1947).
21. Nicholas Slonimsky, *Lexicon of Musical Invective: Critical Assaults on Composers since Beethoven's Time* (New York: Coleman-Ross, 1965), p. 52.
22. Slonimsky, *Lexicon*, p. 46.
23. Slonimsky, *Lexicon*, p. 50.
24. Joyce Kilmer, "Trees," in *Collected Poems*, ed. Robert Cortes Holliday (New York: George H. Doran, 1914), p. 180.
25. Bill Henderson, *Rotten Reviews: A Literary Companion* (Wainscott, N.Y.: Pushcart Press, 1986).
26. Henderson, *Rotten Reviews*.
27. Paul Ziff, *Antiaesthetics: An Appreciation of the Cow with the Subtile Nose* (Dordrecht, Netherlands: D. Reidel, 1984), pp. 62–63.
28. From a review by Bernard Holland, *New York Times*, October 24, 1985.
29. John Hospers, *Understanding the Arts* (Englewood Cliffs, N.J.: Prentice-Hall, 1982), p. 331, quoting a review of Robert Altman's film *Quintet* in the *Los Angeles Weekly*, February 15, 1979.
30. John Mendelsohn, "Black Oak Arkansas," *Rolling Stone*, May 27, 1971, p. 48.
31. D. Marsh, ed., *The Rolling Stone Record Guide* (New York: Random House, 1979).
32. D. Young, "Language: The Poet as Master and Slave," in *A Field Guide to Contemporary Poetry*, ed. S. Friebert and D. Young (New York: Longman, 1980), p. 160.
33. *Robert Rauschenberg* (Washington, D.C.: National Collection of Fine Arts, Smithsonian Institution, 1976), pp. 8, 34.
34. Michelle Huneven, "The Great San Jose Art Mystery," *California*, April 1987, pp. 74, 88, 106.
35. Joseph Alsop, "Art into Money," *New York Review of Books*, July 17, 1986, pp. 42–43.
36. From a column by Donal Henahan, *New York Times*, April 13, 1985.
37. From a review by Jack Anderson in *New York Times*, July 13, 1986.
38. Rudolph Arnheim, *Art and Visual Perception: New Version* (Berkeley and Los Angeles: University of California Press, 1974), p. 1.

INDEX

AARON (computer program),
136–138
Acquisition of stolen art, 162
Additive aesthetic value, 210
Adoration of the Lamb, 82–83
Adorno, Theodore, 19
Advance of the Broken Arm, 9
Aeschylus, 143
Aesthetic attitude theorists, 6
Aesthetic of Ugliness, The, 41
Aesthetics
  equivalence and, 23
  experience and, 42–46, 49
  pleasure and, 199
  quality and, 152
  values related to beauty, 37–38
Agamemnon, 143
Aguado, Dionisio, 128
Albee, Edward, 129–130
Aldrich, Virgil
  on aesthetic experience, 45
  on beauty, 35
Alexander, Samuel, on ugliness and
  beauty, 40
Alienation of art from society, 158
Allison, Richard, 126, 128
Alsop, Joseph, 214
"And Did Those Feet in Ancient
  Time," 65–66, 74
Angelico, Fra, 155
Antiessentialism, 7–8
Aristotle, 89
  on beauty, 36–37
  on functions of objects, 159–160
  imitation theory of art, 67–68
  on presentation of the ugly, 40–41
  on the role of the poet, 111
  on tragedy, 211
  on tragic art, 197–198
Arnheim, Rudolf, on talk about art,
  217
Art and Illusion, 75
Artist
  authority of, 117
  character and work relationship,
  155
  influence on value of art, 214

interpretation by, 98
relationship to works, 14–15
Aspection and aesthetic
  experience, 45
Asphalt Rundown, 162
Attribution
  credit for performance, 134–135,
  136
  and value, 87–88, 150, 214–215
Auden, W. H., 144
Audience
  and meaning in dance, 83–84
  perception and interpretation,
  94–98
  perceptions of beauty, 28–30
  role in creation, 116–117
  role in defining art, 10, 22
  role in defining beauty, 47
Augustine, Saint, on beauty, 39–40
Authorized reproduction, 138–140
Avey Shhakim, revision and meaning, 86

Babbage, Charles, 79–80
Bach, Johann Sebastian, 9
Bacon, Francis, beauty in the
  works of, 40
Bannard, Darby, 56
Barthes, Roland, on audience par-
  ticipation, 116
Bateson, F. W., on relevance, 66
Baudelaire, Charles, ugliness re-
  lated to beauty, 41
Beardsley, Monroe, 198–199
  on aesthetic experience, 45
  on audience collaboration, 116
  on creativity, 113
Beauty, 28–40
Bed, 210
Beiderbecke, Bix, 19–20
Bell, Clive, 155
  defining art, 5
Berenson, Bernard, interpretation
  and intent, 91
Berlioz, Louis Hector, 102
Billy Budd, illusion of reality,
  52–53